012372337

D1610501

CIVIL RIGHTS,
THE CONSTITUTION,
AND CONGRESS, 1863–1869

CIVIL RIGHTS, THE CONSTITUTION, AND CONGRESS, 1863–1869

Earl M. Maltz

University Press of Kansas

Published by the University Press of Kansas (Lawrence, Kansas 66045), which was
organized by the Kansas Board of Regents and is operated and funded by Emporia
State University, Fort Hays State University, Kansas State University, Pittsburg State
University, the University of Kansas, and Wichita State University

Library of Congress Cataloging-in-Publication Data

Maltz, Earl M., 1950–
   Civil rights, the Constitution, and Congress, 1863–1869 / Earl M.
Maltz.
     p. cm.
   Includes bibliographical references.
   ISBN 0-7006-0467-7 (alk. paper)
   1. United States—Constitutional law—Amendments—13th-15th—
History. 2. Civil rights—United States—History. 3. Afro-
Americans—Civil rights—History. I. Title.
KF4757.M29 1990
342.73′085—dc20
[347.30285]

90-32818
CIP

British Library Cataloguing in Publication Data is available.

Printed in the United States of America
10 9 8 7 6 5 4 3 2 1

Contents

Tables

Preface

The constitutional amendments adopted during the Reconstruction era provide the cornerstone for much of modern constitutional law. Controversial Supreme Court decisions involving issues such as school desegregation, racial discrimination in employment, voting rights, affirmative action, abortion, and criminal procedure are all tied in one way or another to the Thirteenth, Fourteenth, and Fifteenth Amendments. It is thus not surprising that the original understanding of those who drafted these amendments has been the subject of a substantial body of scholarship.

The debate over the original understanding proceeds on two different levels. Legal theorists have sharply differing views on the relevance of the original understanding to contemporary constitutional jurisprudence. Some constitutional theorists—known as originalists—contend that courts should consider themselves bound by the original understanding. Other scholars—nonoriginalists—often concede that the original understanding is relevant to constitutional analysis but argue that other considerations are also pertinent to judicial decisionmaking.

Originalism is currently unfashionable in the academic world. Nonetheless, as I have discussed in detail elsewhere, my own sympathies lie generally with those who would focus on the original understanding.[1] The Constitution requires that two-thirds of the members of each house of Congress affirm their support for any proposed additions such as the Reconstruction amendments; in the absence of this support, the Constitution remains unaltered. Yet if a change in language is later given a meaning different from the understanding of those originally voting, support for the different meaning will never have been demonstrated. Thus in effect the Constitution will have been changed by a process totally inconsistent with the structure created by the document itself. Only an originalist approach avoids this problem.

Given this perspective, the search for the original understanding of the drafters of the Reconstruction amendments becomes critical to proper constitutional analysis. Many of the legal scholars dealing with this issue have focused their attention almost entirely on section one of the Fourteenth Amendment.[2] In some respects this focus is entirely understandable; after all, much of contemporary constitutional law is

ix

based upon this provision. In other ways, however, an undue emphasis on section one can distort the inquiry.

The Fourteenth Amendment was not a sudden, isolated alteration of the American constitutional structure; indeed, scholars such as Jacobus tenBroek and Harold M. Hyman and William Wiecek have argued that section one was simply a restatement of the Thirteenth Amendment.[3] At most, the Fourteenth Amendment was simply part of a process of reallocation of constitutional authority that projected federal power into areas hitherto reserved exclusively to the states. This process constitutionalized the portion of the Republican party program dealing with the legal status of blacks—a program that by the end of the Civil War included not only freedom for slaves but citizenship and suffrage for free blacks. The constitutional realignment began with the adoption of the Thirteenth Amendment in 1865, an event that invoked federal power to destroy the state-created institution of slavery. It continued with the Civil Rights Act of 1866, which declared free blacks to be citizens and defined the rights appurtenant to that status. Adopted by Congress later that year, section one of the Fourteenth Amendment did not represent a radical advance from earlier congressional action. Instead, it reaffirmed the principles of the Thirteenth Amendment and the Civil Rights Act as part of an omnibus proposal defining the conditions under which the defeated southern states could regain their representation in Congress. Finally, in 1869 Congress passed the Fifteenth Amendment, which prohibited racial discrimination in voting rights. The Fifteenth Amendment completed the new constitutional framework; later civil rights measures would have to be justified within that framework.

The key point is that the adoption of section one of the Fourteenth Amendment was simply a part of the evolution of a new constitutional structure developed to meet the challenges of the post–Civil War era. To focus on any single part of the new structure without also scrutinizing other, equally important components is to ignore the significance of context in historical analysis. Thus, the essential features of the new federal approach to civil rights issues are best considered together.

Studies of the new structure might proceed from a variety of perspectives. For example, works by such scholars as Eric L. McKitrick and Michael Les Benedict have examined in detail the political crosscurrents that determined not only the content of congressional actions on civil rights but also the overall shape of Reconstruction policy in the immediate post–Civil War era;[4] LaWanda Cox and James L. Cox have focused particularly on the political forces that shaped the controversy over civil rights.[5] Taking a different approach, Harold Hyman has brilliantly studied the impact of the Civil War and Reconstruction on attitudes toward constitutionalism generally[6] and (together with William

Wiecek) has applied his analysis to the drafting of the Reconstruction amendments.[7]

Each of these works is immensely valuable and provides necessary background for any study of the Reconstruction amendments. None, however, focuses directly on the issue of greatest import to lawyers—the question of what changes in the law the members of Congress believed they were making by proposing constitutional amendments and adopting other civil rights measures. This book is an attempt to answer that question.

The nature of the inquiry dictated the sources relied upon. In particular, I concluded that extensive examination of private correspondence would be of little value to the inquiry. The drafters were not acting as private citizens; instead, they were performing a public function—lawmaking. Moreover, in interpreting statutes and constitutional amendments, judges will typically have access only to the public record. It is this record that formed the basis of my conclusions. Of course, any analysis of the public record must begin with an examination of the language ultimately chosen. To properly evaluate these choices, however, a variety of factors must be considered.

First, one must understand the legal culture in which the drafters operated. Critically important concepts such as slavery, civil rights, equal protection, due process, and privileges and immunities had all been extensively discussed in prior case-law and legal commentaries. Most of the key players on both sides of the debate were legally trained. Moreover, during the debates both supporters and opponents of civil rights measures made copious references to these standard legal sources in attempting to bolster their respective positions. The measures that ultimately emerged can therefore only be understood as an embodiment of preexisting legal concepts.

Second, the significance of language *not* chosen cannot be overestimated. In each case the language of the Civil Rights Act, the Fourteenth Amendment, and the Fifteenth Amendment was chosen only after earlier formulations had been offered and rejected in Congress; alternative language was also presented during the debate over the Thirteenth Amendment. The reasons for the rejection of the alternatives were often either obvious or explicitly stated. In many instances, these reasons related directly to potential judicial interpretations of the discarded language—interpretations that the drafters found undesirable. One can reliably conclude that the drafters did not believe that they were inviting these same undesirable constructions in the language they ultimately did adopt.

Finally, the basic ideology of the Republican party on issues of race and federalism must be considered. The Republican concept of racial equality was, by modern standards, incomplete; at the same time, the party's commitment to states' rights remained strong even after the Civil War. These two factors limited the potential scope of any national civil rights initiatives.

All together, these factors paint a relatively clear picture of the original understanding of the Reconstruction amendments. The drafters were faced with specific problems, and they adopted new statutory and constitutional measures to address those problems. At the same time, however, sensitive to state prerogatives, the drafters consciously sought to limit expansions of federal authority; they did not intend to grant sweeping new authority to the federal government to enforce open-ended concepts of liberty and equality. Taken together, these two somewhat conflicting goals shaped the congressional approach to civil rights issues in the period from 1863 to 1869.

Acknowledgments

Some sections of this book have previously been published in article form. Parts of chapter one appeared in "Fourteenth Amendment Concepts in the Antebellum Era," *American Journal of Legal History* 32 (1988): 305; and "The Concept of Equal Protection of the Laws—A Historical Inquiry," *San Diego Law Review* 22 (1984): 501 (© 1985 San Diego Law Review Association; reprinted with the permission of the *San Diego Law Review*). Substantial portions of chapters two through five were published as "Reconstruction without Revolution: Republican Civil Rights Theory in the Era of the Fourteenth Amendment," *Houston Law Review* 24 (1986): 221. Most of chapter six is derived from "The Fourteenth Amendment as Political Compromise—Section One in the Joint Committee on Reconstruction," *Ohio State Law Journal* 45 (1984): 933 (© 1984 Ohio State University). Permission to use materials from these articles is gratefully acknowledged.

Many people have read all or part of this book at various stages and have made helpful suggestions that have improved the final product immensely. To acknowledge each individually would require another full-length book. I would be remiss, however, if I did not specifically note the important contributions of Herman Belz, Peter Hoffer, Natalie Hull, Jim McClellan, Forrest McDonald, and Bill Nelson. Summer Research Grants from Rutgers Law School financed the completion of the manuscript. The secretarial staff of the law school—particularly Celia Hazel and Mary Perrine—were unstinting in their support. Brad Geyer provided invaluable research assistance. Most important, my wife, Peggy, provided continuous support and encouragement, and my son, David, helped keep my feet firmly planted in the real world.

1
Republicans and Black Rights prior to Reconstruction

THE ANTEBELLUM ERA

No single source reflects the full variety of antebellum Republican views on race-related issues, but the Lincoln-Douglas debates of 1858 provide an excellent snapshot of the moderate Republican position.[1] The occasion was the contest for the control of the Illinois state legislature and with it the right to elect a senator to serve in the next Congress. In a preview of the presidential election of 1860, the representatives of the two dominant northern parties engaged in a series of one-on-one discussions that covered the important issues of the election. Race figured prominently in the debates. Throughout, Lincoln sought to portray Douglas as proslavery; conversely, seizing on Lincoln's opposition to the Supreme Court's decision in *Dred Scott v. Sandford*,[2] Douglas argued that Lincoln was an abolitionist and an advocate of true racial equality. Douglas's line of attack was typical of Democratic rhetoric on the race issue:

> If you desire negro citizenship, if you desire to allow them to come into the State and settle with the white man, if you desire them to vote on an equality with yourselves, and to make them eligible to office [and] to serve on juries . . . then support Mr. Lincoln and the Black Republican party, who are in favor of the citizenship of the negro.
>
> . . . .
>
> [Lincoln] holds that the negro was born his equal and yours.[3]

In short, Douglas charged Lincoln with favoring the elimination of all legal distinctions based on race—a position that might be described as ''total racial equality.''

Some prominent radical Republicans, including Charles Sumner of Massachusetts and Salmon P. Chase of Ohio, had in fact embraced the doctrine of total racial equality.[4] Others, while perhaps not accepting the doctrine fully, believed that free blacks should be considered citizens, entitled to the protection of the privileges and immunities clause of Article IV of the Constitution—the comity clause.[5] Indeed, five

1

northern states had granted blacks the right to vote in the antebellum period and one—Massachusetts—allowed them to serve on juries as well.[6] A number of factors, however, prevented the theory of total racial equality from becoming the basic Republican position on race issues before the Civil War.

First, in a society infected with widespread, deeply rooted racism, advocacy of total racial equality was politically hazardous. The danger was particularly strong in a state such as Illinois—a border state that, although it had never allowed slavery, had a long history of antiblack legislation; as late as 1853 Illinois had adopted legislation making it criminal for blacks to settle in the state. If Republicans were to succeed in such states, they could not be viewed as the party advocating racial equality. Moreover, for many Republicans the objections to the concept of total racial equality—even in a simply legal sense—transcended simple expedience. Republicans themselves were subject to the same racist sentiments prominent in the population as a whole. These sentiments emerged in a variety of contexts. For example, opposition to the extension of slavery to the territories was frequently portrayed as a device to preserve the territories for the use of whites. The logic was simple: Most American blacks were slaves, and therefore a prohibition on the importation of slaves would also ensure that the black population was low.[7]

The influence of these factors was apparent in Lincoln's response to Douglas's attack on the race issue. Lincoln stated that his ideal solution to the problem of slavery would be to have the slaves freed and sent to Liberia.[8] Later he asserted:

> I am not, nor have ever been, in favor of bringing about in any way the social and political equality of the white and black races . . . I am not nor have ever been in favor of making voters or jurors of negroes, nor of qualifying them to hold office, nor to intermarry with white people; and I will say in addition to this that there is a physical difference between the white and black races which I believe will forever forbid the races living together on terms of social and political equality.[9]

Lincoln's analysis of the citizenship issue is particularly enlightening. On this point, his main quarrel with the *Dred Scott* decision was not based on the view that free blacks should be citizens; instead, he argued that Taney's opinion was flawed because it denied to the states the *power* to confer citizenship on former slaves.[10] Thus Lincoln's argument was based on principles of federalism rather than racial equality.

In the political context of 1858, Lincoln's state-centered concept of citizenship was not surprising. From an antislavery perspective, the theory of a strong central government seemed to have few attractions. No mainstream politician believed that the federal government had authority to abolish slavery in the existing states. At the same time, increases in federal authority posed very real threats to the effectiveness of antislavery activity in the free states—particularly in an era in which proslavery forces generally controlled the federal government.

The festering dispute over the enforcement of the Fugitive Slave Act of 1850 is illustrative. Adopted by Congress as part of the Compromise of 1850, the act was tilted strongly in favor of slaveholders, who claimed that blacks in free states were in fact runaway slaves who should be returned to their masters. Northern state legislatures responded by adopting "personal liberty laws," which provided additional protection for the blacks, claiming that they were not runaways.[11] The tension between the two legislative regimes reached its zenith in *Ableman v. Booth*.[12]

Booth was a Wisconsin resident who had been arrested and charged under the Fugitive Slave Act of 1850 for obstructing the return of a fugitive slave. While in federal custody, but before his trial, Booth applied to the Wisconsin Supreme Court for a writ of habeas corpus. A justice of the Wisconsin court freed Booth on the grounds that the Fugitive Slave Act was unconstitutional,[13] and this judgment was affirmed by the entire state supreme court.[14] While an appeal from this judgment to the United States Supreme Court was pending, Booth was rearrested and convicted in federal district court. Once more, the Wisconsin Supreme Court issued a writ of habeas corpus ordering his release from federal custody. In one of Chief Justice Taney's most famous and well-respected decisions, he overturned the writs and forcefully asserted the principle of federal judicial supremacy.[15]

Although not all Republicans agreed with the action of the Wisconsin Supreme Court in its attempt to nullify the Fugitive Slave Act, the act nonetheless stood as impressive evidence of the power and willingness of the federal government to aid the proslavery forces. The possible implications of *Dred Scott* were even more troubling. The Court in that case had held that Congress had no authority to outlaw slavery in the territories. As Lincoln pointed out in the debates, Republicans feared that the next step would be for the Court to hold that as a matter of federal law, northern states could not prevent slaveholders from bringing their slaves into the free states and continuing to hold the slaves there.[16] Once again, the federal government was cast as a potential obstacle to the antislavery movement.

Lincoln's response to Douglas's attack also reflects the ambivalence of the antebellum Republican position on race and the importance of the citizenship question in the popular mind.[17] Even if the status of citizenship carries with it no particular rights, designating a person a citizen necessarily connotes full partnership in political society. In order to effectively avoid the charge of being in favor of total racial equality, Lincoln was compelled to deny that blacks should be citizens.

At the same time, however, Lincoln averred that free blacks were entitled to equality with whites in certain respects:

> There is no reason in the world why the negro is not entitled to all the rights enumerated in the Declaration of Independence, the right to life, liberty, and the pursuit of happiness. I hold that he is as much entitled to these as the white man . . . in the right to eat the bread, without the leave of anybody else, which his own hand earns, *he is my equal and the equal of Judge Douglas, and the equal of every living man.*[18]

This passage accurately captures the core of the antebellum Republican position on the rights of blacks. Republicans were committed to the idea that all men were equally entitled to a limited set of natural rights. Blacks were entitled to these rights not because racial discrimination was wrong; instead, their claim was based on what might be called a theory of "limited absolute equality"—that all men, whatever their condition or attributes, were entitled to a certain minimum level of rights. As one prominent Republican put it, with respect to natural rights—the rights to life, liberty, and property—"it is a question of manhood, not of color."[19]

Republicans often spoke of these rights in terms that would later emerge in the Fourteenth Amendment. For example, they claimed that the Fugitive Slave Act and the establishment of slavery in the territories deprived free blacks of liberty without due process of law.[20] Similarly, a provision of the Oregon Constitution that denied free blacks access to the courts was said to be inconsistent with the right of all persons to have the protection of the law.[21]

The basic concept of limited absolute equality was not a product of the antislavery movement; on this point, Republican ideology was simply adopting a theory that was deeply imbedded in more general American political thought. It was recognized not only in the Declaration of Independence but also in the constitutions of both slave and free states. The Pennsylvania Constitution captured the idea succinctly, providing "that all men are born equally free and independent, and have certain inherent and indefeasible rights, among which are those of enjoying and defending life and liberty, of acquiring, possessing, and protecting property and reputation, and of pursuing their own happiness."[22]

Further, while declining in influence in private law in the early nineteenth century,[23] natural rights remained an important, recurrent theme in the development of judicially created public law. Admittedly, in 1837 the decision of the Supreme Court in *Charles River Bridge v. Warren Bridge*[24] eviscerated the concept of natural law as an element of federal constitutional constraints on state action. But throughout the antebellum era, courts in states both slave and free continued to rely on natural law theories to check legislative action. For example, in 1849, in striking down a married woman's property act insofar as it purported to abrogate preexisting property rights, a New York judge stated that "the security of the citizen against such arbitrary legislation rests on the broader and more solid ground of natural rights, and is not wholly dependent upon those negatives upon the legislative power contained in the Constitution."[25]

Occasionally the natural rights concept was interpreted quite broadly. In 1855 in *Beebe v. State*, the Indiana Supreme Court found that a prohibition on the right to manufacture and sell liquor was inconsistent with natural law.[26] More often, however, natural rights were limited to those described by Chancellor James Kent: "the right of personal security, the right of personal liberty, and the right to acquire and enjoy property."[27]

Once blacks were conceptualized as people, then their entitlement to these rights followed ineluctably. Hence the core of the antebellum Republican position was simply that blacks were people rather than property. During the Civil War, this position was replaced by a new consensus among Republicans—that blacks were entitled not only to the rights of persons but also to those that derived from citizenship. Many Republicans included access to the ballot box in those rights.

THE CIVIL WAR ERA

During the early stages of the Civil War, little progress was made toward removing racially discriminatory legislation at the state level. Particularly in the Midwest, fears that the conflict would free large numbers of slaves who would emigrate north had exacerbated racial tensions.[28] In such an atmosphere, even those legislatures controlled by the Republican party recognized that moves toward racial equality were political suicide. Moreover, in the elections of 1862 Democrats made substantial headway, gaining control of state legislatures in Illinois and Indiana.[29] The prevailing mood was perhaps best symbolized by the 1862 referendum on a proposed new constitution in Illinois; while the constitution was defeated by a margin of 16,051 votes, the electorate favored a provision prohibiting the immigration of blacks by a majority of 107,650. In addition, a clause barring blacks from voting and holding office was approved by a margin of almost six to one.[30] Such results reflected a negrophobic consensus that cut across party lines.

At the federal level, the picture was somewhat brighter but still mixed. Republicans were firmly in control and at times used that control to substantially improve the legal position of free blacks in areas controlled by the national government. In 1862 Congress established schools for District of Columbia blacks and simultaneously provided that persons of all colors should be subject to the same laws and ordinances.[31] In the same year, however, Congress appended a voluntary colonization scheme to the District of Columbia emancipation bill, refused to allow blacks to become letter carriers, and provided that state laws should govern the admission of testimony in all cases in federal court[32]—even in states that prohibited free blacks from offering evidence.

As the war progressed, blacks made substantial legal progress. A variety of factors contributed to this development. Successes on the military front enhanced the fortunes of the Republican party (now temporarily renamed the Union party); in the elections of 1864, Republicans scored a sweeping triumph.[33] Moreover, the performance of black soldiers on the battlefield generated increased respect among the white population.[34] At the state level, the impact of these factors was manifested by some important actions. The Illinois legislature repealed both the black exclusion laws and the ban on black testimony in courts of law; in Iowa and Ohio, blacks were made eligible to receive public assistance.[35] The United States Congress mirrored this trend: It refused to appropriate funds for the voluntary colonization program, effectively killing the plan.[36] Congress also equalized the pay for white and black soldiers[37] and, reversing earlier decisions, adopted measures allowing blacks to carry the mail[38] and testify freely in federal courts.[39] Finally, District of Columbia street railroad companies were expressly forbidden to exclude blacks from their cars.[40]

The changes in attitude emerge clearly from the evolution of the Republican approach to the emotional issues of citizenship and suffrage. The citizenship question operated on different levels. First, citizenship could be seen as a problem of tangible rights. Presumably, citizens possessed certain rights that were not available to others occupying some different noncitizen status. Under this view, to find that free blacks were citizens would necessarily imply that they had such rights. This approach to the citizenship issue had been used *against* Republicans before the Civil War; indeed, it formed the cornerstone of the proslavery argument during the antebellum era. The two most important expositions of this position were Chief Justice Taney's majority opinion in *Dred Scott* and the 1821 opinion of Attorney General William Wirt which interpreted a statute giving the right to command certain vessels to "citizens of the United States." In each case, the author contended that because free blacks were routinely denied many of the most important rights normally possessed by citizens, only whites could be said to enjoy that status in the United States.[41]

The difficulty with the tangible rights analysis lay in identifying the rights that were the *sine qua non* of citizenship. Some equated the rights of citizenship with Kent's list of natural rights;[42] this approach to the problem, however, seemed to drain the concept of citizenship of independent significance. The additional rights most often mentioned were political—the rights to vote and to hold office.[43] The problem was that these rights were not denied only to blacks; they were routinely withheld from other groups, such as white, native-born women and children, who clearly were citizens. In addition, some states allowed aliens to vote. Use of political rights as a benchmark for citizenship therefore posed insoluble theoretical problems.[44]

A connection between citizenship and tangible benefits was not, however, the only sense in which the concept was critical to the debate over the status of free blacks. Even if no other benefits were conferred, designating a person a citizen meant that person was a member in good standing of political society. Thus Democrats could effectively charge that on an important symbolic level, advocacy of black citizenship was equivalent to an assertion of racial equality.[45]

Finally, the debates over both the tangible rights and the symbolic content of black citizenship were complicated by uncertainties in federal-state relations. Under the American system, questions of a person's citizenship raise not one but two issues. One issue is whether the person is a citizen of a state; the other is whether the person is a citizen of the nation as a whole. Theoretically, this problem could be resolved in several ways. First, the two types of citizenship might be viewed as entirely independent. Second, one might argue that national citizenship is an incident of state citizenship (except for those who are residents of the United States but not of any state). Third, one could conclude that state citizenship is an incident of national citizenship.

As already noted, antebellum Republicans typically argued that state citizenship was paramount and that national citizenship was only a secondary incident thereof.[46] With the outbreak of the Civil War, this position became untenable. Previously, the slavery issue had been the central focus for the Republican party. But after secession, the prosecution of the war and the maintenance of the Union became (for the moment, at least) dominant. A state-centered view of citizenship was not entirely compatible with the positions that states had no right to leave the Union and that support for the Confederate cause was treason.

It was against this background that Attorney General Edward Bates analyzed the status of free blacks in an opinion issued on November 29, 1862.[47] The question was the same as that which Wirt had analyzed in 1821. Bates rejected the state-centered view of citizenship; instead, he declared that national citizenship was solely a matter of federal law and that all citizens of the nation were also citizens of the respective states in which they were domiciled.[48] Further, Bates concluded that all native-born free blacks were citizens of the United States, characterizing the contrary conclusion of the majority in *Dred Scott* as *"dehors the record* [i.e., dictum] and of no authority as a judicial decision."[49]

Taken alone, these conclusions might have formed the basis for a claim that states were under an obligation to grant free blacks a variety of basic rights. But another prominent feature of the opinion was its rejection of the tangible rights theory of citizenship. Bates noted that white, native-born infants and females were considered citizens despite the fact that they possessed few if any of the rights normally associated with that status;[50] he also observed that even those who were sold into involuntary servitude as a punishment for crime retained their citizenship.[51] Thus, he reasoned, "I can hardly comprehend the thought of the absolute incompatibility of degradation and citizenship."[52] Drawing on authorities such as Kent and Blackstone, Bates espoused a quite different definition of citizenship:

> In my opinion, the Constitution uses the word citizen only to express the political quality of the individual in his relations to the nation; to declare that he is a member of the body politic, and bound to it by the reciprocal obligation of allegiance on the one side and protection on the other.[53]

He explicitly concluded that this right to "protection" was not inconsistent with the denial of other important rights.[54] The status that Bates posited for blacks was primarily of symbolic importance.

Even with its limited scope, Bates's opinion was not universally accepted by Republicans. As late as 1864, its premises were questioned by Republican senators such as John Henderson of Missouri and Peter Van Winkle of West Virginia.[55] Nonetheless, the fact that a Republican administration openly embraced even a narrowly defined black citizenship constituted an important advance for free blacks.

Congressional voting patterns during 1864 suggest that as the war progressed, black suffrage also gained increasing support within the Republican party. In the Thirty-eighth Congress, the issue first emerged in the discussions of the bill for the organization of the Montana Territory. As initially passed by the House of Representatives and reported from committee in the Senate, the bill provided that in territorial elections the franchise should be limited to white male inhabitants.[56] On the Senate floor, however, Morton S. Wilkinson of Minnesota moved to amend the bill to enfranchise "every free male citizen and those who have declared their intention to become such."[57] Obviously, the aim was to eliminate the color barrier to voting in the territory.

Despite its clarity of purpose, the actual impact of the Wilkinson amendment was somewhat uncertain. Under its terms, the proposal would have limited suffrage to citizens and those eligible to achieve that status. Under the Bates opinion, this requirement would not exclude blacks, but the inconsistency of Bates's view with that of Taney in *Dred Scott* remained a problem. If *Dred Scott* was still good law, the Wilkinson amendment would have had no practical effect.

Initially, Democrat Reverdy Johnson of Maryland seemed to concede the citizenship issue, opposing Wilkinson because "the effect of the amendment . . . is to admit to the elective franchise in the proposed Territory black men as well as white."[58] Later Johnson revised his position, arguing that the *Dred Scott* decision had settled the question of black citizenship and that therefore the Wilkinson amendment "will not accomplish his purpose."[59] Even so, Johnson and other Democrats continued to oppose the amendment, contending that it would create uncertainty regarding the rights of blacks and that even the possibility that nonwhites would be allowed to vote was distasteful.[60]

Notwithstanding the verbal fencing over citizenship, the Wilkinson proposal was clearly understood to be a test of sentiment on the suffrage question. The amendment was adopted by a vote of 22 to 17.[61] The bill as a whole then passed by a 29 to 8 margin;[62] the nays were a protest against the recognition of the principle that free blacks should be entitled to vote.[63] Both houses then agreed to a conference to resolve the differences between the two versions of the Montana bill.

The first resolution reached by the conference committee embodied the Senate version of the suffrage provision. The House, however, refused to accept this report; after a motion to table failed on a tie vote,[64] the conference report was defeated 85 to 54.[65] By a 75 to 67 margin, the House then instructed its conferees not to accept any version that enfranchised blacks.[66] Faced with such intransigence, a majority of Senate Republicans reluctantly retreated; on a vote of 26 to 13, the upper house passed a Montana bill which, while not explicitly mentioning race, left blacks unenfranchised by reference to the requirements for voting in the Idaho territorial bill.[67]

A later attempt to provide for impartial suffrage in the District of Columbia met a similar fate. When a bill seeking to change the voter registration laws in the District reached the Senate floor, Charles Sumner attempted to attach a proviso "that there shall be no exclusion of any person from the register on account of color."[68] James Harlan of Iowa moved to limit the Sumner proviso to those blacks who had served in the armed forces. This alteration carried easily by a vote of 26 to 12.[69] As amended, the Sumner proviso was initially adopted without a roll-call vote;[70] however, on a later vote it was defeated by a 20 to 18 margin.[71]

A number of points emerge clearly from the Montana and District of Columbia discussions. First, despite the ultimate defeat of black suffrage in both cases, a substantial majority of Republicans in Congress supported the basic principle that at least some blacks should have access to the ballot. In the Senate vote on Montana, twenty-two of the thirty-one Republicans voting backed the Wilkinson amendment; in the House of Representatives, fifty-four Republicans supported the initial conference committee report, and only twenty voted against it. Similarly, when the issue was raised in the District of Columbia context, Republican senators approved the modified Sumner proposal by a margin of 18 to 10; moreover, five senators who had voted in favor of black suffrage for Montana were absent for the District of Columbia vote.

The Republican majority failed in their efforts because the more conservative party members were able to form an effective coalition with the minority Democrats to block action granting black suffrage. The potentiality of such a coalition gave conservative Republicans an influence on policy disproportionate to their numbers. In general, only policies that were acceptable to a substantial number of these conservatives had a chance of being adopted by Congress as a whole.

Moreover, even those who might favor enfranchising blacks in principle were at times hesitant because of political concerns. Lyman Trumbull emphasized the political dangers inherent in embracing the concept of black suffrage, arguing that "you give men who are really opposed to the Government something to go to the people upon, and get up divisions and distractions, when we want no divisions."[72] The New York Times echoed this theme, asserting that

> the untimely and unseemly zeal with which [black suffrage] is urged is only calculated to excite dissatisfaction with emancipation. Nothing is surer to produce against a cause than an attempt to carry it beyond its proper scope.[73]

Finally, extraneous issues sometimes reduced the support for specific black-suffrage measures. The debate on Sumner's District of Columbia proposal provides a dramatic example. Lot Morrill of Maine and James Grimes of Iowa had supported enfranchising blacks in Montana and had announced that they also favored the same principle in the District of Columbia. Both Morrill and Grimes, however, believed that the registration bill before the Senate was an inappropriate vehicle for making such a significant change in voting requirements; they preferred to have the issue await consideration of the comprehensive restructuring of the

District of Columbia charter, which had been reported from Morrill's District of Columbia Committee.[74] The negative votes of these two senators provided the margin by which the Sumner amendment to the registration bill was defeated.

Analogous factors combined to deal the proponents of black suffrage an overwhelming defeat during the consideration of the Wade-Davis Reconstruction Bill.[75] The Wade-Davis Bill was the centerpiece of a congressional effort to gain control of the Reconstruction process during the Civil War. In December 1863, President Lincoln had outlined the conditions he viewed as necessary and sufficient for the restoration of the rights of conquered Confederate states. Initially, Lincoln's plan— which did not require black suffrage—was supported by many Republicans. As the program was implemented in Louisiana and Arkansas in 1864, however, opposition from within the party began to mount. The Wade-Davis Bill embodied the plan of the dissident Republicans.

The debate over the Wade-Davis Bill focused on two key issues: the stringency of the conditions to be imposed on the ex-Confederate states and the question of whether Congress or the president would control the Reconstruction process. In the form that the bill passed the House of Representatives, no provision was made for the imposition of black suffrage on the former Confederate states. The Senate Committee on Territories voted to add a clause enfranchising blacks. By the time the bill reached the Senate floor, however, it had become clear that the addition of such a provision would probably doom the measure. Even radicals such as Benjamin F. Wade of Ohio and John P. Hale of New Hampshire found it necessary to "waive . . . conscientious scruples and go for expediency" by opposing the black-suffrage requirement.[76] The amendment was defeated by a vote of 32 to 5.[77] Thus the Thirty-eighth Congress failed to take any significant action to expand the right of blacks to vote.

Despite these setbacks, one should not underestimate the shift that the Civil War generated in the Republican attitude toward free blacks. Before 1861 both the citizenship and suffrage issues were highly controversial within the party. By the end of 1865, in contrast, both black citizenship and black suffrage were openly espoused by most party leaders. Although it is apparent that the use of blacks in the military was of some importance to this shift in opinion,[78] the causes of the change in attitude have never been fully explored. But for whatever reason, a new consensus on black rights was emerging among Republican legislators.

An analysis of referenda on state constitutional amendments dealing with the suffrage issue shows this clearly. For example, in Wisconsin 54.67 percent of the voters supported the Republican candidate for governor, whereas only 46.72 percent voted for the black-suffrage amendment. Assuming (logically, given the politics of the time) that virtually all of those who supported black suffrage were Republicans, these figures indicate that *over 80 percent* of the Republicans voting supported enfranchising blacks. Similar voting patterns emerged in both Minnesota and Connecticut.[79] Thus, while a majority of the electorate as a whole was anti–black suffrage, most *Republicans* were in favor of the concept.

At the same time, however, the failure of black-suffrage proposals during the latter stages of the Civil War reflected a dynamic that was to recur repeatedly during the early Reconstruction era. Majority support among Republicans was not enough to carry civil rights measures in Congress; taken together with solid Democratic opposition, even a relatively small number of Republican defections could doom federal initiatives. Conservative Republicans would consistently exercise an influence on policy that was out of proportion to their numerical strength.

Moreover, virtually all Republicans felt constrained by traditional American conceptions of the role of the federal government in society. Until nearly the end of the Civil War, there was no thought of displacing the predominant role of the state governments in the protection and definition of rights; instead, proposals were generally limited to those narrow areas in which the federal government had plenary authority either because of the war power or because no state governments existed. The Thirteenth Amendment was the first break with this pattern.

2
The Coming of
the Thirteenth Amendment

THE FEDERAL GOVERNMENT AND SLAVERY
DURING THE EARLY WAR YEARS

With the secession of the southern states and the abandonment of the federal legislature by their representatives, the Republican party dominated the Thirty-seventh Congress.[1] Given the ideological origins of republicanism, one might have expected immediate, decisive federal action against slavery. Yet such action was not forthcoming; indeed, in an effort to forestall civil war during the final days of the Thirty-sixth Congress, a number of Republicans supported a constitutional amendment that would have forever guaranteed to the states the right to maintain slavery within their borders.[2] Once secession became an unalterable fact, Republicans were eager to portray the Civil War as a struggle for the Union rather than an armed campaign against slavery. Thus in 1861 Congress did not confront the issue of emancipation directly. A Confiscation Act was passed in that year, depriving masters of the right to the labor of slaves used in the rebellion. However, that act studiously avoided any specific attempt to change the legal status of confiscated slaves.

The year 1862 saw far more vigorous federal action. Congress attacked slavery on two fronts. First, slavery was abolished in areas that had historically been under federal control. In April, compensated emancipation was decreed in the District of Columbia, and slavery was outlawed in the federal territories. Although the latter was clearly inconsistent with the majority opinion in *Dred Scott*, neither action interfered with the internal institutions of any state. Thus, the basic structure of federalism was not affected.

The potential implications of the assault on slavery in the rebellious states were far greater. In July, Congress adopted the Confiscation Act of 1862, which provided that three classes of erstwhile slaves were "forever free": those who had escaped from rebel masters to the Union lines, those who had been captured from or abandoned by rebels, and those who were found in places occupied by Union armies. Even more significantly, on September 22 President Lincoln issued the preliminary Emancipation Proclamation, which provided that all slaves held in areas still in rebellion on January 1, 1863, were to be "thenceforward, and forever free." On January 1, he finalized the proclamation.

The second Confiscation Act and the Emancipation Proclamation injected federal power directly into local affairs whose oversight belonged to the states. Both measures could therefore be viewed as fundamentally inconsistent with the basic structure of antebellum federalism. At the same time, however, the assumptions that undergirded the emancipation measures of 1862 were inherently self-limiting. The source of authority justifying federal intervention was not a general right to protect the rights of those within the borders of the nation, but rather the war power. In theory, once the Civil War was concluded, the way remained open for a return to the antebellum division of governmental power. It was only during the next Congress that such a possibility was finally laid to rest.

THE DRAFTING OF THE THIRTEENTH AMENDMENT

Despite some setbacks in the Midwest in the elections of 1862—setbacks often attributed to Democratic attacks on the race issue[3]— Republicans in the Thirty-eighth Congress determined to press for a final solution to the slavery problem. Some radical Republicans adopted a position that before the war had been almost universally rejected by mainstream politicians. They argued that Congress possessed authority under the Constitution to abolish slavery by statute. The views of this group were embodied in a bill introduced on December 14, 1863, by Cong. Owen Lovejoy of Illinois, which relied on the Declaration of Independence as a source of power to require emancipation even in loyal slave states.[4] Other radicals relied on the war power for the requisite authority.[5]

The statutory solution had the advantage of relative simplicity. A constitutional amendment would have to be proposed by a two-thirds majority from each house of Congress and ratified by three-quarters of the states. Republicans held less than the requisite majority in the House of Representatives. Moreover, under the proposition that the states of the Confederacy had no constitutional authority to secede, the ratification process would require that these states also approve the proposal. Proceeding by statute would avoid these problems.

However, the more conservative Republicans firmly rejected the constitutional philosophy behind the statutory solution. For example, in introducing the resolution that was later to become the Thirteenth Amendment in the Senate, Lyman Trumbull specifically addressed the war power argument:

Some . . . say that we may pass an act of Congress to abolish slavery altogether. . . . I am as anxious to get rid of slavery as any person; but has Congress authority to abolish slavery everywhere?
. . . .
It is a convenience [for prosecution of the war] some will say. Sir, it is not because a measure would be convenient that Congress has authority to adopt it. The measure must be appropriate and needful to carry into effect some granted power, or we have no authority to adopt it.[6]

John B. Henderson of Missouri echoed similar sentiments, noting the clear lack of congressional authority to abolish slavery in the loyal states and bemoaning the difficulties inherent in proceeding by constitutional amendment.[7]

Faced with such opposition, no statute had a chance of passage; if slavery was to be abolished throughout the nation, a constitutional amendment would be necessary. Thus, on the same day that Lovejoy proposed his antislavery bill, James M. Ashley of Ohio[8] and James F. Wilson of Iowa[9] each introduced emancipation amendments in the House. One month later, Henderson introduced a similar measure in the Senate.[10] In February 1864, Charles Sumner proposed an antislavery amendment that was phrased somewhat differently than those of Ashley, Wilson, and Henderson.[11]

In pressing for constitutionally mandated emancipation, Republicans relied primarily on two lines of argument. The first was a moral attack on the institution of slavery. As floor manager of the amendment in the House of Representatives, Ashley quoted Abraham Lincoln's familiar statement that *"if slavery is not wrong, nothing is wrong."*[12] Isaac M. Arnold of Illinois aptly summarized the Republican position by contending that adoption of the proposed constitutional amendment would truly make the United States *"the home of the free."*[13]

At least equally prominent were Republican claims that the constitutional amendment was an important peace measure. For example, Sen. Henry Anthony of Rhode Island claimed that emancipation would remove the "disloyal cause of the troubles which afflict the land."[14] Reporting the proposed amendment from the Senate Judiciary Committee, Lyman Trumbull expressed similar hopes, asserting that "all the causes of our troubles, and of the distress, desolation and death which have grown out of this atrocious rebellion . . . sprung from slavery" and that "this measure will secure to us future peace."[15]

The reference to *"future peace"* was a crucial element of the Republican argument. Obviously, Republicans could not claim that emancipation would settle the Civil War that was raging in 1864; indeed, the proposed amendment would have no impact in the disloyal states until the armed struggle was pressed to a successful conclusion. Their point was that permanent abolition of slavery was required to prevent the eruption of a new conflict at some future date. Henry Wilson of Massachusetts put the argument succinctly, maintaining that "so long as slavery shall live, it will infuse its deadly poison into the southern brain, heart and soul."[16] In essence, Republicans saw the constitutional amendment as a necessary first step in the process of reconstructing the Union.

In evaluating this argument, we must recognize that during the debate Republican references to "slavery" included not only the institution itself but also the "slave power." In the Republican view, the slave power was composed of the slaveholders as a class who, it was argued, had dominated both national politics and the governments of the slave states in the antebellum era. Republicans contended that slaveholders had used their power to preserve a hierarchical society in their own states and to improperly deny the opponents of slavery their rights as American citizens.[17] The close linkage between slavery and the slave power in the Republican mind is illustrated by the remarks of Cong. William D. Kelley of Pennsylvania:

> It was slavery that denied the right of asylum to the beautiful and accomplished daughter of Samuel Hoar, of Massachusetts, and expelled that venerable scholar, jurist and statesman from the limits of South Carolina, who went to argue a great cause in her courts. It was slavery that did not deny the right of asylum to William Lloyd Garrison, but offered $20,000 to the man who would kidnap him and carry him to that State [to be tortured]. . . . It was slavery that by threats and demonstrations of violence twice banished that friend of the Union and of mankind, George Thompson, from the limits of our country.[18]

In his argument Kelley used the term "slavery" as a synonym for the slave power. From the Republican perspective, the slave power was the generative force behind the secession movement; they believed, as Sen. Daniel Clark of New Hampshire contended, that "this rebellion is slavery in arms."[19] By striking at slavery, Republicans hoped not only to destroy the hated institution itself but also to remove the underpinnings of slave power authority and thus forestall future rebellions.

By 1864 all Republicans accepted the force of these arguments. In the Thirty-eighth Congress, however, mere unanimity among Republicans was insufficient to secure passage of a constitutional amendment. The party had the necessary two-thirds majority in the Senate, but the

Democrats had enough votes to block an amendment in the House of Representatives. The fate of the antislavery proposal thus depended on the ability of Republicans to convince a substantial number of Democrats to give their support.

Like its Republican counterpart, the Democratic party of 1864 was not a monolith. Its leaders ranged widely in their allegiances: For example, Sen. Reverdy Johnson of Maryland was an antislavery War Democrat, while Cong. Fernando Wood of New York was a militant Peace Democrat who defended slavery as a positive good.[20] Although most were more moderate than Wood, a large majority of congressional Democrats joined him in resisting the proffered amendments.

Anti-amendment Democrats attacked the Republican proposals from a variety of angles. Some, such as Alexander M. Coffroth of Pennsylvania and Andrew J. Rogers of New Jersey, claimed that it was unfair to destroy the property rights of citizens of loyal states.[21] Another common contention was that the time was not ripe for a profound change in the American system of government. This argument took two forms. Some suggested that consideration of the slavery question should await calmer times; as Daniel W. Voorhees of Indiana put it, "such an act should not be consummated amid the fiery passions and vehement hates engendered by civil war. It should be the work of calmness and of peace."[22] Other Democrats agreed with Charles A. Eldridge of Wisconsin, who argued that the adoption of an emancipation amendment would prolong the war by stiffening the resistance of southern slaveholders:

[Passage of the amendment] will furnish the rebel leaders another argument by which to win the doubting and to arouse the lukewarm; it will aid them in raising other armies to fight against the Union; it will enable them to prolong this bloody and terrible war by embittering and intensifying the hatred of these people against the abolitionized North.[23]

The most powerful Democratic arguments, often intertwined, were based on claims that the proposed constitutional change was inimical to both the proper conceptions of race relations and the basic structure of American federalism. On the race relations issue, some joined Wood in taking the position that the maintenance of slavery per se was desirable.[24] Democrats who were less willing to adopt an explicitly proslavery stance based their objections on the fear that the amendment would lead to black citizenship and suffrage—rights that Joseph K. Edgerton of Indiana argued were "logically involved in the proposed amendment."[25] William S. Holman of Indiana suggested that the emancipation amendment itself would make blacks citizens *and* grant them the right to vote.[26] By contrast, Samuel S. Cox of Ohio seemed to concede that emancipation alone would not raise the freed slave to the level of citizen or elector, yet he feared that liberation was only a first step:

> If we may change the relation of the blacks to the whites in one respect, may we not in another? May we not change the Constitution to give them suffrage in States in spite of all State laws to the contrary? Must we not amend the Constitution to allow the importation of free blacks into States like Illinois and Indiana? Must we not declare all State laws based on their political inequality with the white races null and void?[27]

Cox's argument combined the specter of black equality with concerns about federalism. The concept of federalism itself inspired two arguments against the Republican proposal. Many Democrats contended that the power to amend contained in Article V was not broad enough to encompass an emancipation amendment. Chilton A. White of Ohio claimed that

> the very term "amendment" is itself a word of limitation. [The proposed amendment] is not a change, an alteration, a modification, an enlargement, or a diminution of any provision already existing in the Constitution, but it is a supplement added to the Constitution—a separate, independent, distinct, substantive clause, disconnected with any grant or delegation of power written down in the Constitution.[28]

The argument of George H. Pendleton of Ohio was more focused: "You cannot, under the power of amendment, contravene the letter and spirit of the Constitution; . . . you cannot subvert republicanism; . . . you cannot destroy the liberty of the States; . . . you cannot decide the status of the citizens of the States."[29]

Cox and other Democrats were willing to concede that Congress possessed the power to adopt an emancipation amendment, but they argued that its adoption would lead to undesirable consolidation of authority in the government. Holman warned that the proposal would grant Congress the authority "to invade any state to enforce the freedom of the African in war or peace."[30] Robert Mallory of Kentucky believed that emancipation was a step onto a slippery slope of centralization: "Give up our right to have slavery if we choose . . . and in what right are we secure? One after another will be usurped by the President and Congress, until all State rights will be gone."[31]

Despite these arguments, the overwhelming Republican majority in the Senate assured the passage of the emancipation amendment. On

April 8, 1864, the proposal was approved by a vote of 38 to 6. Every Republican present supported the amendment, as did Democrats Johnson and James W. Nesmith of Oregon.[32] By contrast, in the House of Representatives a protracted political struggle ensued. As already noted, the Republican strength in the House fell well short of the two-thirds majority required for passage of a constitutional amendment. The antislavery proposal could therefore succeed only if a substantial number of Democratic votes could be attracted. When the initial ballot was taken on June 15, 1864, the Republican effort to attract crossover support was revealed as an almost total failure; only four Democrats—Joseph Bailey of Pennsylvania, Ezra Wheeler of Wisconsin, and John A. Griswold and Moses F. Odell of New York—voted for the amendment. The 93 to 65 tally was thirteen votes short of the constitutionally mandated requirement for passage.[33]

The battle was far from over, however. When it became clear that the amendment would not win the necessary votes in the House of Representatives, James Ashley switched his vote from "yea" to "nay." This parliamentary maneuver left him free to move for reconsideration when the Thirty-eighth Congress reconvened for its second session in 1865. By the time Ashley made this motion in January of that year, a number of factors had intervened to change the political dynamic, the most important of which was the overwhelming Republican victory in the national elections of 1864. Not only was Lincoln reelected, but it was guaranteed that in the upcoming Thirty-ninth Congress, Republicans would have the necessary votes to pass the emancipation proposal. Democratic resistance was therefore futile; moreover, as Democrat Anson Herrick of New York pointed out, opposition would allow Republicans to portray the Democratic party in future elections as proslavery.[34] In the free states, such a label would be extremely damaging.

Other factors included the moves by Maryland and Missouri to abolish slavery by state action. This not only increased the antislavery momentum generally but also reduced the force of the argument that adoption of a federal emancipation amendment would unfairly take the property of some citizens of loyal states. Finally, the Lincoln administration engaged in an intense lobbying effort to convince wavering Democrats to support the proposed amendment, or at the very least to abstain.[35] At times the effort involved complex political maneuvers. The case of Andrew Jackson Rogers—first term Democrat from New Jersey—provides an illuminating example.

Among a group of men not known for their racial tolerance, Rogers stands out for the violence of the verbal abuse that he heaped on blacks from the floor of the House. Indeed, he was so vituperative that Republicans often goaded him to speak at length, believing that Rogers's remarks would supply them with political ammunition. Later, during the Thirty-ninth Congress, Rogers would "thank god" that he had never voted for the Thirteenth Amendment.[36] Indeed, he both voted against the proposal the first time it was brought before the House of Representatives and spoke strongly against Ashley's motion to reconsider. Yet when the vote was retaken during the second session of the Thirty-eighth Congress, Rogers absented himself from the floor. How does one account for such behavior?

The probable answer lies in Rogers's close connection with the Camden and Amboy Railroad Company. In the mid-1860s, the Camden and Amboy had a monopoly on railroad transportation between New York and Philadelphia. During the first session of the Thirty-eighth Congress, the House of Representatives had passed a bill which would have opened the route to competition from the rival Raritan and Delaware Bay Company. In return for aid in blocking the bill in the Senate, the Camden and Amboy offered to use its influence to induce Democrats to either vote for the Thirteenth Amendment or abstain when the vote was taken.[37] Rogers later denied any wrongdoing; the facts remain, however, that he was not present for the vote and that the Senate never considered the railroad bill, despite the strenuous efforts of its champion, Charles Sumner.

Rogers was only one of a number of targets of administration lobbying—part of an effort that provided the margin of victory for the constitutional amendment. When the vote was taken on January 31, eleven Democrats who had opposed the constitutional change in 1864 now voted in favor, and seven others did not vote at all. These shifts in position were sufficient to change the ultimate result. The margin was 119 to 56; with two votes to spare, the antislavery amendment thus passed Congress.[38]

THE CONTEMPORARY UNDERSTANDING
OF THE AMENDMENT

As adopted by Congress, the language of the Thirteenth Amendment is deceptively simple. The text reads:

> Section One. Neither slavery nor involuntary servitude, except as a punishment for crime whereof the party shall have been duly convicted, shall exist within the United States or any place subject to their jurisdiction.
> Section Two. Congress shall have the power to enforce this article by appropriate legislation.

The apparent simplicity of the phraseology conceals formidable difficulties of interpretation. Foremost among these are two related questions. The first is whether section one by its terms guarantees any
rights beyond the freedom from physical restraint. The second is the
scope of authority granted to Congress by section two.[39]

The congressional debates on the Thirteenth Amendment provide
only fragmentary evidence regarding the intent of the drafters on these
points. Given the context of the debates, the dearth of evidence is not
terribly surprising. The basic issues before Congress were whether the
master/slave relationship should be outlawed in the United States and
whether the federal government was the appropriate agency to decree
this abolition. Resolution of these issues did not require a definition of
the nature of slavery in the abstract or a description of the difference
between "slavery" and "freedom" at the margins. The existing evidence does suggest some difference of opinion among the drafters. This
evidence is derived from three sources: the language of the amendment, the explanations of supporters, and the related contemporary
discussions of the slavery issues.

The Language of the Amendment

The argument based on the language of the amendment focuses on the
fact that section one prohibits only slavery and involuntary servitude
and does not (at least on its face) guarantee any additional rights. The
language was discussed in the Senate after Charles Sumner of Massachusetts moved to amend the proposal, to wit:

> All persons are equal before the law, so that no person can hold an-
> other as slave; and the Congress shall have power to make all laws
> necessary and proper to carry this declaration into effect every-
> where within the United States and the jurisdiction thereof.

The proposed alteration was rejected without even a vote. The rationale
for the rejection was expressed clearly by Jacob Howard of Michigan, a
member of the Senate Judiciary Committee that had drafted the Thirteenth Amendment:

> I should like [Senator Sumner], if he is able, to state what effect
> [his proposal] would have in law in a court of justice. What signif-
> icance is given to the phrase "equal" . . . before the law in a
> common-law court? It is not known at all.
>   Besides the proposition speaks of all men being equal. I suppose
> before the law a woman would be equal to a man, a woman would
> be as free as a man. A woman would be equal to her husband and as
> free as her husband before the law. . . .

I prefer to . . . go back to the old Anglo-Saxon language employed by our fathers in the ordinance of 1787, an expression which has been adjudicated upon repeatedly, which is perfectly understood both by the public and by judicial tribunals. . . . I think it is well understood, well comprehended by the people of the United States, and that no court of justice, no magistrate, no person, old or young, can misapprehend the meaning and effect of that clear, brief and comprehensive clause.[40]

These remarks suggest that the proposal as adopted was intended to embody the prohibition on slavery contained in the Northwest Ordinance—no more and no less. Yet the language from that ordinance had been incorporated into a number of state constitutions and had not been viewed as an obstacle to the inclusion of the grossest restrictions on the rights of free blacks. As late as 1857, for example, the state of Oregon had adopted a constitution which banned slavery in language almost identical to that of the Thirteenth Amendment but which also barred free blacks from making contracts, holding property, or even entering the state.[41] A black-exclusion provision was enforced in Illinois—another free state—as late as 1864.[42] On this basis, one might easily conclude that the "well understood, well comprehended . . . meaning" of the amendment's language was very narrow indeed.

This view might be fortified by reference to the legal status of manumitted blacks in the South immediately before the Civil War. Although entitled to the basic right to protection of the law, they were rarely accorded any of the other rights that demonstrate full participation in society. The situation was aptly described by the Georgia Supreme Court in *Bryan v. Walton*:

The *status* of the African in Georgia, whether bond or free, is such that he has no civil, social or political rights or capacity, whatever, except such as are bestowed on him by Statute; that he can neither contract, nor be contracted with; that the free negro can act only by and through his guardian; that he is in a state of perpetual pupilage or wardship; and that this condition he can never change by his own volition. . . . The act of manumission confers no other right but that of freedom from the dominion of the master, and the limited liberty of locomotion.[43]

The leading southern treatise on the subject disagreed with the *Walton* court's reasoning, arguing that absent contrary statutory prohibitions, "free persons of color . . . may make contracts, and dispose of their estates by will." The same document, however, also noted that in general slave states had severely restricted the rights of free blacks legislatively:

> Public policy has made it necessary for the slaveholding States, by statute, to impose . . . restrictions upon free persons of color. They have been forced to extend over them their patrol and police regulations, to deny to them the privilege of bearing arms, to require of them the selection of a guardian, who shall stand as patron, and contract for them; to restrain their acquisition of negro slaves as property; to place them on the same footing with slaves as to their intercourse with white citizens; such as purchasing spirituous liquors, &c. These various restrictions . . . place the free negro but little above the slave as to civil privileges.[44]

Of course, in the free states the statutes that abolished slavery in the early nineteenth century had also clothed the freed blacks with fundamental civil rights.[45] The point is that Howard and the other drafters of the Thirteenth Amendment must have been aware of regimes in which freed slaves were denied almost all rights except that of freedom *simpliciter*.

The difficulty with using these arguments as evidence of intent is that in his response to Sumner, Howard was not primarily interested in describing the rights that would be protected by the antislavery amendment. Instead, he was concerned with preserving the specific language that had been adopted by the Senate Judiciary Committee. This phrasing had particular significance because it was drawn from the Northwest Ordinance. For many Republicans, the ordinance had almost mystical significance; they viewed it as embodying the true antislavery sentiments of the framers of the Constitution, unsullied by the proslavery compromises made to win approval for the Constitution as a whole.[46] Moreover, as Howard noted, the committee language was "peculiarly near and dear" to the residents of the states that had been created from the Northwest Territory.[47] By contrast, the substitute language was especially offensive because it was not even American in origin; in typical fashion, Sumner traced his proposal to the French Declaration of Rights.[48] Thus, although this colloquy is suggestive, it is not dispositive on the question of the intended scope of the Thirteenth Amendment.

Discussions by Supporters

Generally focusing on the issues of citizenship and suffrage, some supporters of the antislavery proposal evinced an extremely narrow view of its scope. Pro-emancipation Democrat George H. Yeaman of Kentucky, for example, argued that passage of the amendment would leave Democrats free to ''go before the country on the questions . . . of raising the negro to citizenship and suffrage contrary to State law.''[49] Republican Peter Van Winkle of West Virginia also voiced his opposition to the concept of black citizenship.[50] John Henderson of Missouri expressed a similar understanding of the emancipation amendment in his statement that the proposal gave to an erstwhile slave ''no right except his freedom, and [left] the rest to the States.'' Henderson was referring specifically to citizenship and suffrage.[51]

In one sense, these opinions might be regarded as a self-selected sample. Yeaman, Van Winkle, and their associates were on the conservative edge of the coalition that generated the Thirteenth Amendment; hence, they might well be expected to hold more narrow views of its scope than other members of the coalition. But in another sense, the views of the Yeaman/Van Winkle group were particularly crucial. It was this group that the pro-emancipation forces had to convince in order to have the amendment adopted. They were thus in a position to demand the narrowest possible interpretation as a condition for their support. Even though the conservative emancipationists did not formally make such a demand, it is vital to recognize that any broader understanding of the Thirteenth Amendment would have led to the defeat of the proposal in Congress.

Regardless, some supporters seemed to take that broader view. In assessing the opinions of these Republicans, one must distinguish carefully between the effect of the amendment itself and its expected incidental impact on southern society. As already noted, by destroying the institution of slavery, Republicans hoped also to break the grip of the slave power. Thus James Ashley of Ohio claimed that slavery

> has for many years defied the Government and trampled upon the national Constitution, by kidnapping, imprisoning, mobbing and murdering white citizens of the United States guilty of no offense except protesting against its terrible crimes. It has silenced every free pulpit within its control, and debauched thousands which ought to have been independent. It has denied the masses of poor white children within its power the privilege of free schools, and made free speech and a free press impossible within its domain.[52]

In this he was speaking metaphorically of the slave power rather than about slavery itself.

At the same time, some Republicans did believe that emancipation per se would vest all blacks with important basic rights. James Harlan of Iowa and E. C. Ingersoll of Illinois took very similar positions on this point. Harlan listed as ''incidents'' of slavery the prohibition of family relationships and the denial of the rights to acquire and hold property, to be a party and witness in court, and to freedom of speech and press.[53] Ingersoll asserted that the amendment

> will secure to the oppressed slave his natural and God-given rights. I believe that the black man has certain inalienable rights, which are as sacred in the sight of Heaven as those of any other race. I believe he has a right to live, and live in a state of freedom. He has a right to breathe the free air and enjoy God's free sunshine. He has a right to till the soil, to earn his bread by sweat of his brow, and enjoy the rewards of his own labor. He has a right to the endearment and enjoyment of family ties.[54]

In short, the congressional discussions of the Thirteenth Amendment are somewhat unclear regarding its intended scope. The same ambiguity is reflected in related materials as well.

Related Activity in the States

Indiana. The actions of the Indiana legislature in 1865 point to a limited interpretation of the Thirteenth Amendment. The same legislative session that ratified the proposed constitutional amendment also affirmatively decided to retain (at least in large measure) the state's ban on black testimony in courts.[55] Apparently, the state legislature saw no inconsistency between these actions. The legislators could hardly have taken such a position if they had believed that the abolition of slavery automatically vested the freed blacks with basic rights.

Although obviously important, the significance of these concurrent votes should not be overstated. Indiana was one of the most racist of the free states; the views of its state legislature—Republican-controlled or not—on the meaning of the Thirteenth Amendment may not have been typical of those of more advanced Republicans in other states. Neither did the decision to retain the black code necessarily reflect the opinions of the majority of Indiana Republicans; since the legislature still contained substantial numbers of Democrats who would generally oppose any liberalization of the rights of blacks, the defection of even a few Republicans would block such liberalization. Thus the Indiana action does not conclusively prove that the broad view of the Thirteenth Amendment was rejected by most of the proposal's supporters there or elsewhere.

Missouri and Maryland. Contemporary discussions in state constitutional conventions suggest that the narrow understanding of the Thirteenth Amendment was at least controversial. During the

Civil War, the two loyal states of Missouri and Maryland adopted constitutional amendments that abolished slavery. In both states, the evidence provided by the debates over the proposed amendments is somewhat equivocal on the issue of the rights the freed slaves would possess.

In Missouri, the question of what rights would be conferred automatically by emancipation proposals was never directly addressed. Much of the debate concerned the precise *form* of emancipation—whether abolition would be immediate or at some later date and whether the freed slaves would be subject to a period of mandatory apprenticeship. However, the implications of some of these discussions could be seen as supportive of a narrow reading of the Thirteenth Amendment. For example, while not adopting a provision for the deportation of the newly freed blacks, the members of the convention apparently saw no inconsistency between such a provision and the concept of emancipation.

At the same time, statements were frequently made that suggested that freedom would imply more than simply the dissolution of the master/servant relationship. One opponent of emancipation believed that freedom would probably confer citizenship automatically on the former slaves.[56] Some of the antislavery delegates were more specific. One stated that the freedman could acquire property, establish domestic relations, and enter into contracts. Another argued that the

> great leading distinction between slavery and freedom is that [even as an apprentice, an ex-slave] would have the right of serving in a court of justice, of acquiring and holding property of every description, goods, chattels, land and tenements; whatever he might acquire by labor, by gift or by descent would be his.[57]

The Maryland convention of 1864 addressed the issue more directly. At that gathering it was clearly understood by all delegates that slavery would be a central issue. Anticipating the success of the pro-emancipation forces, extreme negrophobes sought to append to the state bill of rights the following provision:

> Nothing in this article shall be construed to prevent the legislature from passing all such laws for the governance, regulation and disposition of the free colored population of this state as they deem necessary.[58]

Proponents of this motion contended that in the absence of the additional provision, the state government would not be allowed to discriminate against the freed slaves. They wished to ensure that the government could take all actions necessary to deal with the "problem" of freed slaves, including (but not limited to) the institution of an oppressive apprenticeship system such as that inaugurated for freed slaves by Nathaniel Banks during the reconstruction of Louisiana.[59]

The proposal was supported by some antislavery delegates. Moreover, those opposed to the addition to the bill of rights argued that emancipation would not deprive the legislature of the power to deal effectively with freed slaves. William T. Purnell took the position that abolition of slavery would do no more than simply sever the master/slave connection and that the erstwhile slaves would remain subject to the state's stringent laws regulating free blacks.[60]

Archibald Stirling took a more moderate view, holding that a post-emancipation legislature could pass any special laws not inconsistent with the freed slaves' "status as freedmen." Such legislation could include the establishment of an apprentice system "consistent with personal liberty," defined to include rights "to life, liberty, to protection of property [and] to appeal to the laws of the land." Implicit in this argument was the theory that possession of certain fundamental rights was essential to the status of being a freedman rather than a slave.[61]

In short, the evidence does not definitively establish the intentions of the drafters of the Thirteenth Amendment generally. Some supporters no doubt believed that the amendment would only abolish involuntary servitude per se without granting any additional rights to blacks. Others, however, took an opposing view, vesting the abolition of slavery with a broader significance. The question of which view was dominant in 1864 and early 1865 is simply not answerable; indeed, many of the backers of the amendment may not have even thought about the problem.

One point does seem clear. Given the closeness of the vote in the House of Representatives, the amendment could not have been adopted without the support of men like Yeaman who took the narrowest possible view of its significance. Put another way, an amendment that was clearly understood to go beyond the simple abolition of slavery could not have passed Congress. If this is accepted as the appropriate measure of the original understanding, then the Thirteenth Amendment should be construed narrowly.

In any event, the dispute over the proper understanding of the anti-slavery amendment crystallized at the federal level and divided the first session of the Thirty-ninth Congress when it convened in December 1865. Even before the Freedmen's Bureau Bill and the Civil Rights Bill were introduced, one finds many mainstream Republicans expressing the belief that the Thirteenth Amendment guaranteed freedmen natural rights. Such statements came not only from radicals such as Henry Wilson of Massachusetts but also from conservative moderates such as John Sherman of Ohio, William Stewart of Nevada, and Lyman Trumbull of Illinois.[62] They were opposed by Andrew Johnson and both pro- and anti-emancipation Democrats, as well as by a small number of Republicans, including Edgar Cowan of Pennsylvania and John Bingham of Ohio.[63] All of the opposition argued that the Thirteenth Amendment did no more than dissolve the master/slave relationship and that section two gave Congress no power to grant blacks any other rights. This dispute provided one of the major themes in the early Reconstruction era.

3

The Reconstruction Dynamic

THE NATURE OF THE ISSUES

By 1865 virtually all congressional Republicans believed that blacks should have the rights generally enjoyed by citizens, as well as the right to vote. The key question was one of federalism—what role the federal government should play in guaranteeing those rights—and was inextricably linked to the issue of Reconstruction. Indeed, in a very real sense Reconstruction was entirely a problem of federalism.

Republicans in 1865 generally contemplated federal action on civil rights only as an aspect of Reconstruction policy. They were admittedly concerned by unjust treatment of blacks in the Union states;[1] in fact, the *National Anti-Slavery Standard* proposed a constitutional amendment that would have barred "any distinction in Civil Rights and Privileges . . . on Account of Race, Color or Descent."[2] But such proposals for generally applicable federal action were rare. Republicans typically called only for federal action governing the ex-Confederate states; indeed, they justified their calls by reference to the unusual status of those states.[3]

In addressing the problem of Reconstruction, Republicans were faced with the task of drawing a balance between two conflicting pressures. On one hand, most wished for a speedy return of authority to the state governments of the defeated Confederacy; on the other, they wished to assure that the restored state governments would be in loyal hands and would adequately protect the interests of both white unionists and freedmen. The editorials of *Harper's Weekly*—an influential centrist Republican organ—reflected the tension between these goals. At one point the editors asserted that "it is desirable, upon every account, that there shall be as little delay as possible in intrusting the local government of the States to their own loyal inhabitants."[4] On another occasion, they noted that "the important point is not speedy reorganization, but sure reorganization. . . . [I]t is better that Virginia should be governed as a territory for half a century rather than that she should be recognized as a State by the spirit of State Sovereignty and caste that produced the rebellion."[5]

The task was further complicated by the Republicans' firm attachment to the basic structure of American federalism. From the time of the secession of the first state, the objective of the Republican party had been in fact reconstruction—not revolution or even a substantial alteration in the allocation of governmental authority. Republicans were strongly in favor of the Union, but theirs was not the Union of the 1980s, in which the federal government plays a dominant role in the lives of the citizenry. Instead, they conceptualized the Civil War as a struggle to restore each state to the position of prime responsibility and power that it had occupied in the antebellum era. The statement of John Sherman in 1863 is typical: "The main purpose [of the war] is, the preservation and perpetuity [of] the State governments and the national Government, with all the rights of each State intact, with all the rights of the national Government intact."[6] Of course, the prosecution of the war itself had a centralizing effect, with the federal government assuming powers undreamed of earlier. But this aggrandizement of national authority was always considered temporary, with the cessation of hostilities to be rapidly followed by a return to "normalcy"—the dominance of state governments in most local affairs.

Some commentators have downplayed the significance of this state-centered world view, arguing either that federalism was not a relevant concern in the formulation of Reconstruction policy[7] or, at the very least, that the Civil War had established the proposition that "Congress possessed plenary authority to protect [natural] rights in whatever manner it deemed appropriate."[8] The core of these arguments is the indisputable fact that Republicans viewed the war as having conclusively discredited the Confederate theory of state sovereignty.

In evaluating the meaning of the universal Republican rejection of state sovereignty, one must have a clear understanding of the precise concepts involved. Two points are particularly crucial. First, Republicans drew a sharp distinction between the erstwhile Confederate states and the states remaining loyal to the Union. Unlike Pres. Andrew Johnson, mainstream congressional Republicans believed that Congress retained broad authority over the affairs of the defeated states until the national legislature declared them once again fit to resume their rights and responsibilities as constituent members of the Union. To justify this conclusion, Republicans relied on the guaranty clause and on a variety of more general theories bearing such labels as "grasp of war," "state suicide," and "forfeited rights."[9] But all parties to the debate clearly recognized that in the congressional theory, the southern states stood in a different relationship to the federal government than did their northern counterparts. In the context of civil rights measures, the general concept of states' rights would become relevant only in those states that either had never attempted to leave the Union or had been restored to the status they had enjoyed in the antebellum era.

Second, one must carefully define the nature of the "heresy" that the Republicans found so repugnant. As Phillip S. Paludan has pointed out, there was no necessary inconsistency between a rejection of the southern view on state sovereignty and an acceptance of the notion that the national government should have only very limited powers.[10] For the key to the Confederate position was that the states were *exclusively* sovereign—that the federal government exercised authority only as an "agent" of the states. A number of important corollaries follow. First, the rights of a citizen in the commonly held territories (including the right to hold slaves) were a function of the law of the citizen's home state. Second, each state possessed authority to determine if a given federal action was constitutional and to secede from the Union if the federal government persisted in unconstitutional action. Finally, any allegiance a person owed to the United States was due only by virtue of the relationship of his state government to the federal authority, and the state government could therefore absolve the citizen from that allegiance.[11]

Although in some respects it actually led to greater centralization,[12] in general the southern theory obviously implied that most authority would remain with the states. But to reject this idea was not tantamount to endorsing the concept of a strong, centralized federal government. For the major competing antebellum analysis did not view all sovereignty as vested in the federal government. Instead, this analysis concluded that the sovereignty of the national entity was divided between the federal and state governments. An exchange in the Senate between James M. Mason of Virginia and Lyman Trumbull of Illinois on December 20, 1860, illustrates this point. Mason contended:

The State governments are as sovereign at this day as they were when they formed the Constitution of the United States; and being so, the State governments have the power of absolving their citizens from their obligations to the Federal compact which the State entered into; and when the State absolves its citizens from their obligation to the Federal compact . . . they become as completely foreign to this Government as France or England.

Trumbull responded:

I deny that the States are as sovereign as when they formed this Government. The States are sovereign as to their reserved rights; but the rights they surrendered up to the Federal Government do not now belong to the States. [It was agreed that the Constitution] should be the supreme law of the land, any law or constitution of [any] State notwithstanding. . . . Is that superior to the [State constitutions]? You have surrendered up that power, and you have no power to absolve yourselves from that allegiance.[13]

Clearly, Trumbull's position was not inconsistent with the view that the federal government possessed authority only over a very narrow range of issues. One could simply contend that "the rights . . . surrendered up to the Federal Government" were very limited and the reserved rights of the states quite broad. This approach would still differ from that of state sovereignty theorists on three key points. First, federal rather than state instrumentalities would have ultimate authority to determine whether particular federal actions were constitutional. Second, the federal government would have a paramount claim to the allegiance of the citizens of a state. Third, the states would not have the constitutional right to terminate their association with the federal union. It was these issues that formed the broad political framework for the Civil War.

The differences between the secessionist and unionist positions on state sovereignty should not be allowed to obscure the similarities in their respective views on the nature of federalism. In the antebellum era, all but the most radical of abolitionists agreed that each state government possessed the exclusive authority to protect the fundamental, natural rights of its own citizens. Occasionally one might find an argument that the federal Constitution guaranteed these rights in the abstract;[14] but even those who endorsed this position, such as John A. Bingham, agreed that the national government had no general power to enforce the guarantee.[15]

The Civil War wrought no great change in the attitude of Americans toward the possibility of being governed primarily by the federal government. Condemnations of the idea of centralization reverberated throughout the Reconstruction debate. For example, archradical Wendell Phillips declared, "I love State Rights; that doctrine is the cornerstone of individual liberty."[16] Similarly, the *Nation* described the "Lessons of War" in the following terms:

Our institutions of local freedom are but so many roots to feed and strengthen our common nationality. . . . [A] nation thus vitalized . . . cannot be compressed into a centralized power even under the stupendous weight of war. [The watchword is] sovereignty without centralization.[17]

In opposing a plan for federal action to prevent the spread of cholera the following year, the influential senator James W. Grimes of Iowa was even more explicit:

> During the prevalence of the [Civil War] we drew to ourselves here as the Federal Government authority which had been considered doubtful by all and denied by many of the statesmen of this country. That time, it seems to me, has ceased and ought to cease. Let us go back to the original condition of things, and allow the States to take care of themselves as they have been in the habit of taking care of themselves.[18]

Grimes's basic argument—that only the war power justified the interference of the federal government in the internal affairs of the states—was a common theme during the early Reconstruction era.

The corollary to the fear of centralization was a continuing emphasis on the constitutional rights of the state governments. At times, mainstream Republicans reverted to the antebellum theory of divided sovereignty. For example, in his annual message to the Illinois legislature in January 1865, Gov. Richard Yates (soon to be one of the most radical members of the Senate) declared:

> I am for unlimited state sovereignty in the true sense, in the sense that the State is to control all its municipal and local legislation and I would be the first to resist all attempts upon the part of the Federal Government to interpose tyrannical usurpation of power in controlling the legislation. The States are sovereign in every sense in which it is desirable they should have sovereignty.[19]

Adopting the same terminology, Wendell Phillips described his proposal to bar state discrimination on the basis of race as "a restriction on State Sovereignty."[20] Similarly, in the debate over the Civil Rights Act of 1866, Republican Thomas T. Davis of New York asserted:

> This Government is one of delegated powers, and . . . every law enacted is circumscribed by the limitation of the Constitution. The States have reserved all sovereignty and power which has not been expressly or impliedly granted to the Federal Government.[21]

Other Republicans distinguished sharply between state *sovereignty*, the political philosophy of the Confederate cause, and states' *rights*, an essential aspect of American federalism.[22] For example, the influential *Springfield Republican* contended that those who confuse the notion of states' rights with the southern doctrine of state sovereignty "only confess their own lack of brains."

It is well for the tranquility of the country and for the right direction of party politics that it should be considered a settled thing that the "states rights" recognized and guaranteed by the constitution are still sacred, and will be maintained as scrupulously as the authority of the federal government itself.[23]

In the same vein, in 1868 Oliver H. P. T. Morton asserted:

I am an inveterate enemy of the blood-stained doctrine of State sovereignty [but] I still recognize the doctrine of State rights. There are rights that belong to the States, secured by the same Constitution that secures the rights of [the federal] Government, and therefore they are equally sacred. The States have their rights recognized by the Constitution of the United States as clearly and distinctly as that Constitution builds up this Government; and to the same extent, by the same power that sustains this Government, those rights are to be sustained. . . . It was the abuse of the doctrine of States rights that led to the doctrine of State sovereignty; and it will be another abuse if we run to the other extreme, and say that the States have no rights which cannot be taken away by act of Congress.[24]

Other forces, however, worked against a model of Reconstruction that would have provided for a simple restoration of the Union in its pure antebellum form. The Civil War itself had created situations entirely outside the ambit of the mid-nineteenth-century theory of federalism. In the rebellious states the *only* wartime governments were those that were loyal to the Confederacy. When a state (or portion thereof) was conquered by the Union armies, that government perforce collapsed. Thus until a new framework could be constructed, the federal government was forced to become in effect the local government of an area that was in theory the responsibility of an existing state. Such an assumption of authority was inconceivable to mid-nineteenth-century political leaders.

While theoretically awkward, this quandary could have been dismissed as an anomaly, deriving from the unique emergency generated by the rebellion. With the ultimate victory of the Union forces, however, another serious problem loomed. The Republican defense of the war effort rested on the premise that the seceding states had no constitutional authority to leave the Union. This theory implied that the ex-Confederate states had the right to both govern themselves and be fully represented in the national legislature. Given the widespread popular support the rebellion had enjoyed in the South, the postwar governments of the southern states would doubtless have sought to recreate as closely as possible the political, economic, and social conditions of the antebellum era. The difficulty was that those conditions were inimical to the basic ideology of the Republican party.

One simple device to avoid this problem was suggested by radical elements in the Republican party. They argued that since states had no right to secede, by attempting to do so the adherents to the Confederacy had reduced themselves to the status of territories.[25] Hence, the federal government could directly control the reconquered southern states while maintaining the posture of noninterference with the local affairs of any extant state. Further, since admission of territories had always been within the absolute discretion of Congress, the seceded ''states'' could be excluded until a government that adhered to Republican principles had become firmly entrenched.

For a variety of reasons, however, the territorial justification was generally rejected.[26] Republicans were thus left with the options of accepting the prewar status quo (however distasteful) or making some modifications in the structure of federalism. All mainstream Republicans agreed that some such structural changes were necessary. Nonetheless, in mid-1865 their continual commitment to the concept of states' rights sharply limited the alternatives that Republicans were willing to consider.

These limitations were often manifested in the expressed vision of the role of the federal government (or lack thereof) in the post-Reconstruction South. Richard Henry Dana's famous speech articulating the grasp-of-war theory of congressional power over the defeated Confederate states provides a classic example. Dana emphasized the need to force the southern states to amend their *state* constitutions to guarantee freedmen the rights to testify, hold land, become educated, and make contracts. As he reasoned:

> It must be remembered that, under the [federal] constitution, most of these subjects are entirely matters of state jurisdiction. Once withdraw the powers of war, and admit a state to its full functions, *and the authority of the nation over these subjects is gone.*[27]

The *National Anti-Slavery Standard* took a similar position:

> Every one familiar with our State and Federal system of government knows that all the essential rights of individual citizens depend on State laws and action. . . . Once admit South Carolina to Congress with all her state rights, on the system of her being governed entirely by white men, and slavery under another name will be immediately reestablished there, *while the Federal Government must look on powerless to prevent it.*[28]

Of course, neither of these passages warns against excessive federal activity in the Reconstruction process itself; to the contrary, both caution the national authority to ensure that sufficient safeguards are in place before the ex-Confederate states are readmitted. At the same time, however, they reflect the widely shared belief that after the states were returned to their rightful place in the Union, the role of federal government in the protection of individual rights would be minimal at best.[29]

THE BLACK-SUFFRAGE OPTION

In 1865 many Republicans saw black suffrage as a critical component in the solution to the Reconstruction dilemma. The basic concept was endorsed not only by radical organs such as the *National Anti-Slavery Standard*[30] and *New York Tribune*[31] but also by more moderate periodicals including *Harper's Weekly*,[32] the *Nation*,[33] and the *Germantown Telegraph*.[34] Indeed, the *Springfield Republican* proposed a constitutional amendment to accomplish this goal.[35] But on this point the *Republican* took a minority view; most party members advocated federal action on suffrage limited to the ex-Confederate states. By dealing only with the rebellious states, black-suffrage proponents hoped to defuse federalism-based objections. Thus, while recognizing that Congress lacked the power to regulate suffrage in the loyal states, *Harper's Weekly* argued that the national government could exercise this power in states such as Mississippi "for the same reason that an apple is not a pear. . . . [Mississippi] is not a State of the Union exactly as New York is."[36]

Black suffrage also promised to solve other political problems faced by Republicans in the Reconstruction process. All Republicans were determined to preserve their control over the national legislature. In the absence of additional protections, restoration of southern representation could threaten this control. Indeed, postwar southern legislative power was potentially even greater than that which had existed in the antebellum period. In the original Constitution, for representation purposes, each slave counted as only three-fifths of a person.[37] With the enactment of the Thirteenth Amendment, however, each freed slave would be fully counted. The number of congressmen allocated to the southern states would accordingly be increased. If only whites were allowed to vote, the southern representatives would almost certainly be Democratic; by contrast, many Republicans confidently predicted that the freedmen would support the party of emancipation. Further, the freedmen's votes could help maintain the state legislatures in loyal hands. Unlike the majority of southern whites, blacks had not actively participated in the rebellion. Therefore, Republicans reasoned, they were far more likely to favor pro-Union elements in the state political machinery.[38]

Despite its attractions, not all Republicans favored proposals to force black suffrage on the South as a precondition for Reconstruction. Some—perhaps most notably Jacob D. Cox, Republican candidate for governor of Ohio—remained opposed to black suffrage on principle.[39] More often, however, opposition was based on other grounds. For example, the *New York Times* conceded that black suffrage was desirable but contended that the structure of federalism did not allow federal action on the subject, even in the ex-Confederate states. The argument of the *Times* was simple and straightforward: Since the southern states had had no right to secede, they were still states of the Union. As states, they had the right to determine suffrage qualifications without federal interference.[40]

The less conservative John W. Forney—secretary of the Senate and editor of the *Washington Chronicle* and *Philadelphia Press*—made a related argument. While supporting black suffrage in theory, Forney contended that the final decision on the issue should be left in the hands of southern loyalists—the group that had risked most by their continued support of the Union. Forney argued that to deprive southern loyalists of control over suffrage would leave them with fewer rights than their counterparts in the states that did not secede.[41]

Black-suffrage advocates countered that black suffrage provided a mechanism by which the basic rights of freedmen could be protected at the same time the basic federal structure was preserved. The theory was that if state constitutions were amended to grant blacks the vote and give them other basic rights, federal action would not be necessary to protect them after the southern states had been readmitted. Instead, the freed slaves could use their political power to protect *themselves* against white oppression.[42] The black-suffrage option was thus in many ways a quite conservative approach to the Reconstruction problem.

TOWARD A CONTINUING FEDERAL ROLE

As 1865 progressed, the purely state-centered model of Reconstruction began to lose its appeal for Republicans. The catalyst for the change in attitude was the perceived intransigence of the southern states. No doubt encouraged by the leniency of Andrew Johnson's approach to Reconstruction, both southern leaders and the populace at large behaved in a manner that led Republicans to believe that the South was ''conquered, not converted''[43] and that hatred of the North remained ''still strong and defiant.''[44] This attitude manifested itself in both symbolic and substantive acts. Two patterns were of particular concern to the Republicans.

The first was the election of former Confederate high officials to public office. For example, James L. Orr, onetime Confederate senator, was elected provisional governor of South Carolina; Benjamin G. Humphreys, who was elected governor of Mississippi, had served as a brigadier general in the Confederate army. Perhaps most galling of all, Alexander H. Stephens, former vice-president of the Confederacy, was designated a United States senator by the Georgia state legislature. From a southern perspective, such choices were entirely logical; after all, most of the ablest leaders in each state had joined the Confederate cause. But from a Republican perspective, these men were symbols of a sustained disloyal spirit.[45]

The other disturbing pattern was the continuing mistreatment of both freedmen and Union sympathizers generally. Carl Schurz's report on the condition of the South summarized the situation: ''There appears to be [a] popular notion prevalent in the south . . . that the negro exists for the special object of raising cotton, rice and sugar *for the whites*, and that it is illegitimate for him to indulge, like other people, in the pursuit of his own happiness in his own way.''[46] He also quoted a Union army officer's belief that '' 'there is no doubt whatever that the state of affairs would be intolerable for all Union men, all recent immigrants from the north, and all negroes, the moment the protection of the United States troops were withdrawn.' ''[47]

This attitude found formal legal expression in the adoption of the infamous Black Codes.[48] Beginning in mid-1865, the provisional legislatures of the ex-Confederate states began adopting statutes that dealt comprehensively with the status of freedmen. These laws typically imposed a range of restrictions on the rights of blacks, including limitations on their rights to contract and testify in court. Taken together, the restrictions clearly relegated the freedmen to an inferior legal status.

Republicans reacted strongly against the Black Codes.[49] Even the conservative *Cincinnati Commercial* declared that freedmen must have ''enjoyment of rights essential in their new relations to the State and Government, [and] shall not be the subject of exceptional and oppressive laws designed to defraud them of Civil Rights and Immunities.''[50] Republicans were not only concerned with the rights of freedmen per se; they also feared the establishment of a social structure that would lead to a reinvigoration of the slave power. In this vein, *Harper's Weekly* asserted that ''a population educated in the midst of a large class disfranchised in obedience to the most hateful prejudice grows up haughty, unjust, insolent and most dangerous to the general welfare."[51] On December 2, 1865, the same publication concluded that, given the existing atmosphere, "it is plain that the freedmen cannot be honorably left to the local state legislation."[52]

Differences among Republicans on the nature of federalism became critical with the realization that national legislation might well be needed to protect the freedmen even after the southern states were restored. Though all mainstream Republicans agreed that some modification in the antebellum system was necessary, they were not in accord on the appropriate line between the delegated powers of the federal government and the reserved rights of the states. The question of the power of the national authorities to define and protect natural rights was particularly divisive. Some argued that since the Civil War had conclusively determined that American citizens owed paramount allegiance to the federal government, that government had both the concomitant duty to safeguard the natural rights of the citizens and the plenary authority to do all that was necessary to discharge that duty.[53] Others took a different view; conceding that national citizenship carried with it certain fundamental rights, they argued that the Constitution nonetheless placed sharp restrictions on congressional enforcement authority.[54]

Even Samuel Shellabarger, radical Republican from Ohio, had substantial qualms regarding the power of Congress to secure natural rights. Shellabarger argued strongly that in return for the allegiance of its citizens, the federal government possessed the duty and authority to ensure that those citizens received protection in their fundamental rights. At the same time, as late as 1866, he questioned the constitutional power of Congress to secure some of the rights enumerated in the Civil Rights Bill.[55] Moreover, when drafting his own bill to punish private invasions of basic rights, Shellabarger confined its applicability to actions taken against "such as seek to or are attempting to go either temporarily or for abode from their State into some other." The proposal did not cover wrongs committed between two citizens of the same state—a limitation designed to bring the bill within the ambit of the comity clause and thereby to avoid "doubtful exercise of power by the United States and not to assume or trench upon the powers of the States."[56]

Shellabarger might well have applauded a constitutional amendment clearly establishing congressional authority over fundamental rights. Other mainstream Republicans, however, were tenaciously attached to the concept of states' rights on a more general ideological level. Legislators such as Thomas Davis, Roscoe Conkling, Giles W. Hotchkiss, and William M. Stewart vigorously attacked a proposed constitutional amendment that they feared would unduly expand the competence of the federal government over basic rights.[57] In the political context of the early Reconstruction era, the position taken by such men was to prove decisive.

THE POLITICAL SITUATION

The struggle for power between the Republicans and Democrats and within the Republican party itself had a strong influence on the shape of the policies adopted during the early Reconstruction period. At all times, Republicans had a clear majority in both houses of Congress. Yet Democrats also played an important role in defining freedmen's rights, a role that emerged most clearly in the adoption of the Thirteenth Amendment. In the Thirty-eighth Congress, Republicans had lacked the necessary two-thirds majority to pass a constitutional amendment. Thus, only by maintaining party unity *and* attracting Democratic votes could the Republicans have hoped to outlaw slavery.

The political dynamic that governed the Thirty-ninth and Fortieth Congresses was dramatically different from what had prevailed during the war. The size of the Republican majority increased substantially in the election of 1864 and was maintained in the elections of 1866; in both the Senate and the House of Representatives, well over two-thirds of the membership were affiliated with the party of Lincoln. United, the Republicans could pass any measure they chose.

This does not mean that the Democratic party had become irrelevant. On one level, the Democrats added to the pressure for party unity among Republicans. The existence of such an opposition was a reminder of the potential fate of republicanism (as well as individual Republicans) if the party either fell out of favor with the populace or tore itself apart in internal bickering.[58] Further, even a drastically reduced Democratic party provided an important check on the policymaking options available to the Republicans. In the civil rights area, Democrats would unanimously oppose any new Republican proposals; as a result, even a relatively small number of Republican defections could doom such an initiative. In cases where a two-thirds majority was necessary, Republican consensus was especially critical. Obviously, by their very nature constitutional amendments fell into this category, but the presence of Andrew Johnson made supermajorities essential even for statutory initiatives.[59]

Johnson was a Democrat from Tennessee who had been the only senator from a seceding state to stay on and continue to participate in Congress. He was sent by Lincoln to Nashville in 1862 to become military governor of the reconquered portions of his home state—a post in which he served with distinction, ruling with an iron hand in the most trying of circumstances. In considering a running mate for Lincoln in 1864, the Republicans sought to broaden the electoral base of the Union coalition and to pacify the still-loyal border slave states. At the time, Johnson seemed to fit the bill nicely. Good politics in 1864 proved to be a near disaster in 1866; after the assassination of Lincoln, Republicans in Congress soon recognized that the man in the White House had returned to his political roots and that they were in essence forced to deal with a Democratic chief executive. Not surprisingly, a bitter political battle ensued.

The enmity between Johnson and the Republican mainstream developed gradually from mid-1865 to mid-1866. Initially, the new president enjoyed support from a wide variety of Republicans; for example, the *Springfield Republican* asserted that "he is heartily devoted to the Union and the cause of liberty" and that "while his known severity of feeling toward the rebel chiefs will be a guaranty against any weak leniency, at the same time the influences brought to bear upon him will prevent the enforcement of any harsh and aggravating measures toward the Southern people."[60] Even radicals initially backed Johnson, encouraged by his performance in Tennessee and his statement on the day after Lincoln died that "treason must be made odious and traitors impoverished."[61] The Washington correspondent of the *National Anti-Slavery Standard* assured his readers that "we can trust [Johnson] to defend the rights of the colored people of the South a great deal better than we can the people of the North with the rights of the same class of people there."[62] It soon became apparent, however, that the president had serious differences with congressional Republicans on two critical issues.

One of these issues was the general course of Reconstruction. In part this dispute turned on the question of control; Johnson saw Reconstruction as an executive prerogative, while Congress wished to assert its authority over the process. Substantive policy differences were equally important. Unlike most Republicans, Johnson wished to readmit the southern states with few guarantees of good behavior. He would have required only that new state constitutional conventions void the secession ordinances, ratify the Thirteenth Amendment, and renounce the Confederate war debt. In Johnson's view, any ex-Confederate state that satisfied these conditions was entitled to representation in Congress.[63]

Johnson also broke with most Republicans on the desirability of federal action on civil rights. One of the distinctive features of his administration was his repeated use of the veto power against congressional action to protect the rights of freedmen. For obvious reasons, this was a continuing source of friction between the president and the congressional majority; indeed, LaWanda Cox and John H. Cox view the civil rights issue as the most important source of the split between the president and Congress.[64]

The historiography of the resultant political struggle has undergone a substantial change in the modern era.[65] Until relatively recently, the contest was seen as two-sided, with the villainous radical Republicans defeating the heroic President Johnson and imposing their will on the South.[66] Later accounts have rehabilitated the radicals, attacked Johnson, and focused on a third force—moderate Republicans—as holding the balance of power between the two extremes.[67]

Even this more sophisticated explanation understates the complexity of the political dynamic of Reconstruction. Although in a certain sense the conflict was between three clearly defined visions of the Reconstruction process, many subtle distinctions were also significant. Certainly, some of the key players fit comfortably into one of the three well-established models—radical, moderate, or conservative. For example, the positions of Charles Sumner and the *National Anti-Slavery Standard* virtually defined radical republicanism. Others, however, developed highly individualized approaches to the problem. The differences are particularly apparent when one considers the group generally labeled "moderate Republicans"; they were less a coherent force than a group of men, each of whom was willing to embrace some but not all of the principles endorsed by their more radical colleagues. Within this group, even such close political allies as Sen. James W. Grimes of Iowa and William Pitt Fessenden of Maine could have important policy disagreements over critical issues such as black suffrage. Fessenden was one of the early proponents of a constitutional amendment guaranteeing the right to vote, yet Grimes was one of a handful of Republicans who at one point voted against adoption of the Fifteenth Amendment. The same phenomenon—admittedly to a lesser extent—also can be detected even among the radicals and the Democrats.[68]

The point is that the development of congressional policy on civil rights (as well as Reconstruction policy overall) was not simply the product of a conflict between well-defined groups but rather the interaction between the preferences of many individuals, each driven by a different set of ideological and political imperatives. These individuals can often be appropriately characterized as belonging to identifiable political groups supporting certain basic positions. But especially at the margins, members of the same group could hold divergent positions. Hence it is not surprising that the statutes and constitutional amendments that eventually emerged would reflect a series of delicate compromises among competing views. Moreover, because of the political dynamic governing the legislative process of the era, the compromises were generally designed to placate those of a more conservative bent.

4
Preliminary Skirmishing

THE WILSON INITIATIVE AND
DISTRICT OF COLUMBIA SUFFRAGE

With the convening of the Thirty-ninth Congress, attempts to provide federal statutory protection for the rights of blacks began almost immediately. Noting the passage of the first of the Black Codes by the newly reconstituted state legislatures of Georgia and Mississippi, Henry Wilson, radical senator from Massachusetts, introduced the first civil rights initiative of the new Congress on December 13, 1865. Wilson's bill would have outlawed state-imposed racial discrimination in "civil rights and immunities" in all states that had joined in the rebellion. Apparently relying on the war power, Wilson declared that "our right to pass this bill I cannot doubt."[1] John Sherman and Lyman Trumbull, by contrast, preferred to wait for ratification of the Thirteenth Amendment before taking any action on civil rights. Each viewed section two of the amendment as granting Congress authority to legislate throughout the nation to secure to the freed slaves rights essential to the status of freedmen. Trumbull described those rights as "the privilege to go and come when they please, to buy and sell when they please, [and] to make contracts and enforce contracts."[2] Sherman added the rights to testify, to acquire and hold property, to be protected in their homes and family, and to be educated. He also complained that Wilson's bill might go beyond these specifics and prohibit *all* state-imposed racial discrimination—a course of action that Sherman saw as unwise, if not beyond the power of Congress.[3] In any event, no action was taken on Wilson's bill, and it disappeared from sight.

The first civil rights measure to receive full consideration from the House of Representatives did not directly involve Reconstruction but instead dealt with the right of blacks to vote in the District of Columbia. The bill was an ideal test of Republican sentiment on the black-suffrage question; since Congress has plenary authority over the District, questions of federalism did not complicate the issue. The reaction to the proposal demonstrated the Republican consensus on the right of blacks to vote. The bill was endorsed even by the conservative *New York Times*[4] and *Cincinnati Commercial*[5] and drew near-

43

Table 4.1 Chronology of Congressional Civil Rights Actions during the First Session of the Thirty-ninth Congress, December 1865–June 1866

Wilson Initiative	Dec. 13 Introduced						
D. C. Suffrage		Jan. 10 Reported to House		Jan. 18 Passes House			
Apportionment			Jan. 16 Joint Committee adopts apportionment amendment		Jan. 31 Passes House	Mar. 9 Defeated in Senate	
Freedmen's Bureau Bill		Jan. 12 Reported to Senate	Jan. 25 Passes Senate	Feb. 5 Passes House	Feb. 19 Vetoed	Feb. 20 Overrule attempt fails in Senate	
Civil Rights Bill		Jan. 12 Reported to Senate		Feb. 2 Passes Senate			Mar. 9 Recommitted to House Judiciary Committee
Bingham Amendment			Jan. 16 Introduced in Joint Committee		Feb. 10 Adopted by Joint Committee	Feb. 28 Postponed indefinitely by House	
Fourteenth Amendment							

Table 4.1 Continued

Mar. 13 Amended bill passes House	Mar.15 Amended bill passes Senate	Mar. 27 Stockton unseated; Johnson veto	Apr. 6 Senate overrides veto	Apr. 9 House overrides veto

		Apr. 21 Owen plan introduced in Joint Committee; Bingham proposal added	Apr. 25 Bingham proposal removed	Apr. 28 Black Suffrage removed; disenfran-chisement added; Bingham substitute adopted; Committee adopts plan	May 10 House passes amendment	June 6 Senate passes modified amendment	June 11 House concurs

unanimous support from Republican congressmen. The maneuvering over the final shape of the bill, however, also revealed deep philosophical divisions in the party regarding the *form* of suffrage to be granted to blacks. On this issue, Republicans fell into three groups. The differences between the respective approaches of these groups reflected a long-running debate in American society over the nature of voting rights generally.

First, there were those who favored *universal* suffrage—either true universal suffrage or manhood suffrage. Members of this group maintained that the right to vote was either a natural right, a necessary concomitant of citizenship, or a right whose possession was essential in order to protect one's fundamental rights. But whatever rationale they employed, the common element was the belief that, at the very least, the vote should be given to all competent male citizens over the age of twenty-one (with the possible exception of adherents to the southern rebellion).[6]

A second major group of Republicans advocated *impartial* suffrage; i.e., that suffrage was a purely conventional right whose exercise could properly be limited by one or more of a variety of factors. Some suggested that the right was a *quid pro quo* for either service in the military or the payment of taxes. Others contended that the vote should be limited to those who could exercise it intelligently and thus would have imposed some sort of educational requirement. But all agreed that race (or at least being black) was not an appropriate reason for withholding the franchise from an otherwise qualified individual.[7]

Finally, some Republicans argued for *qualified* black suffrage. Though conceding that not all blacks should be excluded from the franchise, this group held that special safeguards were necessary because granting blacks the right to vote posed special dangers to the electoral process.[8] The model for this position was the antebellum New York Constitution, which required that blacks, but not whites, possess property worth $250 in order to be enfranchised.[9]

The skirmishing among these various factions actually began before the District of Columbia bill reached the House floor. By a wide margin the Republican caucus voted in favor of impartial rather than universal suffrage.[10] Nonetheless, the Committee on the District of Columbia chose to report a universal suffrage bill introduced by radical William D. Kelley of Pennsylvania.[11] The bill also received strong support from such prominent radicals as James F. Wilson of Iowa and George W. Julian of Indiana.[12]

More conservative Republicans argued for less sweeping reform. John A. Kasson of Iowa noted the political dangers involved in taking an unduly extreme position on the black-suffrage issue and also suggested with obvious distaste that the "great mass of [District of Columbia blacks] are ignorant and unable to tell when the ballot they vote is right side up.''[13] He suggested that new voters should either be taxpayers, have served in the armed forces, or be able to read and write. These new requirements were to be race-blind; however, Kasson also argued that to apply these qualifications to already registered voters would be fundamentally unjust. He therefore proposed that all those who had qualified under previous law would remain eligible to vote.[14] In essence, this proviso exempted a large proportion of the white population from the new requirements. Thus, while cast in the language of impartial suffrage, Kasson's proposal in practice would have provided only qualified black suffrage.

Robert Hale of New York—one of the most conservative Republicans in the House—then offered an amendment embodying many of Kasson's ideas. But the Hale amendment differed in one important respect: It would have imposed the new qualifications on *all* voters in the District of Columbia, thus creating a regime of impartial suffrage.[15] Like Kasson, Hale argued that the right to vote did not constitute a vested right and that limiting the franchise was desirable on its own merits; at the same time, however, he contended that having different qualifications for whites and blacks was intrinsically odious.[16]

Even among those who favored only impartial suffrage, the plan to discriminate on the basis of property ownership was controversial. Thus, on motion of Robert C. Schenck of Ohio, the property qualification was eliminated from the Hale amendment.[17] Against this background, Republicans then faced the critical choice between impartial and universal suffrage.

The actions of the House reflected both the agreement among Republicans on certain basic issues and the divisions within the party on important subissues. After an attempt by conservative Republicans to postpone the entire suffrage question attracted only thirty-four votes,[18] fifty-three Republicans voted for the Hale amendment, while eighty preferred to leave the original Kelley bill intact. The balance of power was held by thirty-seven Democrats. Seeking either to defeat the suffrage bill altogether or to force the Republicans into a radical position, the Democrats voted en masse against the Hale amendment, assuring its defeat.[19] Faced now with the choice between universal suffrage and total exclusion of blacks, conservative Republicans left no doubt as to their preference; with only sixteen exceptions they joined their more radical brethren to pass the suffrage bill.[20] As the *New York Times* would later comment, Republicans thus demonstrated that when the alternatives were universal suffrage and complete black exclusion, ''the Republican Party cannot hesitate in its choice.''[21]

Despite the overwhelming endorsement from House Republicans, the District of Columbia Suffrage Bill was not immediately taken up by the Senate. The question of Reconstruction soon came to a head and dominated the political landscape for the remainder of the session.

CIVIL RIGHTS AND RECONSTRUCTION POLICY

In early 1866, Reconstruction-related civil rights proposals originated in two different congressional committees, both chaired by influential moderate Republican senators. The Senate Judiciary Committee was led by the redoubtable Lyman Trumbull of Illinois, who virtually defined the conservative edge of the Republican mainstream. Sen. William Pitt Fessenden of Maine led the Joint Committee on Reconstruction, whose mission was to "inquire into the condition of the States which formed the so-called Confederate States of America and report whether they, or any of them are entitled to be represented in either House of Congress." Working separately, the two committees produced a number of measures which dealt with the civil rights problems generated by Reconstruction. Between January and March 1866, Congress dealt with three of these measures. The results reflected both Republican attitudes toward the role of the federal government in protecting blacks and the dispute between the president and Congress.

The Freedmen's Bureau Bill

The Bureau of Freedmen, Refugees and Abandoned Land had been created in March 1865.[22] Vested with "control of all subjects relating to refugees and freedmen in the rebel states," its existence was to end one year after the termination of hostilities. On January 12, 1866, however, the Senate Judiciary Committee reported a bill to extend the life of the bureau indefinitely. In addition, the bill expanded the jurisdiction of the bureau, in some respects allowing it to protect freedmen throughout the country rather than only in the erstwhile Confederate states. Finally, the bill authorized the president to set aside large tracts of land in Florida, Mississippi, and Arkansas for the use of freedmen and "loyal refugees"; the commissioner of the bureau was to parcel out the land in forty-acre plots, to be rented and then purchased by those whom the agency was assigned to protect.

Democrats launched a series of attacks on the bill. Among the most frequent targets were the two sections that provided that "in any state or district in which the ordinary course of judicial proceedings has been interrupted by the rebellion," the military was to ensure that blacks were protected in their civil rights and that those who violated such rights under color of state law were to be subject to criminal penalties. Opponents expressed fears that this provision would be interpreted as applicable in loyal states that had been subject to invasion; in any event, they claimed that the civil rights component was an unconstitutional enlargement of federal power at the expense of states' rights.[23] Republicans, however, replied that sections seven and eight would clearly have effect only in those states that had seceded. Focusing on the temporary nature of the bill, they defended its constitutionality as a reasonable extension of the extraordinary war power under which Civil War measures had been justified.[24] Republicans also claimed that authority for the measure could be found in the enforcement clause of the Thirteenth Amendment.[25]

Widely perceived as a moderate Reconstruction proposal, the Freedmen's Bureau Bill passed the Senate with no difficulty by a vote of 37 to 10 on January 25.[26] In the House, moderates easily defeated radical efforts to add provisions for the confiscation of rebel lands and free education for blacks; the bill passed easily on February 6.[27] At this stage, however, both the political power of the president and his determination to use that power against federal civil rights legislation became a factor. Johnson vetoed the bill on February 19; moreover, he couched his veto message in the strongest language, not only arguing that such a measure was generally beyond the power of Congress but also suggesting that the bill was invalid because representatives of the southern states had not been allowed to vote on its passage.[28] Thus, in essence the president challenged the entire principle of congressional control over Reconstruction.

Nonetheless, Congress failed to override the veto. The opposition of the president was sufficient to convince eight Republican senators to withdraw their support of the bill when put to the test. The vote in the Senate was 30 to 18—two votes short of the necessary two-thirds majority.[29] The Thirty-ninth Congress's first effort to protect the civil rights of blacks ended in failure. Moreover, the circumstances of the failure demonstrated that only those civil rights measures which could appeal to the most conservative of mainstream Republicans were likely to become law.

Suffrage and Representation

The first initiative reported from the Joint Committee on Reconstruction dealt obliquely with black suffrage. As already noted, one of the primary concerns of all Republicans was the maintenance of their control over the national legislature, and granting freedmen the right to vote was perceived as an important step in that direction. In early 1866, however, political support for a constitutional amendment enfranchising blacks was insufficient to gain passage of such a measure. Thus,

among Republican Joint Committee members, only Fessenden and radical Sen. Jacob M. Howard of Michigan supported a proposal to prohibit
racial discrimination in "political or civil rights or immunities."[30]

The remaining option was to reduce the representation of those
states that did not enfranchise blacks. One proposed solution was a
constitutional amendment to change the basis of representation from
population to legal voters.[31] This proposal, however, had some serious
drawbacks. First, because women were generally not enfranchised, the
alteration would affect the balance of power not only between North
and South but also among the various Union states as well; in particular, basing representation on voters would favor the western states,
which had a smaller percentage of women.[32] Second, there were fears
that the proposal would encourage states to unduly broaden the suffrage to include such groups as aliens and children.[33] Finally, some border states might be less likely to disenfranchise rebel sympathizers—a
prospect disturbing to many Republicans.[34]

These problems led the Joint Committee to offer a more limited constitutional amendment—one that continued to base representation on
population but also provided that "whenever the elective franchise
shall be denied or abridged in any State on account of race or color, all
persons of such race or color shall be excluded from the basis of representation."[35] Since relatively few blacks lived in the North, the committee proposal was well suited to Republican purposes; assuming that
the southern states did not enfranchise the freed slaves, the outcome
would have been reduced southern representation without an alteration in the balance of power among the Union states.

Nonetheless, the committee amendment was vulnerable to a number of criticisms. First, on its face the proposal was a crass, punitive
measure designed to serve the narrow political ends of the Republican
party.[36] Second, it implicitly conceded the right of states to exclude
blacks from voting. This concession was anathema to some radicals;
they claimed that a government that did not allow black suffrage was
not "republican in form" as required by Article IV, Section 4 of the
Constitution.[37] Thus, when the committee proposal was introduced in
the House on January 22, it came under attack from a variety of different groups. Democrats and Johnson Republicans argued that there was
no need to amend the Constitution at all;[38] radicals complained that
the Joint Committee plan legitimated restrictions on black suffrage;[39]
and western Republicans agitated for an amendment that would base
representation on voters.[40] The various Republican positions were embodied in a bewildering tangle of parliamentary motions to amend the
proposal and to recommit it with instructions.[41]

On January 29, published reports of President Johnson's position intervened to change the political dynamic of the situation. Johnson ex-

pressed the view that any further constitutional changes were unwise but suggested that he might be willing to accept an amendment that— unlike the Joint Committee proposal—based representation on the number of eligible voters in each state.[42] This statement seemed to convince House Republicans to unite around a single proposal. On January 30, the amendment was recommitted without instructions;[43] the following day it was reported back to the House floor with only minor modifications. An attempt by Samuel Shellabarger of Ohio to substitute an amendment along the lines suggested by Johnson garnered only twenty-nine votes—all Republicans.[44] The Joint Committee proposal then passed easily, with only twelve Republicans dissenting.[45]

Most Republicans supported the measure in the form that emerged from the House. The *New York Tribune*, for example, argued that it was "right in itself, and . . . will commend itself to every fair mind,"[46] and the *Evening Post* stated that it "seems to us just."[47] Some radical elements continued to demur, however, holding out for action that would directly enfranchise blacks. Although conceding that the proposal "is undoubtedly a matter upon which true men may differ," the *Boston Commonwealth* announced its opposition to the representation amendment.[48] The condemnation of the *National Anti-Slavery Standard* was much stronger: "God has not bought the freedom of four millions of its children at the cost of a million human lives, to be defrauded in the purchase by such compromise, cowardice and criminality even, as generally lie at the basis of legislation like this."[49]

As was often the case, the champion of the radical position in the Senate was Charles Sumner of Massachusetts.[50] The debate on the Senate floor brought a classic confrontation between Fessenden and Sumner (whose differences were not only political but personal) and exemplified their respective approaches to Reconstruction problems. Fessenden rested the argument for the committee proposal on purely pragmatic considerations. The chairman of the Joint Committee averred frankly that he would have preferred a black-suffrage amendment; at the same time, however, he urged approval of the proposed amendment as the best substitute currently attainable:

> The argument that addressed itself to the committee was, what can we accomplish? What can pass? If we report a [black-suffrage amendment] is there the slightest possibility that it will be adopted by the States and become a part of the Constitution of the United States? It is perfectly obvious that there could be no hope of that description.[51]

Sumner, by contrast, characterized the proposal as a "*constitutional recognition of an Oligarchy, Aristocracy, Caste and Monopoly, founded on color.''*[52] Scorning arguments based on expediency, he sought the high ground of pure principle:

> I had hoped that the day of compromise with wrong had passed forever. Ample experience shows that it is the least practical mode of settling questions involving moral principle. A moral principle cannot be compromised.[53]

However, Sumner did indicate that he would accept an apportionment amendment that did not explicitly suggest that states were allowed to prevent blacks from voting.[54]

Sumner refused to retreat from his position. After failing to convince the Senate to adopt a direct black-suffrage amendment,[55] he and four other radical senators voted against the proposed amendment when the final roll call was taken on March 9. Thus, although the supporters of the Joint Committee proposal garnered a 25 to 22 majority, they fell far short of the two-thirds vote necessary for passage.[56] Sumner's position earned him the enmity of many of his Republican colleagues; indeed, he is usually credited with killing the representation amendment.[57] Yet a close examination of the voting record reveals that Sumner's defection did not determine the fate of the proposed amendment. Even if all five dissenting radicals had supported the Joint Committee, the vote would have been only 30 to 17 in favor—still short of the two-thirds requirement.

As with the Freedmen's Bureau Bill, the critical factor was the opposition of conservative Republicans who supported President Johnson. Of the Senate Republicans who had sustained Johnson's veto of the bureau bill, only Edwin D. Morgan of New York voted for the Joint Committee amendment. Further, Morgan's defection was counterbalanced by the negative vote of James H. Lane of Kansas, who had opposed the president on the bureau issue. If Lane and all of the Republicans who had withdrawn their support of the Freedmen's Bureau Bill after the veto had ratified the apportionment amendment, the amendment would have been adopted despite the opposition of the radicals. Thus, the defeat of the Joint Committee proposal demonstrated once again that conservative Republicans held the balance of power on Reconstruction issues. Given Johnson's resistance, civil rights measures could be passed only if this faction were placated.

The Bingham Amendment

In the midst of the congressional deliberations on a variety of Reconstruction- and civil rights-related items, the Joint Committee on Reconstruction reported a proposed constitutional amendment that would have explicitly enlarged the authority of Congress over civil rights. The plan attracted considerably less public attention than either the Freedmen's Bureau Bill or the Civil Rights Bill of 1866. Nonetheless, an in-depth grasp of the debates over this proposal is essential to understanding the basic constitutional theory eventually embodied in the Fourteenth Amendment. First, the language of the suggested amendment is quite similar to that eventually adopted as section one. Second, both section one and the earlier congressional-power proposal were championed by the same man—John A. Bingham of Ohio. Finally, the debates over the initial Bingham amendment contain the only extended congressional discussion of the desirability of granting Congress the authority to regulate private action.

Bingham was well known as a speaker, but his fame did not rest on the trenchance of his argument; style was his strong suit. As one commentator noted, ''His strength as an orator is in the beauty of his diction, not the force of his logic. He is a master of a pretty imagery as applied to political topics, and is never at a loss for choice language, even to express common-place ideas.''[58] Arrogant and egotistical—one contemporary asserted that ''a more opinionated and vain old maid does not exist''[59]—Bingham at times seemed motivated by pique rather than political expediency or devotion to principle. He was consistent, however, on one point: the need to arm Congress with the power to force the states to recognize and protect the rights of their respective residents.

Bingham's initial proposed amendment was submitted to the first session of the Thirty-ninth Congress on December 6, 1865. The plan would have amended the Constitution to empower Congress to pass ''all necessary and proper laws to secure to all persons in every State of the Union equal protection in their rights of life, liberty, and property.''[60] Bingham gave a detailed explanation of the purpose of the measure in a speech delivered on the House floor on January 9, 1866. The speech was a response to a Democratic discussion of a message from President Johnson, in which Johnson had declared himself in favor of ''equal and exact justice to all men.'' After accusing the Democrats of being in favor of equal and exact justice only for white men, Bingham continued.

> The spirit, the intent, the purpose of our Constitution is to secure equal and exact justice to all men. That has not been done. It has failed to be done in the past. It has failed in respect of white men as well as black men. . . . Time was within the memory of every man now within hearing of my voice, when it was entirely unsafe for a citizen of Massachusetts or Ohio who was known to be the friend of the human race, the avowed advocate of the foundation principle of our Constitution—the absolute equality of all men before the

law—to be found anywhere in the streets of Charleston or in the streets of Richmond.

To be sure, it was not because the Constitution of the United States sanctioned any infringement of his rights in that behalf, but because in defiance of the Constitution its varied guarantees were disregarded. . . .

When you come to weigh these words "equal and exact justice to all men," go read, if you please, the words of the Constitution itself: "the citizens of each State (being ipso facto citizens of the United States) shall be entitled to all the privileges and immunities of citizens (supplying the ellipsis 'of the United States') in the several states." [This guarantee] was utterly disregarded in the past by South Carolina when she drove with indignity and contempt and scorn from her limits the honored representative of Massachusetts, who went thither upon the peaceful mission of asserting in the tribunal of South Carolina the rights of American citizens.

I have proposed . . . that hereafter there shall not be any disregard of the essential guarantee of your Constitution in any State of the Union . . . [b]y simply adding an amendment to the Constitution . . . giving to Congress the power to pass all laws necessary and proper to secure to all persons . . . their equal personal rights; and if the tribunals of South Carolina will not respect the rights of the citizens of Massachusetts under the Constitution . . . I desire to see the Federal judiciary clothed with the power to take cognizance of the question and assert those rights by solemn judgment, inflicting upon the offenders such penalties as will compel a decent respect for this guarantee to all the citizens of every State. . . . The divinest feature of your Constitution is the recognition of the absolute equality before the law of all persons, whether citizens or strangers . . . subject only to the exception made by reason of slavery, now happily abolished. The President, therefore, might well say, as he does say in his message, that "The American system rests on the assertion of the equal right of every man to life, liberty, and the pursuit of happiness; to freedom of conscience, to the culture and exercise of all his faculties."

I propose, then, sir, by amending the Constitution, to provide for the efficient enforcement, by law, of these "equal rights of every man," and upon the assertion of which . . . the American system rests.[61]

Several important points emerge from Bingham's actions. The first concerns chronology. Bingham presented his proposal nearly a month *before* Trumbull introduced the Civil Rights Bill. Thus, any argument

that the Bingham amendment was simply an attempt to directly constitutionalize Trumbull's bill or to ensure its constitutionality is
anachronistic. Second, the speech of January 9 totally destroys any contention that Bingham viewed the concept of equal protection merely in
terms of discrimination on the basis of race. Bingham did refer to the
denial of "equal justice" to the freed slaves; the only allusion to specific unconstitutional state behavior, however, was his reference to the
celebrated Samuel Hoar affair—a case in which the state of South Carolina allegedly persecuted a *white* man for attempting to challenge the
state's Negro Seaman's Act.[62] Since Bingham explicitly stated that his
amendment would empower the federal government to protect men
like Hoar, the proposal could hardly be viewed as aimed only at racial
discrimination. Instead, his amendment clearly embodied the theory
of limited absolute equality.

Finally, throughout his January 9 speech, Bingham evinced a belief
that the proposed constitutional change would not enable Congress to
impose any new obligations on the states. Rather, he argued that the
amendment would just allow Congress to enforce preexisting constitutional constraints on the states—in particular, those constraints imposed by the comity clause. These assertions were entirely consistent
with Bingham's antebellum constitutional theory, which he had set
forth in the debate over the admission of Oregon.[63] Further, he plainly
implied that the notion of "equal and exact justice" he had in mind did
not encompass the right of blacks to be free from all racial discrimination; instead, he suggested that blacks in common with other citizens
simply had an absolute right to judicial enforcement of their rights to
"life, liberty, and the pursuit of happiness; to freedom of conscience, to
the culture and exercise of all [their] faculties." His proposed constitutional amendment would merely permit the federal government to step
in if the states did not provide the necessary judicial enforcement.

Soon after this speech, Bingham's amendment was considered by the
Joint Committee on Reconstruction, of which Bingham was a key
member. After considerable maneuvering over the precise language to
be used,[64] the Joint Committee reported a proposed constitutional
amendment that was quite similar to Bingham's original draft of
December 6:

The Congress shall have power to make all laws which shall be
necessary and proper to secure to the citizens of each State all privileges and immunities of citizens in the several States and to all
persons in the several States equal protection in the rights of life,
liberty and property.[65]

Even before the proposal reached the House floor, there were indications that it would face considerable difficulties. Within the Joint Committee, the measure was opposed not only by Democrats but also by two of its more conservative mainstream Republican members—Ira Harris and Roscoe Conkling. Moreover, on January 26, the *Springfield Republican* asserted that it was doubtful the Bingham amendment would pass because "people are not likely to give any such general power to Congress."[66]

The strength of the opposition became clear during debates on the House floor on February 26, 27, and 28. Although Giles Hotchkiss of New York urged an amendment that would directly require states to respect fundamental rights,[67] such objections, taken alone, would not have been fatal. For example, Thaddeus Stevens, who had sponsored an amendment in the form suggested by Hotchkiss,[68] also supported the Bingham proposal.[69] The more serious challenge was focused on the potential breadth of the Bingham amendment. Democrat Andrew Rogers condemned any expansion of federal power.[70] Republican foes were more selective in their attacks. They found no fault with the grant of authority to secure privileges and immunities.[71] Instead, their criticisms were aimed at the equal protection component of the proposal.

Some Republicans contended that the amendment would give Congress authority to force all states to grant identical protection to life, liberty, and property. The main critique, delivered by Robert S. Hale of New York, took a slightly different tack:

> The language [of the proposal] in its grammatical and legal construction . . . is a grant of the fullest and most ample power to Congress to make all laws "necessary and proper to secure to all persons in the several States protection in the rights of life, liberty and property" with the simple proviso that such protection shall be equal. It is not a mere provision that when the States undertake to give protection which is unequal, Congress may equalize it; it is a grant of power in general terms—a grant of the right to legislate for the protection of life, liberty, and property, simply qualified with the condition that it shall be equal legislation. . . . We all know it is true that probably every State in this Union fails to give equal protection to all persons within its borders in the rights of life, liberty and property. . . . Take the case of the rights of married women; did anyone ever assume that Congress was to be invested with the power to legislate on that subject, and to say that married women in regard to their rights of property should stand on the same footing with men and unmarried women?[72]

Thaddeus Stevens attacked the example, arguing that "when a distinction is made between two married women and two femmes sole, then it is unequal legislation; but where all of the same class are dealt with in the same way, then there is no pretense of inequality."[73] Hale, however, would not accept this explanation:

> The language of the section under consideration gives to *all persons* equal protection. Now, if that means you shall extend to one married woman the same protection you extend to another, and not the same you extend to unmarried women or men, then by parity of reasoning it will be sufficient if you extend to one negro the same rights you would do to another, but not those you extend to a white man. I think, if [Congressman Stevens] claims that the resolution only intends that all of a certain class shall have equal protection, such class legislation may certainly as easily satisfy the requirements of this resolution in the case of the negro as in the case of the married woman. The line of distinction is, I take it, quite as broadly marked between negroes and white men as between married and unmarried women.[74]

In summary, then, Hale's argument was as follows. The Bingham proposal was flawed in that it would create a revolution in federalism by granting the federal government plenary authority to perform the most basic function of government, a function previously reserved to the states—the protection of life, liberty, and property. From Hale's perspective, the difficulty with the concept of equal protection was not that it was a bad idea per se but rather that under the Bingham amendment, it would not have imposed a significant limitation on the federal government's ability to legislate generally on the subject of life, liberty, and property.

The same basic theme was reflected in all of the denunciations of Bingham's proposal. Even Hotchkiss was uneasy with the potentially broad scope of the equal protection element of Bingham's amendment and indicated that he favored protecting only those rights to which Bingham himself had referred.[75] Thus, the key issue in the debate was whether the proposal would unduly expand the powers of Congress.

Bingham's defense elaborated on the points of his January 9 speech. After reaffirming that the amendment was intended to protect whites as well as blacks, he reiterated that the equal protection provision would create no new federal powers. Instead, it would simply give Congress the authority to ensure that preexisting rights were protected. When confronted with the claim that his proposal would allow Congress to usurp state control over property, Bingham argued:

Although this word property has been in your bill of rights from the year 1789 until this hour, who ever heard it intimated that anybody could have property protected in any State until he owned or acquired property there according to its local law or according to the law of some other State which he may have carried thither? I undertake to say no one.

As to real estate, everyone knows that its acquisition and transmission under every interpretation ever given to the word property as used in the Constitution of the country are dependent exclusively upon the local law of the State, save under a direct grant of the United States. But suppose any person has acquired property not contrary to the laws of the State but in accordance with its law, are they not to be equally protected in the enjoyment of it, or are they to be denied all protection? That is the question, and the whole question, so far as that part of the case is concerned.[76]

Returning to this theme, he later asserted:

The adoption of the proposed amendment will take from the States no rights that belong to the States. They elect their Legislatures; they enact their laws for the punishment of crimes against life, liberty, or property; but in the event of the adoption of this amendment, if they conspire together to enact laws refusing equal protection to life, liberty, or property, the Congress is thereby vested with power to hold them to answer before the bar of the national courts for the violation of their oaths and of the rights of their fellowmen.[77]

The difficulty, according to Bingham, was that states had defaulted on their obligation to provide the protection of the law for rights derived from the Constitution, natural law, and state law. He referred specifically to the provision of the Oregon Constitution, which denied free blacks access to courts to enforce their rights. He also repeatedly condemned state laws allowing banishment and confiscation. Finally, he saw a need for federal enforcement of the Bill of Rights. Although conceding that the Supreme Court had held the first eight amendments inapplicable to the states in *Barron v. City of Baltimore* and *Lessee of Livingston v. Moore*, Bingham nonetheless contended that the states were at least morally bound to respect the rights created by those amendments. Passage of his proposal, he argued, would allow the federal government to ensure that citizens would be protected in the legal rights guaranteed to them by the Constitution.[78]

Taken as a whole, Bingham's defense of his amendment amounts to a comprehensive restatement of the right to protection of the law.[79]

Bingham was plainly not concerned with problems of classification; instead, he sought to implement the concept of limited absolute equality. His emphasis on the denial of access to courts was an allusion to the most fundamental element of the right to protection by government; his condemnation of banishment statutes reflected a limitation on states' rights to remove the protection of law from persons by declaring them outlaws. The references to confiscation and the Bill of Rights, on the other hand, embodied the right to protection *from* government described by Kent, among others.[80] In this respect, Bingham's view was an entirely orthodox application of widely accepted legal principles.

The major change, of course, was that Bingham envisioned a permanent federal role in making certain that citizens received their basic rights. But contrary to the suggestions of some historians,[81] his views on this point were squarely within the mainstream of moderate Republican Reconstruction theory. First, he did not wish to give Congress general authority to provide protection for life, liberty, and property; he simply sought to ensure that each state granted the protection of the law to its inhabitants. Moreover, this right to protection would not have been guaranteed by a constant federal presence; Congress would be vested only "with power to hold . . . to answer before the bar of the national courts" those state officials who denied their citizens the right to protection of the law. He summarized his position succinctly in the debate over the Civil Rights Bill:

> The care of the property, the liberty, and the life of the citizen, under the solemn sanction of an oath imposed by your Federal Constitution, is in the States, and not in the Federal Government. *I have sought no change in that respect in the Constitution of the country.* I have advocated here an amendment which would arm Congress with the power to compel obedience to the oath, and punish all violations by State officers of the bill of rights, but leaving those officers free to discharge the duties enjoined upon them [by the Constitution].[82]

In other words, Bingham did not intend to give Congress the power to regulate private action, only to punish improper state action.

Despite Bingham's assurances on this issue, he was unable to rally the Republican party behind his proposal. The amendment received substantial support from radicals. Many moderates, however, apparently persuaded by arguments similar to Hale's, opposed Bingham; Thomas T. Davis, Roscoe Conkling, and Sen. William M. Stewart joined Hale and Hotchkiss in attacking the possible breadth of the proposal.[83] The fact that criticisms came from the Republican as well as the Democratic side of the aisle made it clear that the Bingham amendment could not obtain the two-thirds majority necessary for passage. In order to avoid outright defeat, on February 20 Bingham joined in voting to postpone final consideration of his proposal.[84] Commenting on the result, the *Republican* asserted that "no sane man supposes that the states would ratify such an amendment" and that "the people welcome every indication that Congress discards this policy and the leaders who urge it."[85]

Of course, all of "the people" did not agree with the verdict of the *Republican*; the more radical elements of the Republican party certainly would have welcomed the Bingham amendment. In its political context, however, the debate on the amendment had a significance beyond the outcome. The disposition of the Freedmen's Bureau Bill and the apportionment amendment demonstrated that only those civil rights measures that received virtually unanimous support from mainstream Republicans could be adopted. The discussions of the Bingham amendment revealed that a substantial portion of the party—the more conservative moderates—would not accept an open-ended expansion of the authority of the federal government. This point is crucial to the understanding of both the Civil Rights Act of 1866 and the Fourteenth Amendment.

5
The Civil Rights Act of 1866

Although its subject matter was similar to sections seven and eight of the Freedmen's Bureau Bill, the Civil Rights Bill had far more serious implications for the federal structure. The Freedmen's Bureau Bill was sectional; the Civil Rights Bill was national. Even more important, the Freedmen's Bureau Bill was avowedly a temporary measure designed to deal with a war-created emergency, but the structures to be established by the Civil Rights Bill were permanent. Thus the sponsors of the latter could not rely on a war power theory as a source of constitutional authority. These problems led to a protracted struggle over the passage of the bill, during which it underwent important structural changes designed to meet both potential and actual objections. As initially proposed by Lyman Trumbull on January 5, 1866, section one of the bill provided that

> there shall be no discrimination in civil rights or immunities among the *inhabitants* of any State or Territory of the United States on account of race, color, or previous condition of slavery; but the inhabitants of every race and color, without regard to any previous condition of slavery or involuntary servitude . . . shall have the same right to make and enforce contracts, to sue, be parties and give evidence, to inherit, purchase, lease, sell, hold, and convey real and personal property, and to full and equal benefit of all laws and proceedings for the security of persons and property and shall be subject to like punishment, pains and penalties, and to none other.

Section two provided criminal penalties for the deprivation of any of the rights guaranteed by section one "under color of any law, statute, ordinance, regulation or custom."[1]

The extensive enumeration of rights in section one clearly reflected Republican ideology regarding fundamental rights. Basically, the rights conferred by the Civil Rights Bill fall into two classes. The economic rights protected are those essential to meaningful participation in a free labor-based economy. The remaining specified rights are all elements of the rights to protection by and from government.[2] Together, these two sets of rights defined the minimum necessary for active membership in a society operating under the basic Republican ideology.

Identifying a source of authority that clearly authorized federal action was a problem, however. Congressional power to pass the proposal as initially formulated could be found only in the enforcement clause of the Thirteenth Amendment, and reliance on this constitutional provision posed substantial difficulties. First, one had to conclude that the Thirteenth Amendment went beyond mere dissolution of the master/slave relationship and granted Congress the authority to protect a certain class of rights that were essential to the status of a freedman. As already noted, substantial evidence supports the conclusion that this position was consistent with the intent of the drafters of the Thirteenth Amendment; nonetheless, from the language of the amendment, the grant of such power is far from clear.

Moreover, even if one conceded that the Thirteenth Amendment vested power in Congress to protect certain rights, some of the prohibitions in the Civil Rights Bill might have been considered as exceeding that power. Some Republicans believed that the authority of section two extended only to rights intrinsic to being a freedman; that is, if one could be a freedman without a particular right, then Congress could not rely on the authority of the Thirteenth Amendment to protect that right. Although aliens, for example, were not slaves, they had historically been limited in their right to own real property and to inherit intestate. Thus, one could be deprived of those rights and yet not have the status of a slave.[3] Nonetheless, both rights were protected by Trumbull's proposal.

To remedy this problem, even before the bill came before the full Senate, the bill was amended to provide that "all persons of African descent born in the United States are hereby declared to be citizens of the United States." Before its consideration by the House, section one was again modified, this time to provide that racial discrimination in the designated rights was prohibited between citizens, rather than inhabitants.[4] While solving some problems, the addition of the citizenship provision created others. Trumbull continued to insist that the Thirteenth Amendment bestowed ample authority for the exercise of federal power in this regard, arguing that the slaves automatically became citizens when freed. Under this view, Congress would then have authority under section two to guarantee all of the rights appurtenant to that status. The difficulty is that under this interpretation the amendment affected not only slaves but free blacks as well. Color was a bar to citizenship even in many free states during the antebellum era,[5] and in *Dred Scott v. Sandford* the Supreme Court had held that free blacks were not citizens of the United States.[6] Thus, even if one conceded that freedom from slavery entailed possession of natural rights, the Thirteenth Amendment remained a somewhat uncertain source of authority to grant citizenship.

Trumbull also relied on an alternative ground—the power of Congress to provide a uniform rule of naturalization. Again in contravention of *Dred Scott*, he argued that the naturalization power extended to native-born residents as well as to those coming from abroad. Trumbull further contended that the power to create citizens necessarily implied a power to guarantee that the states would ensure the rights of citizenship to the naturalized persons or groups. These rights he defined by reference to judicial decisions interpreting the privileges and immunities clause of Article IV—the comity clause.[7]

Trumbull explicitly recognized that the strictures of the comity clause applied only to cases in which citizens of one state were sojourning in another state.[8] His naturalization power argument, however, clearly implied that Congress could require states to grant all inhabitants the fundamental rights of citizenship. Trumbull revealed his understanding of this point when he responded to the objections of Edgar Cowan of Pennsylvania:

> As a question of power . . . the Federal Government has the power to make every inhabitant of Pennsylvania a citizen. Then could not every inhabitant of Pennsylvania own real estate, and could Pennsylvania deny the right? . . . As a mathematical proposition . . . the Federal Government has authority to make every inhabitant of Pennsylvania a citizen, and clothe him with the authority to inherit and buy real estate, and the State of Pennsylvania cannot help it.[9]

Trumbull's arguments were generally accepted by his Republican colleagues in the Senate. On February 2, the Civil Rights Bill passed the upper house by a vote of 33 to 12. Only three members of the majority party joined the united Democrats in opposition.[10]

The bill did not reach the floor of the House of Representatives until after the Freedmen's Bureau Bill had been vetoed and the Senate had failed to override the veto. The failure of the latter had made Republicans acutely aware of the possible federalism-related problems associated with the Civil Rights Bill. Thus, even before floor debate began, two changes in language were made to quiet the fears of those who found section one overly broad.

The first change eliminated the last vestiges of protection for aliens from the bill. In the Senate debate, Reverdy Johnson had complained that the measure as drafted by Trumbull would prohibit states from discriminating against aliens with respect to the ownership of property.[11]

The House Judiciary Committee addressed the problem by substituting a word: from "there shall be no discrimination among the *inhabitants* of the United States" to "there shall be no discrimination among the *citizens* of the United States." As James F. Wilson—floor manager of the Civil Rights Bill and chairman of the House Judiciary Committee—explained, the change was adopted because "there seems to be some doubt concerning the power of Congress to extend this protection to such inhabitants as are not citizens."[12] Federal action for the protection of rights thus became tied to the status of citizenship.

This point was underlined by reliance on the comity clause as a source of power to adopt the bill. Like Trumbull, Wilson relied on the Thirteenth Amendment and the naturalization clauses; in addition, however, he rejected the antebellum consensus that the comity clause only restrained a state from denying rights to those who were citizens of other states.[13] Instead, he explicitly adopted John Bingham's theory that the comity clause applied to a state's relationship to its own citizens.[14]

Even assuming that the comity clause protected citizens from actions of their own state governments, the Wilson approach still faced some problems. Article IV of the Constitution contains no express enforcement provision, nor is enforcement of its provisions mentioned in Article I, Section 8, which defines the powers of Congress. Bingham himself consistently maintained that Congress had no authority to enforce the comity clause. Moreover, a similar argument had been a mainstay of radical antislavery attacks on the Fugitive Slave Acts; Salmon P. Chase and others had declared that since the acts purported to be enforcing Article IV, Section 3 of the Constitution—the fugitive slave clause—they were unconstitutional because Congress had no power to pass legislation implementing that provision.

Wilson's solution to this problem was relatively simple but ironic. He relied on Justice Story's opinion in *Prigg v. Pennsylvania*—the case that *rejected* the antislavery position and held that Congress possessed authority to adopt legislation implementing Article IV, Section 3.[15] Indeed, Story posited *primary* federal authority to enforce the fugitive slave clause; although state courts could enforce the remedies provided by Congress, under Story's view state legislatures were forbidden from adding to these remedies. Taken together with Wilson's general reliance on the comity clause, this citation might suggest that the Civil Rights Act was intended to turn the antebellum theory of federalism on its head, establishing a regime in which the relationship between the citizen and the federal government was paramount and national authorities were to have primary responsibility for defining and enforcing the rights of the citizenry.

One can easily find evidence to buttress this view in the Civil Rights

Bill debates. The arguments of supporters are replete with references to the obligation of the federal government to protect its citizens from deprivation of their basic rights.[16] A closer examination of the debates, however, reveals that the intended change in the theory of federalism was in fact far more limited. William Lawrence of Ohio, for example, denied that the bill rested on a general congressional authority to punish offenses against life, liberty, and property; rather, congressional intervention was justified "when the States deny . . . the means without which life, liberty and property cannot be enjoyed." In that case, "the nation [may] intervene in behalf of her own citizens . . . to avert the annihilation of citizenship."[17] Although questioning the existing authority of Congress to pass the Civil Rights Bill, Christopher Delano of Ohio declared himself in favor of the policy embodied in the bill and suggested adopting a constitutional amendment "to enable Congress to protect and secure the rights of all her citizens *in any and in every state [which adopts] unjust, unequal and discriminating legislation.*"[18] And Wilson himself remarked that "if the States would all observe the rights of our citizens there would be no need of this bill" and that if all the states would obey the dictates of the comity clause, "we might well refrain from the enactment of this bill into a law."[19]

These and other similar statements suggest an even more ironic twist to Wilson's reliance on *Prigg*; the drafters of the Civil Rights Bill envisioned a federal structure analogous to that described in *Prigg* by Chief Justice Taney rather than by Story. Under Taney's theory the states were to be the primary repositories of responsibility for enforcement of the fugitive slave clause; "the action of the general government [is not] necessary except to resist and prevent [the] violation" of the rights guaranteed by the clause.[20] Likewise, mainstream Republicans in the Thirty-ninth Congress viewed the state governments as the primary bulwarks of fundamental rights, with the federal government stepping in only when the states failed to live up to their obligations. Indeed, one portion of Taney's opinion bears an almost eerie similarity to the post–Civil War Republican argument based on the comity clause.

The Constitution of the United States declares that the citizens of each State shall be entitled to all the privileges and immunities of citizens in the several States. And although these privileges and immunities, for greater safety, are placed under the guardianship of the general government, still the States may by their laws and in their tribunals protect and enforce them. They have not only the power, but it is a duty enjoined upon them by this provision in the Constitution.[21]

In one important respect, however, the Civil Rights Bill was substantially less intrusive on state prerogatives than Taney's approach in *Prigg*. For Taney plainly envisioned a continuing federal effort to enforce the fugitive slave clause no matter what parallel measures might be adopted by the states. By contrast, Lyman Trumbull clearly contemplated that the federal government would be involved only when the states neglected their duty to protect the fundamental rights of free blacks. As he summarized succinctly:

> [The Civil Rights Bill] may be assailed as drawing to the Federal Government powers that properly belong to "States"; but I apprehend, rightly considered, it is not obnoxious to that objection. It will have no operation in any State where the laws are equal, where all persons have the same civil rights without regard to color or race.[22]

The second change in language clearly limited the scope of the bill to matters of racial discrimination. Initially in the Senate, there had been some confusion on this point. The original wording of the bill provided that there shall be "no discrimination in civil rights or immunities . . . on account of race, color, or previous condition of slavery," but section one also mandated that "inhabitants of every race and color shall have the same [enumerated rights]." Although the first language quoted seemingly singled out racial discrimination, the latter clause could plausibly be interpreted to guarantee a minimum level of rights to all citizens. Lyman Trumbull's statement that the Civil Rights Bill "protects a white man just as much as a black man"[23] could be taken to support either view.

The House Judiciary Committee acted to clarify the issue. Section one was amended to provide that "citizens of every race and color . . . shall have the same [enumerated rights] *as [are] enjoyed by white citizens.*"[24] Some outside commentators ignored this new language and still saw the bill as embracing the general prohibitions embodied in the comity clause.[25] Most, however, recognized that only racial discrimination was to be forbidden. On the House floor Samuel Shellabarger of Ohio summarized this point, noting that "the bill does not reach mere private wrongs, but only those done under color of State authority; and that authority must be extended on account of race or color."[26] The *New York Evening Post* expanded on this point, asserting that

> Congress does not say in this bill by what rules evidence shall be given in courts, by what tenure property shall be held, or how the citizen shall be protected in his occupation. It only says to the

states, whatever laws you pass in regard to these matters . . . make them for the benefit of one race as well as for another.[27]

The decision to use the rights of whites as a touchstone not only limited the scope of the bill but also had substantial practical advantages. If Congress had instead attempted to define the protected civil rights in the abstract, it would have been forced to provide a detailed federal code defining punishments for crimes, the rights of women and children, and the various formalities attendant to the making of contracts and the transfer of property. By choosing to refer to the rights granted to white citizens, such matters were left in the hands of the states, preserving the structure of federalism to the greatest degree consistent with the objective of guaranteeing basic rights to freedmen.[28]

Of course, there was a potential danger in this approach. If they so chose, the states could deny the enumerated rights to *all* citizens, thus defeating the basic purpose of the bill. But given the prevalent recognition of the fundamentality of the rights guaranteed, this possibility was so farfetched that no speaker even considered it.

Despite the efforts to limit its scope, the Civil Rights Bill drew opposition not only from Democrats but also from a substantial number of mainstream House Republicans. Unlike the Democrats, mainstream Republicans were generally not concerned with the assertion of congressional authority to confer citizenship on blacks; they all believed that *Dred Scott* had been wrongly decided, and most felt that in any event it had been overruled by the Thirteenth Amendment.[29] But many Republicans feared the effect of the bill on the concept of states' rights. First, the latent implications of the citizenship-based analysis were viewed as inherently dangerous. Unlike those based on the Thirteenth Amendment, such arguments could not logically be limited to matters of racial discrimination. Thus, if Trumbull and Wilson were asserting generalized congressional authority to create citizens and to define and protect the rights guaranteed by that status, in the words of the moderate Christopher Delano of Ohio:

> you render this Government no longer a Government of limited powers; you concentrate and consolidate here an extent of authority which will swallow up all or nearly all of the rights of the States with respect to the property, the liberties, and the lives of its citizens.[30]

The fears Delano vocalized were exacerbated by the language of section one. In addition to the specific rights protected, section one also prohibited discrimination with respect to "civil rights or immunities." Delano and his colleague from Ohio, John Bingham, argued that this general language might guarantee to blacks the right to vote, the right to sit on juries, and other unspecified privileges.[31]

Uncertainty regarding the reach of section one also led to challenges to the constitutionality of section two. Republican opponents claimed that given the potential conflicts between the provisions of the Civil Rights Bill and existing state law, it would be fundamentally unfair to subject state officers to criminal penalties for simply following the pre-existing laws of their own state.[32] Moreover, some contended that to impose criminal penalties on judges for enforcing state laws was an unacceptable infringement on the rights of states.[33] Concerns about the bill's constitutionality were shared even by some of its proponents.[34]

In response to these misgivings, supporters of the bill once again emphasized the narrowness of their intentions. They insisted that the bill was meant to implement, not the theory of total racial equality, but rather the concept of limited absolute equality. The argument of Cong. Martin R. Thayer of Pennsylvania was typical:

> The sole purpose of the bill is to secure to [blacks] the fundamental rights of citizenship; those rights which constitute the essence of freedom, and which are common to the citizens of all civilized States; those rights which secure life, liberty and property and which make all men equal before the law.[35]

Thayer's statement was simply an echo of that of Lyman Trumbull himself:

> [This bill] provides that blacks are to be considered citizens [and that] they will be entitled to the rights of citizens. And what are they? The great fundamental rights set forth in this bill: the right to acquire property, the right to go and come at pleasure, the right to enforce rights in the courts, to make contracts, and to inherit and dispose of property. These are the very rights that are set forth in this bill as appertaining to every freeman.[36]

Despite these assurances, many House Republicans still objected to the bill. The depth of the opposition was demonstrated in the voting pattern on two motions to recommit the Civil Rights Bill to the House Judiciary Committee. The first motion would have instructed the committee to delete the general reference to "civil rights or immunities" from section one and to replace the criminal penalties of section two with civil penalties. The motion was defeated by a large majority, the result of the fact that the opposition included twenty-nine Democrats who wished to leave the bill in a form that was objectionable to more conservative Republicans. Thirty-seven Republicans—many of them

firmly within the party mainstream—voted in favor of the motion.[37] On
a motion to recommit without instructions, they were joined not only
by the Democrats but by an additional eighteen Republicans, and the
motion therefore carried.[38]

When the Civil Rights Bill reemerged from committee, it reflected a
compromise among Republicans anxious to agree on at least some type
of measure that would advance the Reconstruction process.[39] Moderate
opponents of the original proposal agreed to leave questions of constitutionality to the Supreme Court, in return for substantial conces-
sions. First, a provision was added which ensured quick resolution of
the constitutional issues. Second, protection was included for state officials who refused to enforce laws that were inconsistent with the bill.
Finally, and most important, the reference to discrimination in "civil
rights or immunities" was eliminated. The alteration was aimed specifically at fears that the proposal would be construed to involve suffrage. James Wilson commented, "I do not think [the deletion] materially changes the bill," and also noted that the change in language
destroyed any possibility of the bill being viewed as open-ended in any
respect.[40] As revised, the bill gained the support of all but a small handful of Republicans.[41]

Like the Freedmen's Bureau Bill, the Civil Rights Bill was generally
perceived as a moderate measure.[42] Indeed, the radical *National Anti-
Slavery Standard* sharply attacked the proposal, stating that it "meanly,
as well as unjustly, restrict[ed] suffrage to white men. . . . What are civil
rights worth that do not include suffrage?"[43] At first, there was some
hope that President Johnson would sign the bill. As a veto became increasingly certain, however, Senate Republicans recognized the tenu-
ousness of their position and moved to avoid a repeat of their earlier defeat. One Democrat had not voted on the Freedmen's Bureau Bill veto;
and though Republican James H. Lane of Kansas had voted to override, it
was rumored that he had been prepared to support the president if necessary in order to sustain the veto. In addition, Lane had voted against the
representation amendment. Thus, in order to be certain of victory Republicans were required to find somehow four additional votes.

Two of the votes could come from Waitman T. Willey of West Vir
ginia and William M. Stewart of Nevada. On the Senate floor Willey
had indicated that he would not support a Civil Rights Bill veto,[44] and
Stewart believed Johnson had personally promised him that he would
not veto the bill.[45] The struggle for the remaining votes centered around
John P. Stockton of New Jersey and Edwin D. Morgan of New York.

Stockton was a conservative Democrat who had been selected by a
somewhat irregular method.[46] He had been provisionally seated, and
the Senate committee investigating his credentials had recommended
that he be permanently seated. Ordinarily, this would have more or less

ended the matter, but some members of the Republican leadership saw an opportunity to remove a Johnson supporter. Led by Lyman Trumbull, however, the Republican members of the Judiciary Committee vigorously defended their view that Stockton should be confirmed. The maneuvering on the roll calls reflected both the closeness of the vote and the recognition that the Stockton decision might have a profound impact on the resolution of critical issues. Stewart, who had originally supported Stockton in the Judiciary Committee, deliberately absented himself from the Senate floor. At the instigation of Sumner and Fessenden, Lot Morrill of Maine broke a pair to vote against Stockton, whereupon Stockton voted in favor of himself. Initially, Stockton seemed to have survived by a narrow margin, but after a resolution that his vote not be counted, he was unseated by a 23 to 20 margin.[47]

As feared, Johnson vetoed the Civil Rights Bill on March 27. Further, his veto message left little room for compromise; rather than simply attacking the specifics of the bill, the message denied in broad terms congressional authority to protect the civil rights of freedmen. When the vote was taken in the Senate on April 6, the spotlight was on Lane and Morgan. The basis of Lane's affinity for the president has never been fully explained, but Morgan's problem was clear. On the one hand, he was committed to the concept of federal protection for freedmen; on the other hand, he was a political associate of Thurlow Weed and Secretary of State William H. Seward, who were closely allied with Johnson.[48] After strenuous efforts to reach a compromise failed, Lane ultimately resisted party pressure and supported the veto, but Morgan deserted his New York ties and voted to override. By a slim 33 to 15 margin (Johnson supporter James Dixon of Connecticut being absent because of illness), the veto was overridden in the Senate. The House of Representatives followed suit, and the Civil Rights Bill of 1866 was thereupon enacted into law.[49]

In the modern era, the most important issue with respect to the Civil Rights Act has been its intended effect on private discrimination. Those who conclude that the act was aimed only at state action and those who reject this position have each marshaled a variety of arguments to support their respective contentions.

THE ARGUMENT AGAINST
A STATE-ACTION LIMITATION

Public Accommodations

Discussions of public accommodations provide the strongest direct evidence against a state-action limitation on the reach of the Civil Rights

Act. The overblown rhetoric of Democratic Sen. Garrett Davis of Kentucky exemplifies the allegations of the opposition on this point:

> On ships and steamboats the most comfortable and handsomely furnished cabins and state-rooms, the first tables, and other privileges; in public hotels the most luxuriously appointed parlors, chambers, and saloons, the most sumptuous tables, and baths; in churches not only the most softly cushioned pews, but the most eligible sections; on railroads, national, local, and street, not only seats, but whole cars are assigned to white persons to the exclusion of negroes and mulattoes. All these discriminations . . . [t]his bill proposes to break down.[50]

Republican supporters of the Civil Rights Act seem to have been split on the issue. The *Germantown Telegraph*, for example, believed that the act guaranteed blacks the right to ride on public conveyances.[51] Other Republican newspapers took a different view. The discussions of the issue in the *Cincinnati Commercial*—a newspaper on the conservative edge of the Republican mainstream—furnish the most dramatic illustration. Initially the *Commercial* expressed grave doubts about the proposal, fearing that it might be interpreted to require the opening of "hotels, churches and theaters without distinction on the basis of color."[52] Within a month, however, the editors of the *Commercial* abandoned their objections, having been assured by supporters of the bill, including "influential members" of the Ohio delegation, that the prohibitions would not apply to Ohio at all; instead, the bill's provisions would affect only those states that had Black Codes.[53] In other words, having noted the existence of private discriminatory customs and decrying federal efforts to abolish those customs, the *Commercial* supported the Civil Rights Act after being assured that it would have no effect on private discrimination. The *Philadelphia North American* expressed a similar understanding, arguing not only that the act would have no impact on the right to hold office or sit on juries but also that the rights protected did not include the right to "go to any car, coach, hotel, church [or] public place."[54]

In any event, the resolution of the public-accommodations question could not be dispositive on the state-action issue in general. In the mid-1860s, public conveyances, inns, and the like were viewed as a kind of hybrid—privately owned but possessing public attributes.[55] The Supreme Judicial Court of Massachusetts captured the essence of this status in *Inhabitants of Worcester v. Western Railroad Corporation*:

> The establishment of [a railroad] is regarded as a public work, es-
> tablished by public authority, intended for the public use and bene-
> fit, the use of which is secured to the whole community, and con-
> stitutes, therefore, . . . a public easement. . . . It is true that the
> real and personal property, necessary to the establishment and
> management of the railroad, is vested in the corporation; but it is
> in trust to the public.[56]

Given the special nature of public accommodations, the drafters might
well have envisioned a regime in which racial discrimination in such
facilities was prohibited, but private discrimination generally was
unaffected.

Private Discrimination Generally

Proponents of the application of the Civil Rights Act to private discrimination must confront the language of section two of the act. Section
two provides criminal penalties for those who "under color of any law,
statute, ordinance, regulation or custom" deny persons the rights guaranteed by section one of the act. At first glance at least, the application
seems to be limited to state action. In addressing this problem, advocates of the private-discrimination theory use two basic strategies. First,
they deny that section two is in fact limited to state action. Second, they
contend that section one is broader in scope than section two.

The first argument is based primarily on the fact that section two applies to deprivations under color of "custom."[57] As Charles Fairman
has noted, however, in 1866 custom had a specialized meaning that was
entirely consistent with the theory that the Civil Rights Act was intended only to prohibit discrimination by the states.[58] For example, in
1861 the Pennsylvania Supreme Court had stated that "a custom is
something which has the force of law; is law by the usage and consent
of the people."[59] Similarly, four years earlier the Arkansas Supreme
Court had defined custom as "the law established by continued usage."[60] The United States Supreme Court had expressed a parallel understanding; in *Swift v. Tyson*, the Court stated that the "laws of a
State" include "long established local customs having the force of
laws."[61] During the debates over the Civil Rights Bill, Republican
Sen. William M. Stewart of Nevada seemed to evince a similar perception, equating acts done pursuant to "custom" with those "under
color of law."[62]

Further, as Michael Les Benedict observes, a critical difference in the
language of the Freedmen's Bureau Bill supports the conclusion that
"custom" was used as a limited term of art. That bill extended military jurisdiction to areas where rights were denied "in consequence of

any State or local law, . . . custom or *prejudice*."[63] The addition of the term "prejudice" suggests at least the possibility that the concept of rights was to be given a very broad interpretation. Unless totally inadvertent, the omission of that word from section two of the Civil Rights Act indicates that it was intended to have a narrower focus.[64]

The second argument—that section one was viewed as broader than section two—rests almost entirely on negative inference. Since the drafters explicitly restricted section two to state action, it is argued that the failure to provide such a specific limitation in section one must have indicated an intent to allow *civil* suits to remedy private discrimination. Unfortunately, this argument runs afoul of clear signs that Republicans viewed sections one and two as inseparably linked. Section one was seen as simply declaratory, providing no independent enforcement machinery. It is section two that, in Trumbull's words, "is the valuable section of the bill so far as protecting the rights of freedmen is concerned."[65] Thus, in discussing the situation in the state of Georgia, William Stewart focused entirely on the question of whether the strictures of section two would apply there. Contending that no violation of section two was possible in Georgia, he concluded that in that state "[the act] will be simply a nullity, because [the requisite discrimination] will not exist. . . . In Georgia, the bill [will have] no operation."[66]

Those who regard the Civil Rights Act as a prohibition against private discrimination also point to section three of the act. Section three provides for federal court jurisdiction in all cases affecting persons who cannot enforce the rights granted by section one in state court; it further provides for removal to federal court of any action commenced in state court against such persons. Advocates of the private-discrimination theory argue that this section rather plainly applies to private civil suits as well as those commenced by the state governments and that therefore by implication section one also affects private action.[67]

The difficulty with this argument is that it posits an unduly broad view of the intended scope of section three. Responding to Andrew Johnson's claim that section three improperly expanded the jurisdiction of the federal courts,[68] Trumbull gave the following explanation:

The jurisdiction is given to the Federal courts of a case affecting the person that is discriminated against. Now, he is not necessarily discriminated against, because there may be a custom in the community discriminating against him, nor because a Legislature may have passed a statute discriminating against him; that statute is of no validity if it comes in conflict with a statute of the United States; and it is not to be presumed that any judge of a State court would hold that a statute of a State discriminating against a person on account of color was valid when there was a statute of the United States with which it was in direct conflict, and *the case would not therefore arise in which a party was discriminated against until it was tested, and then if the discrimination was held valid he would have a right to remove it to a Federal court—or if undertaking to enforce his right in a State court he was denied that right, then he could go into the Federal court; but it by no means follows that a person [subject to a facially discriminatory statute] would have the right in the first instance to go to the Federal court.*[69]

In other words, section three was only supposed to give the federal courts a kind of quasi-appellate jurisdiction in cases where state courts failed to enforce the provisions of section one. Obviously, there is no inconsistency between such jurisdiction and a state-action limitation on the scope of the Civil Rights Act.

Finally, advocates of the private-discrimination theory often rely upon contextual arguments. They note that the members of the Thirty-ninth Congress received extensive reports of private as well as state-created racial discrimination and that Republicans were greatly disturbed by these reports. Thus, they contend, it is logical to assume that the legislation produced would address private as well as public discrimination.[70]

There can be no doubt that mainstream Republicans were concerned by the possibility that concerted efforts by white southerners would effectively deny the freed slaves those economic opportunities Republicans viewed as a requisite concomitant of freedom.[71] It does not necessarily follow, however, that they would address the problem through a general, direct federal prohibition on private discrimination. Two other factors mitigated against such a solution. First, as already noted, Republicans were strongly attached to the basic antebellum federal structure. Second, although willing to outlaw *legally enforced* racial discrimination in the North, Republicans clearly did not wish to use federal authority to compel any changes in the pattern of northern society—a society in which racism was still rampant (at least by twentieth-century standards).[72]

These competing concerns could be accommodated by a solution that capitalized on the still-uncertain status of the ex-Confederate states. Until the freedmen were established and state governments that could be depended upon to protect their basic rights installed, the defeated Confederacy could be kept under direct federal supervision through the Freedmen's Bureau and (if necessary) the military. Once full local autonomy was restored, restrictions on racially discriminatory state action would ensure that the authorities did not seek to deprive freedmen of their newly acquired status and rights.

This solution might seem the less plausible if no other evidence existed. However, proponents of the view that the Civil Rights Act was intended to apply only to state action can mount powerful, independent arguments in support of that position.

THE ARGUMENT FOR
A STATE-ACTION LIMITATION

The recognition that the Civil Rights Act was meant to embody the theory of limited absolute equality offers one of the strongest arguments for a state-action limitation. For if the guarantees of the rights to make and enforce contracts and to buy and sell property were viewed as encompassing a prohibition on private discrimination, the bill would not only have effected a truly revolutionary change in the federal system but would also have been entirely inconsistent with the very natural rights theory the Republicans sought to implement. Necessarily implicit in the theory that parties should be free to contract and to have the courts enforce voluntarily concluded agreements is the corollary that the parties are also free *not* to enter into contracts if they so choose. This concept formed the basis for the Republican attack on those provisions of the Black Codes that bound freedmen to particular employers.[73] To interpret the Civil Rights Act as a ban on private discrimination would in effect allow the national government to violate this principle by forcing *whites* to enter into contractual agreements with blacks, which the whites found distasteful. Of course, the guarantee of the right to full and equal benefit of all laws and proceedings for the security of personal property entails the requirement for states to protect blacks from private violence and lawlessness. But to infer an intention to interfere with private decisionmaking generally would be inconsistent with basic Republican political theory.

The course of the debates over the Civil Rights Bill reinforces the conclusion that only racially discriminatory state action was intended to be prohibited. The discussions of the problem of intermarriage are probably the most significant in this regard. The claim that the bill would promote miscegenation was an extremely troublesome one for the supporters of the proposal. The right to marry was clearly viewed as fundamental;[74] at the same time, however, laws prohibiting racial intermarriage were common even in the northern states.[75] Democrats vociferously argued that by overturning such laws, the bill would lead to the "mongrelization" of the white race.[76]

William Pitt Fessenden responded to this charge by stating that the Civil Rights Bill would not have any effect on miscegenation laws. He argued that such laws were "equal" because they allowed whites to marry whites and blacks to marry blacks but punished both races for mixed marriages. Thus Fessenden concluded that laws prohibiting interracial marriage were not inconsistent with the Trumbull proposal.[77]

As Reverdy Johnson pointed out, however, this argument had substantial weaknesses. For by their very terms miscegenation laws prohibited blacks from doing what whites were free to do—marry other whites. To claim that such laws did not discriminate on the basis of race therefore seemed at best disingenuous.[78] Perhaps cognizant of the flaws in Fessenden's position, Trumbull pursued a quite different tack. In addition to endorsing the "no discrimination" argument,[79] he contended simply that miscegenation laws were unnecessary to prevent the amalgamation of the races because "we need no law of the kind where no disposition for this amalgamation exists [thus] I do not think there will be any necessity for continuing [miscegenation laws] in my State."[80] In other words, private action could be relied upon to avert the perceived evils of interracial marriage.

Turning to the analogous provision of the Freedmen's Bureau Bill, Republican Cong. Samuel W. Moulton of Illinois was even more explicit. Noting his agreement with Fessenden's position, Moulton also argued:

> I deny that it is a civil right for a white man to marry a black woman or for a black man to marry a white woman. It is a simple matter of taste, of contract, of arrangement between the parties. No man has a right to marry any particular woman, black or white. It is a matter of mutual taste, contract, and understanding between the parties.[81]

At the very least, this argument must assume that private parties may choose to discriminate on the basis of race in selecting their marriage partner.

Although directly addressing only the issue of interracial marriage, the Trumbull/Moulton contention has much broader implications for the interpretation of the Civil Rights Bill. For their argument is based on the premise that marriage is a contract and thus covered by the general prohibition on discrimination with respect to the right to contract. If the bill did not prohibit private discrimination respecting the right to marry, it must also have been intended to leave whites free to choose whether or not to deal with blacks in all completely private transactions.

The private correspondence between two prominent Republicans

THE CIVIL RIGHTS ACT OF 1866

lends additional support for this conclusion. As already noted, later in the session Republican Cong. Samuel Shellabarger of Ohio offered a bill that would have prohibited certain types of private discrimination.[82] In a letter to Lyman Trumbull, Shellabarger asserted that the passage of the Civil Rights Bill did not obviate the necessity for Shellabarger's proposal because Trumbull's bill "punishes *discriminations* 'under *color of law*' and none others."[83]

Finally, the pattern of the opposition attacks on the Civil Rights Bill weakens the private-discrimination theory. No Democratic congressman or senator claimed in debate that the bill would have an impact on private choices outside the area of public accommodations; Johnson's veto measure also failed to make such a claim. The argument that the proposal would outlaw all private discrimination would obviously have made powerful political ammunition. Thus the failure of the opposition to put forward such an argument is best understood as an indication that the claim was simply untenable.

Indeed, the argument of the *Commercial* in its discussion of the public-accommodations issue seems to go even further. By focusing on the existence of discriminatory state *laws*, its analysis appears to suggest that state officials acting in contravention of those laws are not proceeding "under color of law" and thus are not covered by the federal statute. This conclusion also draws substantial support from other sources. For example, William Stewart noted that the state of Georgia had guaranteed the same rights to blacks by state law as those contained in the Civil Rights Act; if other southern states followed suit, he contended that the federal law would become "a nullity" and would have "no operation."[84] Similarly, the *Philadelphia Press* concluded that

> all that a state has to do to avoid operation of [the Civil Rights Act] is to remove every statute in conflict with it. It will not operate in Pennsylvania, New York, Massachusetts or any states the constitution and laws of which are framed in a spirit of Christian freedom.[85]

This evidence takes on particular significance against the background of the Republican approach to race relations at the state level. In state governments, Republicans had consistently advocated the principle of limited absolute equality. Their program included elimination of legal disabilities on blacks, together with protection of the right of equal access to public accommodations and common carriers. In the free states, Republicans had been largely successful in having this program implemented, although pockets of resistance remained in such states as Indiana and Oregon. Yet no state—no matter how radical its legislature—had adopted laws prohibiting purely private racial discrimination. Thus in order to conclude that the Civil Rights Act was intended to outlaw private discrimination, one would have to believe that a statute drafted by one of the most conservative Senate Republicans, and further modified to meet the objections of other conservative Republicans, was intended to dramatically expand all previous Republican commitments to the concept of racial equality. By contrast, if construed as aimed only at state action, the Civil Rights Act would be completely consistent with Republican efforts at the state level. The latter interpretation is surely more plausible.

In short, the arguments against the private-discrimination theory are compelling. The arguments do not, however, suggest that mainstream Republicans believed that with the passage of the act, they had reached the limits of their constitutional authority to protect civil rights. Indeed, despite his restricted interpretation of section three, Trumbull declared that section two of the Thirteenth Amendment

> authorizes us to do whatever is necessary to protect the freedman in his liberty. The faith of the nation is bound to do that; and if it cannot be done without, would have authority to come to the Federal courts in all cases.[86]

On this point Trumbull was supported by even the most conservative mainstream Republicans.[87]

The key question is whether Republicans thought they had the authority to establish the rules by which the courts would decide the cases before them. In the absence of other evidence, one might well conclude that the power to open the federal courts implies such authority. Some Republicans no doubt took this position; the debate over the Bingham amendment suggests, however, that others not only rejected this view but would oppose any attempt to vest the federal government with that power. Hence, one of the critical issues is whether section one of the Fourteenth Amendment was generally viewed as granting broad new powers to the federal government.

6
The Drafting of
The Fourteenth Amendment

The Republican party faced a major political crisis in early April 1866. The terms of Johnson's veto of the Civil Rights Bill had irrevocably alienated him from the party; thus, it seemed highly likely that in the upcoming elections of 1866, the president would lead a movement to end the Republican domination of Congress. The main issue in the election would clearly be Reconstruction. On this point Johnson had a straightforward policy—rapid restoration of the defeated states with few if any new constraints.

By contrast, the Republicans had yet to unite around a firm alternative. No single, comprehensive program had emerged from Congress. Moreover, most of the piecemeal attempts to address specific Reconstruction problems—the Freedmen's Bureau Bill, the apportionment amendment, and the Bingham amendment—had fallen victim to the combination of intraparty strife and Democratic opposition. Although the Civil Rights Bill had been passed over Johnson's veto, standing alone the act was hardly a platform on which an election could be contested. In short, mainstream Republicans badly needed to reach a consensus on a comprehensive Reconstruction program that could be presented as an alternative to Johnson's plan.[1]

THE OWEN PLAN

It was against this background that Robert Dale Owen presented his Reconstruction plan to various members of the Joint Committee on Reconstruction in mid-April. The proposal began with a five-part constitutional amendment. The first section dealt with guarantees of civil rights for blacks. The second section mandated that states grant black suffrage no later than July 4, 1876. The third section provided that until 1876, if a state excluded a portion of its population from the right to vote under criteria based upon race, that portion of the population would not be counted in determining the number of representatives to which the state was entitled in the national legislature. The fourth section required the repudiation of debts incurred to support the Confederate war effort, and the fifth section gave Congress power to enforce all four of the preceding sections.

The Owen plan continued by specifying conditions under which the ex-Confederate states could regain their representation in Congress. Such restoration would occur if and only if (a) the proposed amendment had become part of the Constitution; (b) the relevant state had modified its laws to conform with the amendment; and (c) the elected representatives had taken the appropriate oath of office. In any event, certain classes of ex-Confederate leaders were to be barred from becoming members of Congress until 1876.[2]

As a political statement, the Owen plan fit the needs of the Republican party perfectly. First, it spelled out in some detail the changes the party demanded in both the national and southern political structure. Second, its statutory portion explicitly stated that when the ex-Confederate states agreed to make these changes, readmission would immediately follow. Finally, the amendment format (if not its content) was peculiarly suited to respond to widely shared attitudes of the northern populace. In simple terms, in 1866 most northerners desired some overt confession of southern wrongdoing as a precondition for restoration of the full privileges of citizenship and statehood.[3] No such admission had been forthcoming before 1866. By requiring states to ratify the amendment in order to regain representation in Congress, the Owen plan would exact just such a gesture.

Further, as a potential basis for compromise between moderates and radicals, the Owen plan had much to recommend it. There was something in it for everyone. It began with the one principle upon which the entire Republican party could agree—that blacks should have at least some of the legal rights of citizens. Although moderates might have preferred that the proposed protection be phrased in narrower terms, immediate black suffrage was not included. At the same time, radicals were no doubt pleased by the provision which insured that blacks would eventually be enfranchised. Both groups could agree on the need to ensure that the Congress would not immediately be inundated by the increase in southern representation generated by the freeing of the slaves; they could also concur on the provision in the proposal which required the repudiation of the Confederate war debt. Perhaps of greatest significance to the moderates, the plan set relatively mild but concrete standards for the restoration of the southern states and did not prevent large classes of southern leaders from participating in state government. The radicals, by contrast, would be satisfied by the temporary exclusion of many Confederates from service in Congress. Finally, and perhaps most important in terms of reaching a compromise, the various parts of the Owen plan were seen as inextricably bound up with each other; thus, no faction could attack the sections it found distasteful without endangering the entire program. Thus, on its face, the Owen plan seemed to provide a workable basis for unifying the Republican party.

Despite the apparent promise of the Owen proposal, neither the Joint Committee nor the full Congress adopted the plan intact. The five-part framework of the amendment was retained, but the content of several provisions was altered significantly. The import of some of the changes was obvious: The elimination of all reference to black suffrage was an effort to placate moderates, while the addition of a provision disenfranchising former Confederates was a radical initiative. Yet the meaning of the change in language of section one is far less clear; both the Owen proposal and the final language adopted seem to be couched in quite general terms.

The best source of illumination on this point would be a record of the Joint Committee's actual discussions. Unfortunately, no such record exists. In fact, extensive investigation of private correspondence by a legion of historians has unearthed only the most fragmentary evidence on the issue. There is, however, a journal that records the votes of each of the committee members on the various proposals brought before the committee.[4] By tracing the patterns on key votes dealing with section one and placing those patterns in their political context, one can gain some insight into the question of whether the ultimate language reflected radical or moderate thinking.

Of course, such an analysis would be useless without some understanding of the basic philosophies of the various Joint Committee members on civil rights issues. Clearly, the Democrats on the committee—Reverdy Johnson, Andrew J. Rogers, and Cong. Henry Grider of Kentucky—could be expected to hold the most conservative views. The divisions among the Republicans on the committee, by comparison, is reflected in their votes on civil rights measures that split the party before section one of the Fourteenth Amendment was adopted. Table 6.1 maps these divisions.

The table reveals a Republican delegation divided rather evenly among the various factions of the party. Four members of the committee—Sen. Jacob M. Howard of Michigan and Congressmen George S. Boutwell of Massachusetts, Thaddeus Stevens of Pennsylvania, and Elihu B. Washburne of Illinois—supported radical positions on civil rights fairly consistently. Although more moderate, Cong. Justin S. Morrill of Vermont also demonstrated some sympathy toward those positions. By contrast, Sen. Ira Harris of New York and Congressmen Henry T. Blow of Missouri and Roscoe Conkling of New York were clearly allied with the conservative elements in the Republican mainstream. The remaining committee members—Fessenden, Bingham, and senators James W. Grimes of Iowa and George H. Williams of

Oregon—are best described as center moderates, sometimes supporting conservative positions and other times voting with the radicals. The interaction between these groups generated the final form of section one.

VOTING PATTERNS ON SECTION ONE

The final phase in the development of section one began on April 21, 1866, when the following section was introduced as part of the Owen plan:

> No discrimination shall be made by any state, nor by the United States, as to the civil rights of persons because of race, color, or previous condition of servitude.[5]

Bingham immediately moved to amend this provision by adding:

> Nor shall any state deny to any person within its jurisdiction the equal protection of the laws, nor take private property for public use without just compensation.

This emendation was defeated. Johnson, Stevens, Bingham, Blow, and Rogers voted in favor; Grimes, Howard, Williams, Washburne, Morrill, Grider, and Boutwell voted against;[6] Fessenden, Harris, and Conkling did not participate. The section as proposed was then adopted without a roll-call vote.

On its face, the voting pattern on Bingham's proposal is somewhat surprising. Since his suggestion left the civil rights provisions of the Owen amendment intact and only supplemented them, one might expect that the additions would draw radical support. Moreover, radicals had been the mainstay of Bingham's earlier civil rights amendment. But in this case, radicals were generally displeased with Bingham's proposal; the amendment drew its primary support from the conservative wing of the committee—two Democrats and Bingham and Blow, the two most conservative Republicans voting. Six of the seven "nay" votes, on the other hand, came from more radical elements of the committee—four radicals or moderates with radical leanings (Howard, Washburne, Morrill, and Boutwell) and two center moderates (Grimes and Williams). Adding to the confusion is the fact that the conservative bloc was supported by one committed radical (Stevens) and the radical votes were joined by that of one Democrat (Grider).[7]

The key to understanding this vote lies in the fact that the Bingham amendment would not have added to the constitutional protection for

Table 6.1 Positions on Black Rights

	Congressmen				
	In the Joint Committee				
	Black Suffrage				
	Tennessee 2/20/66 (Yea–R)	Section 2 of amendment 4/21/66 (Nay–X)		Removal of Section 2 4/28/66 (Nay–R)	
Rogers	C	X		C	
Grider	C	X		C	
Bingham	C	M		C	
Blow	NV	M		C	
Morrill	R	M		C	
Washburne	R	M		R	
Conkling	C	NV		C	
Stevens	R	M		C	
Boutwell	R	X		C	

	Federal Power				
	Strike out equal political rights and privileges 1/27/66 (Yea–C)	Report amendment 1/27/66 (Nay–X)	Bingham replacement 2/3/66 (Nay–C)	Agree to amendment 2/3/66 (Nay–C)	Report amendment 2/3/66 (Nay–C)
Rogers	NV	NV	R	C	C
Grider	C	X	C	C	C
Bingham	R	M	R	R	R
Blow	NV	NV	NV	NV	R
Morrill	R	M	R	R	R
Washburne	NV	NV	R	'R	NV
Conkling	C	X	C	C	C
Stevens	R	M	C	R	R
Boutwell	R	X	R	R	R

	In the Full House					
	Black Suffrage					
	Postpone D.C. Suffrage Bill 1/18/66 (Yea–MC)	Limit D.C. Suffrage Bill 1/18/66 (Yea–MC)	Passage of D.C. Suffrage Bill 1/18/66 (Nay–C)	Colorado 5/3/66 (Yea–R)	No new territories to be admitted without black suffrage 5/27/66 (Nay–C)	Nebraska 7/27/66 (Nay–R)
Rogers	U	U	C	NV	C	NV
Grider	U	U	C	C	C	NV

Continued

Table 6.1 *continued*

	In the Full House					
	Black Suffrage					
	Postpone D.C. Suffrage Bill 1/18/66 (Yea–MC)	Limit D.C. Suffrage Bill 1/18/66 (Yea–MC)	Passage of D.C. Suffrage Bill 1/18/66 (Nay–C)	Colorado 5/3/66 (Yea–R)	No new territories to be admitted without black suffrage 5/27/66 (Nay–C)	Nebraska 7/27/66 (Nay–R)
Bingham	U	U	R	C	R	C
Blow	U	MC	R	C	NV	NV
Morrill	U	U	R	R	R	R
Washburne	U	U	R	R	NV	NV
Conkling	MC	MC	R	C	R	C
Stevens	U	U	R	R	R	R
Boutwell	U	U	R	R	R	R

	Black Rights Generally	
	Recommit Civil Rights Bill with limiting instructions 3/9/66 (Yea–MC)	Motion to recommit Civil Rights Bill without instructions 3/9/66 (Yea–C)
Rogers	U	C
Grider	NV	C
Bingham	MC	C
Blow	MC	C
Morrill	U	C
Washburne	U	R
Conkling	MC	C
Stevens	U	R
Boutwell	U	R

	Senators	
	In the Joint Committee	
	Black Suffrage	
	Tennessee 2/20/66 (Yea–R)	Section 2 of amendment 4/21/66 (Nay–X)	Removal of Section 2 4/28/66 (Nay–R)
Johnson	NV	X	U
Harris	C	M	U
Fessenden	NV	M	NV
Grimes	NV	M	U
Williams	C	M	U
Howard	R	M	R

Federal Power

	Strike out equal political rights and privileges 1/27/66 (Yea–C)	Report amendment 1/27/66 (Nay–X)	Bingham replacement 2/3/66 (Nay–C)	Agree to amendment 2/3/66 (Nay–C)	Report amendment 2/3/66 (Nay–C)
Johnson	C	C	NV	NV	C
Harris	C	C	C	C	C
Fessenden	R	R	C	R	R
Grimes	NV	NV	C	R	R
Williams	R	R	R	R	R
Howard	NV	NV	R	R	R

In the Full Senate

Black Suffrage

	Amendment to proposed constitutional amendment on representation 3/9/66 (Yea–R)	Tennessee 7/21/66 (Yea–R)
Johnson	C	C
Harris	C	C
Fessenden	C	C
Grimes	C	C
Williams	C	C
Howard	NV	C

Black Rights Generally

	Amendment providing full equality for blacks (1) 3/9/66 (Yea–R)	Amendment providing full equality for blacks (2) 3/9/66 (Yea–R)
Johnson	C	C
Harris	C	C
Fessenden	C	C
Grimes	C	C
Williams	C	R
Howard	NV	NV

Key:
 R = Radical Position
 C = Conservative Position
MC = Moderate Conservative Position

M = Moderate Position
X = Extreme Position
U = Uncertain Ideological Position
NV = Not Voting

blacks. The original text of the Owen proposal already prohibited discrimination against the freed slaves. Instead, the basic effect of the supplement—particularly its just-compensation clause—was to extend constitutional protection to the rights of whites generally. As previously noted, in the congressional debates on civil rights measures, Bingham had expressed concern over the seizure of the property of white unionists.[8] His amendment was intended to prevent such seizures in the future.

From a radical perspective, the difficulty with the Bingham proposal may have been that it would have protected ex-Confederate sympathizers as well. Many radicals wished not only to exclude the southern aristocracy from the political process but also to destroy the economic power of that class. One idea for accomplishing this was confiscation and redistribution of their lands. If southern radicals were to gain control of the reconstructed governments, the Bingham amendment might stand in the way of a thoroughgoing economic reconstruction. Further, unlike Bingham's earlier, radical-supported amendment that had been postponed by the House on February 28, Congress could not alter the protections provided to whites. Thus, radical votes against the Bingham addition emerge as entirely logical.

From a Democratic perspective, Bingham's proposal created something of a dilemma. On the one hand, it offered some protection for Democratic interests against possible future predations by radical southern governments. On the other hand, adding restrictions on state governments was contrary to the basic Democratic philosophy of states' rights. Consequently, it is not surprising that the Democrats split on the Bingham vote.

This leaves only Stevens's vote to explain. One might have expected Stevens, as a leading proponent of confiscation schemes, to oppose the just-compensation provision. Here political considerations may have been crucial. Throughout the deliberations of the Joint Committee, one of Stevens's major aims was to generate a program for Reconstruction that would unite the Republican party. Given that Bingham was the leading House moderate on the Joint Committee, Stevens's vote on the proposal can be seen as a move designed simply to placate him on a relatively minor matter.

Despite his initial defeat, Bingham remained steadfast in his determination to alter the shape of the original amendment. Later the same day he offered the following as an additional section:

No state shall make or enforce any law which shall abridge the privileges or immunities of citizens of the United States; nor shall any state deprive any person of life, liberty or property without due process of law nor deny to any person within its jurisdiction the equal protection of the laws.

Within the next four days this proposal was voted on three times. The positions of the various committee members changed with almost dizzying speed. On April 21, the committee approved the new section by a vote of 10 to 2.[9] Only Grider and Rogers dissented, while Fessenden, Harris, and Conkling were absent. On a motion to reconsider on April 25, however, the section was removed by a 7 to 5 vote.[10] On the same day, an attempt to offer the Bingham language as a separate amendment drew only the votes of Bingham and the three Democrats.[11]

This voting pattern appears at first to be totally inexplicable. In the space of four days, three roll-call votes were taken on seemingly identical issues—whether Bingham's new section would be proposed in addition to the original Owen plan. Of those who participated in all three votes, every Republican except Bingham voted both for and against the proposal at least once.

In view of the radicals' opposition to the "equal protection/just compensation" formulation, their support for Bingham's second proposal on April 21 seems particularly anomalous. Since both versions would have left intact the initial Owen language prohibiting discrimination in civil rights on the basis of race, both must be viewed as protecting the rights of the citizenry generally, rather than simply banning discrimination against blacks. Indeed, the later proposal from Bingham seems considerably broader in scope in this regard, which would magnify potential radical objections; yet radicals by and large had opposed Bingham's initial suggestion, while Republicans of all stripes united around his later one.

Changes in the political dynamic during the course of the meetings probably explain these seeming inconsistencies in the voting pattern. Between the time of Bingham's first and second proposals, the Joint Committee had considered and approved each of the operative provisions of Owen's constitutional amendment. With the exception of a single vote by Boutwell on the enfranchisement section, the Republicans had unanimously supported each provision.[12] The Owen plan thus gave every indication of being the uniting force Republicans had been seeking. The perceived need to preserve this newly found cohesion might well have been the factor that moved the more radical members of the Joint Committee to reconsider their positions. By April 25—the date of the next crucial vote on Bingham's proposals—the political situation had changed substantially. Influential Republicans from outside the Joint Committee had voiced strong opposition to the inclusion of a black-suffrage provision in the constitutional amendment.[13] The Owen plan's potential as a unifying force was therefore substantially reduced.

Table 6.2 Votes on Section One

	First Bingham Addition 4/21/66	Second Bingham Addition 4/21/66	Motion to Remove Second Bingham Addition 4/25/66	Separate Article 4/25/66	Ultimate Section One 4/28/66
Congressmen					
Rogers (D)	Y	N	N	Y	Y
Grider (D)	N	N	Y	Y	Y
Bingham (R)	Y	Y	N	Y	Y
Blow (R)	Y	Y	N	N	Y
Morrill (R)	N	Y	N	N	N
Washburne (R)	N	Y	NV	NV	Y
Conkling (R)	NV	NV	Y	N	Y
Stevens (R)	Y	Y	N	N	Y
Boutwell (R)	N	Y	Y	N	Y
Senators					
Johnson (D)	Y	Y	Y	Y	Y
Harris (R)	NV	NV	Y	NV	NV
Fessenden (R)	NV	NV	NV	NV	NV
Grimes (R)	N	Y	NV	N	N
Williams (R)	N	Y	Y	N	Y
Howard (R)	N	Y	Y	N	N

The dispute over suffrage indirectly affected the Bingham initiative. Some of the Republicans on the Joint Committee had apparently abandoned opposition to Bingham's proposal in the name of Republican party solidarity. Given the disagreement on the suffrage question, the possibility of reaching consensus seemed increasingly remote. Thus it is not surprising that on April 25, reversing its decision of only four days earlier, the committee voted by 7 to 5 to remove Bingham's provision from the original amendment. The voting pattern was remarkably similar to that on Bingham's initial "equal protection/just compensation" proposal; only Reverdy Johnson and Justin Morrill changed their positions.[14]

The political dynamic also explains the difference in the voting pattern on Bingham's final initiative—the attempt to have his second proposal reported as a separate amendment. When included in the Owen plan, the Bingham proposal would have the effect of cementing the support of Bingham and his allies for the remainder of the amendment. By contrast, when offered as a separate measure the Bingham proposal was potentially very divisive. Democrats could argue that by voting for the separate amendment, moderate Republicans could secure constitutional protection for the basic rights of blacks without also taking on such baggage as black suffrage, which some moderates found distasteful. If the Democrats could convince moderates to support this position, reduction in representation for the South might also be avoided. Using the Bingham proposal in this manner was particularly attractive to Democrats because, once separated from the overall Owen plan, it lacked an enforcement provision. Thus, the way would be clear to argue at some later date that the amendment granted no new powers to Congress. In any event, the potential divisiveness of a separate amendment dealing with civil rights plausibly explains the unanimous Republican rejection of Bingham's final initiative on April 25, as well as the strong Democratic support for it.

At this stage, the outlook for any proposal drafted along the lines advocated by Bingham seemed quite dim. But the Owen plan as a whole also seemed to be in considerable difficulty. By a margin of 7 to 6, the Joint Committee had voted to report to the floor a constitutional amendment along the lines of that proposed by Owen, together with a bill that would have allowed restoration of southern congressional representation when his conditions were met.[15] But the opposition of Republicans as diverse as Boutwell, Conkling, and Blow on the committee hardly augured well for the prospects of gaining either the two-thirds vote in both houses of Congress necessary to propose a constitutional amendment or the approval of the three-quarters of the States necessary to ratify that amendment. The major dispute was not over Bingham's proposals; although controversial, they were apparently not critical, even to him. Instead, as already noted, the issue of black suffrage seemed to be the primary stumbling block to Republican unity. A number of important Republican state organizations had made it clear that they did not wish to conduct an election campaign on the basis of a platform that included the principle of black suffrage in any form.[16]

The unpopularity of black suffrage confronted the radicals with a delicate tactical problem. One possible alternative was to fight for the retention of the suffrage provision even though it placed the entire Republican Reconstruction program in jeopardy. This would be a high-risk strategy, for if the Fourteenth Amendment failed in Congress, Republicans would be left with no coherent plan to present as an alternative to conservative presidential Reconstruction.

Despite the risks, radicals initially seemed determined to pursue this strategy. On April 25, in a motion to reconsider the vote to adopt the Fourteenth Amendment, two of the three radicals participating— Stevens and Howard—voted against reconsideration.[17] Boutwell, the remaining radical, probably voted to reconsider not because he objected to the principle of black suffrage but rather because the amendment as proposed postponed such suffrage until 1876. By contrast, the solid coalition of moderates and conservatives who joined Boutwell to carry the

motion to reconsider were doubtless motivated by an aversion to the suffrage provision.[18]

Shortly thereafter, the House radicals on the Joint Committee seem
to have decided to pursue a different course of action. Rather than consistently pressing for the most radical language possible, they seem to
have agreed to accept a more moderate proposal, which, although incorporating some radical principles, might have a better chance for ultimate adoption. To this end, on April 28, Stevens, the leading House radical, moved to delete the suffrage provision altogether.[19] The motion
carried overwhelmingly, with Stevens being joined not only by all of the
conservative and moderate members of the Committee but also by Justin Morrill, who generally supported radical positions, and the hard-
core radical Boutwell. Only Washburne and radical Jacob Howard dissented.[20] The elimination of the suffrage provision created potential
problems for section two, that dealt with the basis of representation.
Obviously, some permanent change was necessary to reduce potential
southern power; the question was how to draft a proposal that would
avoid the impasse that had ultimately defeated the Joint Committee's
proposal earlier in the session. Finally, the Committee adopted a compromise between a representation amendment based on legal voters and
the Owen provision, which had focused only on racial exclusions. Only
radicals Howard, Stevens, and Washburne dissented.[21]

At this stage the radicals went on the offensive. Boutwell first attempted to include a provision forever disqualifying large numbers of
former Confederates from national office. This measure narrowly failed
to pass the committee.[22] A motion was then made to add as section three
a provision to prevent virtually all previous rebels from voting in national elections until 1870. Although proposed by Harris—one of the
most conservative moderates—the measure drew its primary support
from radicals. At first, the addition was defeated on a vote of
8 to 7;[23] a dramatic shift by Grimes, however, reversed this vote and
added the disenfranchisement provision to the proposed constitutional
amendment.[24]

It was against this background that Bingham made his final effort to
modify the Owen amendment. He moved that the committee replace
Owen's section one with the language used in his second proposal—
concerning equal protection, due process, and privileges and immunities—that had initially been accepted on April 21, but removed on
April 25. The motion carried by a vote of 10 to 3, with Grimes, Howard,
and Morrill dissenting, and Fessenden and Harris not voting.[25]

The voting pattern on the Bingham substitute clearly reflects the
moderate origin of the current language of section one. The more moderate and conservative elements of the committee were virtually unanimous in their support of the proposal; among this group, only Grimes

dissented. One would hardly expect such agreement unless the proposal were interpreted as a move to soften the language of the civil rights amendment.

One immediate problem with this conclusion is the radical voting pattern on the Bingham substitute. A solid negative radical vote would confirm the impression that the substitute was a moderate proposal. But no such clear voting pattern emerged; instead, radicals divided almost evenly on the new language. In political context, such a split is entirely consistent with the premise that the current section one has moderate roots. Radicals voting on the proposal were faced with a tactical problem analogous to the one confronting them on black suffrage. In isolation, radicals might well have preferred the Owen language, but they also had to consider the problem of drafting an amendment that would pass. Mollifying the moderates on the civil rights issue might have sounded especially attractive since the proposed amendment already contained an important radical initiative—the rebel-disenfranchisement provision. In such a situation one might well expect a split between those radicals seeking a political compromise and those adhering rigidly to principle.

If the break in radical ranks were the only available evidence, one might conclude that the major objective of Bingham's proposal was to extend section one beyond the context of racial discrimination. This interpretation, however, does not explain the behavior of the conservative moderates Conkling and Williams or Democrats Johnson and Grider. In earlier tests each had voted against the Bingham language, presumably on the ground that it unduly expanded the reach of constitutional protections.[26] Indeed, Conkling had been one of the two Republicans who had opposed Bingham's original federal-power proposal. Yet on the critical ballot of April 28, all four supported Bingham.

One crucial point explains the change in votes. Unlike earlier votes on the Bingham language, the April 28 roll call was on a *substitute* for section one of the Owen plan, rather than an addition to the protections of that plan. This distinction has two important consequences. First, taken together with the elimination of the black-suffrage provision and the alteration of section two, the change in section one had the effect of creating a Reconstruction plan that never mentioned race. Thus in the upcoming election of 1866, Republicans would not need to run solely as the champion of the rights of blacks. Instead the party could present its platform as guaranteeing the allegiance of the defeated southern states and protecting the fundamental rights of loyalists generally. This prospect must have been appealing to moderates such as Conkling and Williams.

This explanation, however, fails to account for the actions of Grider and Johnson. As Democrats, they would hardly be moved by an appeal to improve the political salability of the Republican platform. Only one explanation for the Democratic shift is also consistent with the Republican voting pattern. Although it extended constitutional protection beyond the problem of racial discrimination, the Bingham substitute must have been aimed at a narrower class of rights than the Owen proposal was. Given Bingham's own previous statements, this class of rights could be no broader than what would be guaranteed under the theory of limited absolute equality.

As an explanation of moderate support for the Bingham language, this theory fits comfortably with the pattern of earlier actions of the Thirty-ninth Congress. For example, in the House, we have seen that moderates only supported the Civil Rights Bill after it had been modified to avoid the possibility of an overly expansive judicial interpretation. Further, the defeat of the early proposal to expand congressional power over individual rights stemmed largely from fears that the proposal was unduly broad. A moderate initiative to narrow the Owen plan's protections would thus be entirely compatible with earlier actions of moderates on the same issue.

In short, to be consistent with the political dynamic of 1866, section one must have been intended to be not only less sweeping than the original Owen proposal but also not subject to the objections that caused the rejection of Bingham's original amendment. It is against this background that one must evaluate the contemporary discussions of the reach of section one.

7

The Intentions of the Drafters of Section One

Section one was not considered by either supporters or opponents of the Fourteenth Amendment to be the most significant feature of the Joint Committee proposal. For example, in introducing the Fourteenth Amendment on the House floor, Thaddeus Stevens referred to section two as "the most important in the article."[1] Later in the debate he snarled, "Give us section three or give us nothing."[2] The bulk of the controversy over the amendment concerned these two sections.[3] Nonetheless, a substantial amount of time was also devoted to discussions of the merits of section one.

Republicans and Democrats expressed radically different views of the scope of the proposed section one. Republican John Bingham, for example, asserted that "this amendment takes from no State any right that ever pertained to it."[4] Democrat George S. Shanklin argued that "the first section of this proposed amendment to the Constitution is to strike down . . . State rights and invest all power in the national government."[5] Admittedly, both proponents and opponents saw the measure as embodying at least some principles similar to those underlying the Civil Rights Act. But Republicans saw this as a positive feature, while Democrats viewed the situation with dismay. Thus, Thaddeus Stevens noted that it was "partially true" that the Civil Rights Act "secures the same things" as section one, but he argued that the constitutional amendment would guard against the repeal of the act.[6] Andrew Rogers, by contrast, condemned the attempt to constitutionally embody "that outrageous and miserable civil rights bill."[7]

In evaluating the different statements about the proposed amendment, a number of factors must be taken into account. First, discovering the intent of the drafters of any piece of legislation from the statements of its adversaries is at best a perilous enterprise. Typically, in attempting to defeat proposed legislation, opponents will bring forth a parade of horribles, greatly exaggerating the effect of the proposals. The more extreme Democratic descriptions of section one may be viewed as falling within that pattern. Of course, one can also argue that advocates of a proposition like section one might tend to minimize its impact in order to gain support. But several contextual points suggest that the Joint Committee formulation was in fact intended to have only a limited impact.

First, section one was part of an omnibus Reconstruction measure designed to unify the Republicans. As the previous actions and debates of the Thirty-ninth Congress had demonstrated, any measure that was understood to undermine the primacy of the states in regulating their internal affairs would have divided the party and thus defeated the main goal of party cohesion. The most logical conclusion is that section one embodied only the basic moderate program of simply providing the federal government with authority to ensure that the states themselves enforced certain fundamental rights.

This conclusion is buttressed by the fact that moderates clearly preferred the ultimate language to two other related formulations. As noted before, the choice to replace the original Owen wording—which would have simply prohibited any racial discrimination by states in civil rights—seemed plainly a move to placate moderates. Similarly, more conservative elements obviously preferred the committee version of section one to the original Bingham proposal. During the course of the floor debates on the committee draft of the amendment, Republicans were by no means shy in suggesting changes in the various sections of the proposal. Moderates were particularly active in criticizing the disfranchisement provisions of section three.[8] Yet only two nominal Republicans—Johnson supporters Edgar Cowan of Pennsylvania and Charles E. Phelps of Maryland—argued that the Joint Committee's tripartite formulation of section one intruded unduly on states' rights.[9] None of the Republicans who had voiced federalism-based concerns regarding Bingham's initial proposal—Conkling, Hale, congressmen Davis and Hotchkiss, and Senator Stewart—expressed similar objections to the committee's version of section one (although Hale would later claim that he had made such objections).[10] Indeed, Stewart was one of those who pressed for augmentation of section one through the addition of a definition of citizenship. Thus in context, Republican protestations of narrow intentions are more credible than contrary Democratic arguments.

The attitude of the *Springfield Republican* is particularly instructive. As we have seen, the *Republican* had strongly attacked Bingham's original congressional-power proposal on the ground that it would have undermined the traditional allocation of authority between state and federal governments. But although the newspaper's support of the new Joint Committee proposal was only lukewarm, its reservations were not based on fears that section one would unduly expand the scope of federal authority; rather, editorials described the tripartite formulation as "superfluous" and "of no practical value" and expressed fears that it would attract attention away from section two, which the *Republican* judged as the truly significant portion of the Joint Committee plan.[11] Such a view is totally inconsistent with an understanding that section one was intended to vest the federal government with sweeping new authority to protect civil rights.

GENERAL DISCUSSIONS

Both in Congress and in the newspapers, much of the debate over section one was conducted in quite general terms without differentiation among its various components. For the Democrats, Shanklin's attack was typical of the genre, as was this statement by Benjamin M. Boyer of Pennsylvania:

> The first section embodies the principles of the civil rights bill, and is intended to secure ultimately, and to some extent indirectly, the political equality of the negro race. It is objectionable also in its phraseology, being open to ambiguity and admitting of conflicting constructions.[12]

Many of the Republican defenses of the proposal were cast in equally broad language. For example, the only direct references to section one in the Report of the Joint Committee on Reconstruction address the necessity of "providing such constitutional . . . guarantees as will tend to secure the civil rights of all citizens of the republic" and of making "changes [in] the organic law as shall determine the civil rights and privileges of all citizens in all parts of the republic." No more precise definition is given of the rights protected. Introducing the proposal on the House floor, Thaddeus Stevens was only slightly more specific. After arguing that each of the three clauses was contained "in some form or other" in either the Declaration of Independence or the Constitution, Stevens continued:

> But the Constitution limits only the action of Congress, and is not a limitation on the States. This amendment supplies that defect [sic] and allows Congress to correct the unjust legislation of the States, so far that the law which operates upon one man shall apply *equally* upon all. Whatever law punishes a white man shall punish the black man in precisely the same way and precisely the same degree. Whatever law protects the white man shall afford "equal" protection to the black man. Whatever means of redress is afforded to one shall be afforded to all. Whatever law allows the white man to testify in court shall allow the man of color to do the same.[13]

The tenor of these discussions reflected the basic philosophy under-girding section one. Like the Thirteenth Amendment before it, the objective of this portion of the Fourteenth Amendment was simply to define the status of various persons and to place that status under federal protection. The equal protection and due process clauses essentially restated the Thirteenth Amendment itself, guaranteeing all persons the legal incidents of freedom. The citizenship and privileges and immunities clauses, by contrast, went beyond the simple prohibition of slavery, defining the class of persons entitled to the status of citizens and guaranteeing to that class the rights consequent to that status. In neither case was the intent to fix the parameters of the rights accompanying a particular status.

This idea is reinforced by the one point that does emerge fairly clearly from the characterizations of section one: Both the Joint Committee in general and Stevens in particular were basically committed to the concept of limited absolute equality rather than total racial equality. As already noted, the Joint Committee report speaks of the necessity to secure the civil rights of "all men." Moreover, the report asserted that this amendment was needed because, in the South, "the general disposition among all classes are yet totally adverse to the toleration of any class of people loyal to the union, *be they white or black.*"[14] Admittedly, Stevens referred to the abolition of racial discrimination in the narrow context of punishment for crimes and access to courts generally. But his main thrust was the claim that the amendment would require states to have laws that applied equally to all men. This assertion is tied to the statement that section one would give Congress the power to enforce constitutional provisions that hitherto had bound only the federal government, an echo of statements made by Bingham and later reiterated by Jacob Howard with respect to the comity clause.[15] These professions in turn reflect the basic concept of limited absolute equality—the idea that *all* men are entitled equally to certain basic rights, rather than that racial discrimination was, in general, wrong.

SPECIFIC ISSUES

The Relationship between "Privileges and Immunities" and "Equal Protection and Due Process"

Basically, section one of the Fourteenth Amendment can be divided into two parts. The first part defines citizenship and guarantees citizens a certain class of rights—privileges and immunities. By contrast, the due process and equal protection clauses apply to noncitizens as well as citizens. Logically, therefore, these clauses should protect a narrower range of interests—those that belong to aliens as well as citizens.

Raoul Berger has argued that this difference in phraseology was inadvertent.[16] However, even a cursory examination of the debates of the first session of the Thirty-ninth Congress reveals that those who framed the Fourteenth Amendment were acutely aware of the differentiation between aliens and citizens and drafted legislation with this distinction in mind. Conkling, for example, noted that the initial representation measure was drafted to refer to ''persons'' rather than ''citizens'' in order to include voting aliens in the basis of representation.[17] Further, as previously noted, the Civil Rights Bill was deliberately changed to protect only citizens; moreover, Bingham attacked this change, arguing that if Congress had the authority to protect the enumerated rights, that protection should be accorded to aliens as well as citizens.[18] Finally, in his presentation to the Senate, Jacob Howard clearly separated the various clauses of the amendment based on the distinction between ''citizen'' and ''person.''[19] In short, to attribute the decision to protect ''persons'' rather than ''citizens'' to an oversight seems inappropriate.

In the modern era, some judges have seized on the fact that the equal protection clause applies to persons as a warrant for judicial activism in cases involving aliens.[20] In the 1860s, however, the different statuses were rather plainly viewed as implying a limitation on the rights guaranteed by the equal protection and due process clauses. The presentation of Sen. Jacob M. Howard is particularly instructive in this regard. Because of Fessenden's illness, Howard was the designated spokesman of the Joint Committee on Reconstruction in the Senate. His speech on the Senate floor was thus the official explanation of the Fourteenth Amendment. Moreover, it was the most detailed contemporary congressional examination of the rights secured by section one.

Howard's presentation reflects well the dichotomy between the privileges and immunities clause and the remainder of section one. He began with an extended discussion of the concept of privileges and immunities, discussing a wide variety of rights that might be guaranteed to citizens by that clause. Adopting Bingham's theory of the comity clause, Howard rejected Wilson's argument that Congress had implied power to enforce that provision of the Constitution. Instead, he asserted that ''they stand . . . in the Constitution, without power on the part of Congress to give them effect; while at the same time the States are not restrained from violating the principles embraced in them except by their local constitutions.'' Howard concluded that ''the great object of [section one together with section five] is . . . to restrain the power of the States and compel them at all times to respect these great fundamental guarantees.''

Howard then expressed his understanding of the equal protection and due process clauses. His remarks were extremely brief, yet Howard did distinguish between those rights belonging to all persons and those that belong only to citizens:

> The last two clauses of the first section of the amendment disable a State from depriving *not merely a citizen of the United States, but any person, whoever he may be, of life, liberty, or property without due process of law or from denying to him the equal protection of the laws of the State.* This abolishes all class legislation in the States and does away with the injustice of subjecting one caste of persons to a code not applicable to another. It prohibits the hanging of a black man for a crime for which the white man is not to be hanged. It protects the black man in his fundamental rights as a citizen with the same shield which it throws over the white man. Is it not time, Mr. President, that we extend to the black man, I had almost called it the poor privilege of the equal protection of the law? Ought not the time to be now passed when one measure of justice is to be meted out to a member of one caste while another and a different measure is meted out to the member of another caste, both castes being alike citizens of the United States, both bound to obey the same laws, to sustain the burdens of the same Government; and both equally responsible to justice and to God for the deeds done in the body?[21]

Taken out of context, this passage might be interpreted quite broadly indeed. It speaks of abolishing ''all class legislation'' and condemns the practice of having ''one measure of justice. . . meted out to a member of one caste while another and a different measure is meted out to the member of another caste.'' Certainly at first glance, these phrases might be construed as prohibiting all forms of racial discrimination and perhaps other types of discrimination as well.

This impression is somewhat misleading, however. The key to understanding Howard's argument is in recognizing that his reference to ''class legislation'' is an echo of the due process analysis of the antebellum era. Many antebellum courts relied on ''due process'' or ''law of the land'' clauses in state constitutions to strike down legislation that singled out individuals or small groups for unfavorable treatment. Apparently related to the concerns underlying the hostility to bills of attainder, such condemnations of class legislation can be traced to Blackstone's definition of law itself. Law, he argues, ''is a *rule*; not a transient sudden order from a superior, to or concerning a particular person; but something permanent, uniform and universal."[22] In *James v. Reynolds*, the Texas Supreme Court provided a more typically American formulation of a similar principle: "the terms 'law of the land' . . . are . . . in their most usual acceptation, regarded as general public laws binding upon all members of the community . . . and not partial or private laws, affecting the rights of private individuals or classes of individuals."[23] Defending its indictment of class legislation, the Pennsylvania Supreme Court argued that

> when, in the exercise of proper legislative powers, general laws are enacted, which bear or may bear on the whole community, if they are unjust and against the spirit of the constitution, the whole community will be interested to procure their repeal by a voice potential. And that is the great security for just and fair legislation.
>
> But when individuals are selected from the mass, and laws are enacted affecting their property, without summons or notice, at the instigation of an interested party, who is to stand up for them, thus isolated from the mass, in injury and injustice, or where are they to seek relief from such acts of despotic power? They have no refuge but in the courts, the only secure place for determining conflicting rights by due course of law.[24]

Under the mid-nineteenth-century understanding of substantive due process, this analysis applied only to denials of the fundamental vested rights of life, liberty, and property.[25] It did not prohibit the exclusion of particular classes from governmental benefits or the deprivation of rights that were not vested. The judicial treatment of legislative alteration of rights to inheritance illustrates this point. A number of courts invalidated attempts to change the allocation of estates *after* the death of the person from whom the inheritance was claimed. The reasoning was that the rights of the heirs had become vested upon the death and that the legislature lacked power to divest them of these rights in favor of other claimants. By contrast, rules altering the dower rights of wives of living husbands were generally upheld. The courts held that the wives had simply an inchoate "expectancy" that they would receive a certain amount of property upon their husband's death; this expectancy did not rise to the level of a constitutionally protected vested right.

This perspective informed the framers' view of the due process and equal protection clauses in section one. Only natural rights or those that had become otherwise vested were protected by these clauses. The grant of other benefits was to remain within the discretion of the state governments.

This point is manifested in Howard's discussion of the suffrage issue.

Howard argued that section one did not confer the right to vote on any class because "the right of suffrage is not . . . one of the privileges and immunities . . . secured by the Constitution."[26] The general import of this statement is clear. Since blacks are citizens, they are entitled to the rights guaranteed by the privileges and immunities clause, including all natural rights. By virtue of section one, states are required to give the protection of law for those rights and to not infringe upon them without due process. But if a right (such as the right to vote) is not within the ambit of privileges and immunities, states are free to act as they please. The remaining clauses of section one were not intended to limit governmental authority in this regard.

The analysis of John Henderson of Missouri in a different context strongly supports this interpretation. Henderson was defending the final version of section three, which disqualified certain Confederate sympathizers from holding office. Opponents charged that this provision amounted to a bill of attainder and *ex post facto* law. In response, Henderson noted first that a constitutional amendment could override these concerns. He then continued:

And again, punishment means to take away life, liberty, or property. These are absolute or inalienable rights. To take them away is an injury to the person. It is what we call punishment. They ought never to be taken away *without due process of law*. Office is the creature of Government. It is true it may be called a right. The right is not absolute but conventional. The Government created it and the Government can take it away.[27]

Like Howard, Henderson's conception of the constraints of due process was based on what today might be described as a right/privilege distinction. Government is limited by due process considerations in relation to its actions regarding fundamental, "inalienable" rights. But with respect to "conventional" rights—those "Government created . . . and . . . can take away"—due process (at least in its substantive guise) is simply not a factor.

Finally, the unanimity of Republican support also suggests that the equal protection and due process clauses were generally viewed narrowly. The focus of the Republican opposition to the original Bingham amendment had been its equal protection component. Typically, the lack of similar resistance to section one has been attributed to approval of the change from the "positive" form of "Congress shall have power to make all laws necessary and proper" to the ultimate "negative" form, which directly prohibited state action and simply granted Congress power to enforce the prohibition. The negative formulation recognized the primacy of the states in defining and maintaining the rights of citizens.

In the Joint Committee, however, moderates and Democrats had preferred the Bingham language to another negative provision—the original Owen proposal. This choice can only be read as reflecting a dislike of open-endedness. In the debate over the Civil Rights Bill, some moderates had complained that the concept of civil rights might be interpreted to encompass all rights, including the right to vote. By contrast, although the term *privileges and immunities* was admittedly vague at the margins, Republicans were certain that it was limited to fundamental rights and, at the very least, did not include the right to vote. Thus for someone like Conkling, elimination of the civil rights language from section one was a clear plus.

Other modifications in the equal protection wording of the original Bingham proposal also contributed to Republican confidence in the narrowness of section one. The proposal initially would have granted Congress power to guarantee ''equal protection in the rights of life, liberty, and property.'' Although Bingham consistently maintained that this was not his intention, the language on its face seemed to transfer to Congress the basic protective function of government. Section one, however, split this phrase into two components—states were forbidden to ''deprive any person of life, liberty or property without due process of law'' and to ''deny any person . . . the equal protection of the laws.'' Neither of these provisions seems to establish any new substantive rights or give Congress the authority to define such rights. Dealing with *preexisting* rights, they simply enjoin the state to grant all citizens ''protection of the laws'' for those rights and to refrain from taking the rights away ''without due process of law.'' This is consistent with the narrow antebellum view of the scope of the right to protection of the laws—a view that, as we have seen, was explicitly adopted by both Bingham and Attorney General Bates. Thus, rather than shifting the locus of basic functions, section one simply directs states to respect specific interests—rights that by consensus belonged to all free men.

The opposition apparently took a similar view. For example, although he disapproved of the privileges and immunities clause, Reverdy Johnson, one of the least conservative Democrats who was the most brilliant opposition theoretician, voted in favor of the equal protection clause in the Joint Committee[28] and stated on the Senate floor that he favored the due process clause.[29] Similarly, Edgar Cowan—a nominal Republican who consistently supported the Democrats on Reconstruction issues—said that he was against making blacks full citizens but was in favor of legally establishing the entitlement of all people (including blacks) to the rights that ''sojourners'' enjoyed, including ''the protection of the laws while [the person] is within and under the jurisdiction of the courts."[30] Finally, the platform of the National Union Convention—a gathering organized by the supporters of President Johnson—explicitly recognized the rights of "all . . . inhabitants [to] equal protection in every right of person and property."[31] Other Democrats did voice objections to the due process and equal protection clauses, but their arguments usually rested on the principle of federalism rather than the content of the rights protected by the two clauses.[32]

In summary, the strong preponderance of the evidence indicates that when compared to the privileges and immunities clause, the due process and equal protection clauses were intended to guarantee a smaller group of rights to a larger class of individuals and that Congress would have only a limited power to enforce these guarantees.

The Problem of "State Action"

The Evidence of a Broad Understanding. On one key issue—the role of "state action" in Fourteenth Amendment analysis—the equal protection clause is critical. During the Reconstruction era, the contemporary state-action issue was not a factor in Reconstruction discussions of the meaning of section one. No one suggested that private action per se could be a violation of the Fourteenth Amendment.[33] Instead, the critical question was the extent of congressional power to pass legislation that had a direct impact on private activities.

Beginning in 1870, a number of statutes were proposed which provided for direct federal intervention against individuals. It was in this context that the debate over the link between section five and state action took place. Three distinct positions emerged. At one extreme were pure state-action theorists, who argued that section five gave Congress authority to regulate only the activities of state officials.[34] At the other extreme was a position based upon what might be called a supplemental protection theory, which argued that where Congress determined that a state was not providing "equal protection of the laws" to some group, the national government could intervene directly under section five authority to provide the needed protection.[35] Those who took an intermediate position contended that Congress could act against private individuals who attempted to interfere with the efforts of state governments to provide the rights guaranteed by section one.[36]

Seizing on the fact that many of the members of Congresses between 1870 and 1875 had also served in the Thirty-ninth Congress, several commentators have suggested that the debates of the later era provide an accurate indication of the intent of the original drafters of sections one and five.[37] If this premise were correct, then those arguing for broad congressional authority would have the stronger position. For despite opposition from some Republicans, a number of measures were ultimately adopted that could only be justified under a supplemental protection theory. Moreover, this theory was advocated in 1871 by John Bingham—the author of section one.[38] Several points, however, reduce the reliability of the 1870–75 debates as evidence of the true aim of the drafters in 1866.

First, the understanding expressed in the late 1860s and early 1870s was far from uniform. For example, James A. Garfield, who had been a member of the Thirty-ninth Congress, argued in 1871 that the final equal protection language did not give Congress broad enforcement authority. Comparing section one with the initial Bingham amendment that had encountered strong Republican opposition, Garfield contended that

the one exerts its force directly upon the States, laying restriction and limitations upon their power and enabling Congress to enforce these limitations. The other, the rejected [equal protection] proposition, would have brought the power of Congress to bear directly upon the citizens, and contained a clear grant of power to Congress to legislate directly for the protection of life, liberty, and property within the States. The [enacted form] limited but did not oust the jurisdiction of the State over these subjects. The [rejected form] gave Congress plenary power to cover the whole subject with its jurisdiction and, as it seems to me, to the exclusion of the State authorities.[39]

Similarly, in 1871 Bingham himself gave a description of equal protection that was consistent with a narrow understanding of the scope of the clause:

[The equal protection clause] means that no State shall deny to any person within its jurisdiction the equal protection of the Constitution of the United States . . . and, of course, that no State should deny to any such person any of the rights which it guaranties to *all* men, nor should any State deny to any such person any rights secured to him either by the laws and treaties of the United States or of such States.[40]

The remarkable aspect of this definition is that Bingham does not refer to classifications at all. Instead, he states that the equal protection clause guarantees (1) *any* person (2) equal protection of (3) rights established either by the Constitution, the laws of the United States, or the laws of the particular state where the person happens to be located. Put another way, by its own force the equal protection clause does not prohibit discrimination in the granting of substantive rights; rather, the clause merely requires that the states make available on equal terms the mechanism necessary to enforce the rights created either by other provisions of the Constitution or by state law.

Of course, all of these statements can be viewed as "law office history." Those who supported the policy of federal intervention argued for broad section five authority; those who opposed such intervention tailored their arguments accordingly. In neither case can the record of the debates be said to reflect an unbiased view of past events.

In the case of the civil rights measures of the 1870s, this problem is exacerbated by the change in the political climate from 1866. As already noted, at first the theory of Reconstruction was to provide conditions under which the state governments could resume their respective roles as primary guardians of individual rights. With the ratification of the Fourteenth and Fifteenth Amendments, the new safeguards to ensure that state governments would meet their responsibilities were in place, and thus most of the states could be readmitted.[41] But by 1870, it was already clear that the state-centered model of Reconstruction was failing. The new southern governments were all too often either unwilling or unable to provide protection for the fundamental rights of blacks and Republicans.[42] Thus the concept needed revising—to include a continuing federal presence. The debate over the scope of section five can be seen as an attempt to fit this new model into the old state-centered Reconstruction framework epitomized by the Fourteenth Amendment.

Analysis of the debates of the early 1870s is further complicated by the political factors that split the Republican party during that period. These controversies led to schisms along lines quite different from those that had divided the party in 1866.[43] Thus, the pure state-action model was adopted not only by the conservative Lyman Trumbull but also by Lot M. Morrill and Carl Schurz—radicals in 1866.[44] Conversely, the more radical supplemental protection theory was embraced by Robert Hale, a former Johnson Republican.[45] In short, taken alone, the discussions of the 1870s are an unreliable guide to the intentions of the drafters in 1866. Other factors, however, point strongly to a narrow original understanding.

The Evidence of a Narrow Understanding. The most important evidence of the narrow understanding of the due process and equal protection clauses is the lack of opposition engendered by the two clauses. We have already seen how, during the debates over the initial Bingham proposal, moderate Republicans focused their attack on the equal protection component of the proposal. At the same time, Bingham consistently denied any intention of granting Congress any authority to define substantive rights of life, liberty, and property; he viewed this power as being appropriately vested in the states alone.[46] Regardless, Republican opposition to the original proposal was based broadly on the fear that it would be seen as embodying a supplemental protection theory. If they had believed that the ultimate wording of section one reflected a similar theory, conservative moderates would have been unlikely to embrace it without protest. Yet no moderate assailed section one of the Fourteenth Amendment. This suggests that by changing from the "positive" to the "negative" form, the drafters intended to vest Congress only with the authority to regulate state action, not to also reach private individuals in cases where the state had defaulted in its responsibilities. At the very least the negative form recognized the states' primacy in establishing and maintaining individual rights, with Congress given authority to intervene only when the states were remiss in fulfilling their obligations.[47]

Bingham's own words also support the pure state-action theory. In a letter to a close friend in early 1866, he outlined his view of the need for new federal power:

National law must protect the privileges and immunities of all the citizens as well as aliens in the Republic. It must prevent any *state* from abridging or denying the inborn rights of every person in its jurisdiction.[48]

This passage seems to indicate that Bingham meant for his proposals to be aimed at the actions of state governments—not those of private individuals.

One problem with the pure state-action theory is its apparent dissonance with Trumbull's discussion of Thirteenth Amendment power in the debate over section three of the Civil Rights Bill. This provision granted jurisdiction to the federal courts in all criminal and civil cases "affecting persons who are denied or cannot enforce in the courts or judicial tribunals of the State or locality where they may be any of the rights secured to them by the first section." According to Trumbull, the specific provision was intended to have only a limited scope; in his response to the presidential veto of the bill, he argued that the federal courts would have jurisdiction only if "the party . . . discriminated against . . . tested [the offending statute] and . . . the discrimination was held valid [or] if undertaking to enforce his right in a state court he was denied that right." Hence, notwithstanding the fact that section three provided for trial *de novo*, this trial effected what was essentially a kind of appellate jurisdiction to correct the errors of state courts—a regime entirely consistent with a pure state-action theory.

Trumbull also claimed that Congress could have gone further if it had chosen to do so:

> If it be necessary in order to protect the freedman in his rights that he should have authority to go into the Federal courts in all cases where a custom prevails in a State, or where there is a statute-law of the State discriminating against him, I think we have the authority to confer that jurisdiction. . . . [Section two of the Thirteenth Amendment] authorizes us to do whatever is necessary to protect the freedman in his liberty . . . if it cannot be done without, [Congress] would have authority to allow him to come to the Federal courts in all cases.[49]

This argument embraces at least a limited version of the supplemental protection theory.

Republican members of the Thirty-ninth Congress never addressed this seeming inconsistency directly. One possible line of reconciliation could have focused on the fact that Trumbull spoke only of opening the courts, thereby limiting the import of his remarks to that situation. Under this interpretation, Congress could not use the equal protection rubric to either define new rights to life, liberty, or property or provide new punishments for private actions in contravention of existing rights. Instead, in this context federal power could only be exercised to enforce state-created rights. The sole limitation on the content of those rights would be provided by a different provision in section one—the privileges and immunities clause.

The most plausible conclusion is that Republicans were probably split on the state-action issue. Radical Republicans who had supported the original Bingham amendment may well have embraced the supplemental protection theory. On the other hand, some of the more conservative party members—members whose backing was critical to congressional approval of the Fourteenth Amendment—very likely adhered to the pure state-action theory. Hence, a constitutional amendment that clearly embraced the supplemental protection theory could not have been adopted in 1866.

PRIVILEGES AND IMMUNITIES

Most of the discussion of section one was aimed at the citizenship and privileges and immunities clauses. This emphasis was partly a reflection of the symbolic importance of granting blacks citizenship. In addition, the privileges and immunities provision was viewed as being the most significant in terms of the rights protected. Thus the focus on this clause is entirely understandable.

The privileges and immunities language was drawn directly from the comity clause of the original Constitution. The scope of this clause had been discussed during the pre–Civil War period in the treatises of Story[50] and Kent[51] and cases such as *Corfield v. Coryell,*[52] *Abbott v. Bayley,*[53] and *Campbell v. Morris.*[54] Republicans were well aware of these authorities[55] and presumably understood that the rights protected by the privileges and immunities clause in section one would be defined by reference to preexisting legal principles.

In describing the privileges and immunities of national citizenship, the antebellum authorities generally tracked the language of the Civil Rights Act closely.[56] However, there were aberrations. For example, in *Corfield,* Justice Bushrod Washington indicated that he considered the right to vote to be one of the privileges and immunities of national citizenship,[57] and in *Dred Scott* (admittedly not the Republicans' favorite precedent) Chief Justice Taney suggested that First Amendment rights had the same status.[58] It is against this background that the original understanding of the privileges and immunities clause must be considered.

Not surprisingly, Democrats repeatedly claimed that with the enforcement provision of section five, the clause amounted to an open-ended invitation to Congress to create and protect a new set of nationally defined interests. Reverdy Johnson had voted in favor of an equal protection provision in the Joint Committee[59] and declared himself in favor of the due process clause, but he found the privileges and immunities language "quite objectionable . . . because I do not understand what will be the effect of that."[60] Andrew Rogers stated the Democratic argument in greater detail:

What are privileges and immunities? Why, sir, all the rights we have under the laws of the country are embraced under the definition of privileges and immunities. The right to vote is a privilege. The right to marry is a privilege. The right to contract is a privilege. The right to be a juror is a privilege. The right to be a judge or President of the United States is a privilege. I hold if that ever becomes a part of the fundamental law of the land it will prevent any State from refusing to allow anything to anybody embraced under this term of privileges and immunities. If a negro is refused the right to be a juror, that will take away from him his privileges and immunities as a citizen of the United States, and the Federal Government will step in and interfere, and the result will be a contest between the powers of the Federal Government and the powers of the States.[61]

For their part, Republicans almost certainly viewed the privileges and immunities clause as guaranteeing only a relatively small, fixed group of rights. Even in the absence of direct evidence on this point, one might well draw this conclusion from contextual factors alone. The fear that Congress was assuming an unrestricted authority to define and protect the rights of citizens generally had provoked substantial Republican opposition to both Bingham's original constitutional proposal and early versions of the Civil Rights Bill. Given this background, the most plausible explanation for the Republican consensus on section one is that the reach of all three clauses was viewed as fixed and limited. As we have already seen, Bingham himself expressed intentions that were inconsistent with the concept of an open-ended privileges and immunities clause. Beginning on January 9, 1866, and continuing throughout the debates, Bingham emphasized that his objective was to provide a mechanism to assure the enforcement of guarantees that in his view were already in the Constitution—particularly those inherent in the comity clause. Rather than achieving this purpose, an open-ended clause would have radically altered the federal/state balance of power—an intention Bingham vigorously and repeatedly denied.

Finally, the debate over Bingham's original proposal provides direct support for a limited concept of the privileges and immunities clause. For although complaining about the potential breadth of the measure generally, Hale, Hotchkiss, and Stewart were careful to note that their arguments only applied to the equal protection component of the proposed amendment; each explicitly stated that he had no quarrel with the privileges and immunities provision.[62] Their shared position on this point is particularly significant since their general discomfort with the proposal reflected an unease with the possibility that the federal government would be granted open-ended authority over matters more properly left to local control. Hotchkiss made this point succinctly:

> I understand the amendment as now proposed by its terms to authorize Congress to establish uniform laws throughout the United States [for] the protection of life, liberty and property. I am unwilling that Congress shall have any such power. . . . It is not indulging in imagination to any great stretch to suppose that we may have a Congress here who would establish such rules in my State as I would be unwilling to be governed by. Should the power of this Government . . . pass into the hands of the rebels, I do not want rebel laws to govern and be uniform throughout this Union.[63]

In the face of such statements, the acceptance of the privileges and immunities clause specifically by Hotchkiss and like-minded Republicans can only indicate confidence that the provision had a fixed, limited import.

The one important mainstream Republican speech which might be taken to support an open-ended theory of the privileges and immunities clause was given by Jacob Howard. Introducing section one in the Senate, Howard first linked the clause to the Bill of Rights and Justice Bushrod Washington's comity clause discussion in *Corfield v. Coryell*. He also stated, however, that the privileges and immunities guaranteed in the clause ''are not and cannot be fully defined in their entire extent and precise nature.''[64] This admission seems to confirm George Boutwell's later observation that Bingham preferred his formulation because ''its euphony and indefiniteness were a charm to him.''[65]

In analyzing these statements, one must distinguish between vagueness and malleability. Howard and Boutwell were clearly suggesting that the content of privileges and immunities was unclear at the margins. They did not, however, mean that the content of the clause could or should change over time. Certainly Bingham's oft-asserted vision of this amendment would be irreconcilable with any such contention. Moreover, Howard's firm assertion that Congress could not use the privileges and immunities clause to require states to grant the right to vote is also inconsistent with the idea of a malleable clause.[66] For if the parameters of the clause could be altered, Howard could not confidently claim that *any* right was excluded. In short, the only plausible conclusion is that Howard—like other Republicans—viewed the concept of privileges and immunities as slightly vague but not malleable.

A fairly lucid picture of the Republican interpretation of the privileges and immunities clause emerges from the debates of the Thirty-ninth Congress. The clause was perceived as guaranteeing a relatively small set of rights which, though somewhat unclear at the margins, was nonetheless fixed for all time in 1866. Given the intention to secure a fixed set of rights, the key question becomes what interests were to be protected by the privileges and immunities clause. Clearly, the rights enumerated in the Civil Rights Act were to be guarded, but the status of other rights is less certain.[67] Three issues have generated considerable controversy in modern commentaries.

Education

Education was a central concern of the Republicans who drafted the Fourteenth Amendment. The origins of this concern predated the Civil War,[68] as evidenced by the famous case of *Roberts v. City of Boston*.[69] *Roberts* was an 1849 challenge to the maintenance of segregated schools in Boston. Arguing for the plaintiff, Charles Sumner relied in part on the provision of the Massachusetts Constitution which read, ''All men are born free and equal and have certain natural, essential, and inalienable rights, among which may be reckoned the right of enjoying and defending their lives and liberties.'' This statement, Sumner contended, established the proposition that whites and blacks were "equal before the law," and since in his view segregated schools were by their nature unequal, the continuance of separate schools violated the state constitution.[70]

Chief Justice Lemuel Shaw, although accepting the argument that the state constitutional provision established equality before the law, rejected the claim that the maintenance of segregated schools was unconstitutional. Shaw concluded:

> The great principle . . . is that by the constitution and laws of Massachusetts all persons . . . are equal before the law. This, as a broad general principle . . . is perfectly sound. . . . But when this great principle comes to be applied to the actual and various conditions of persons in society, it will not warrant the assertion, that men and women are legally clothed with the same civil and political powers, and that children and adults are legally to have the same functions and be subject to the same treatment; *but only that the rights of all, as they are settled and regulated by law, are equally entitled to the paternal consideration and protection of the law, for their maintenance and security. What those rights are, to which individuals, in the infinite variety of circumstances by which they are surrounded in society, are entitled, must depend on laws adapted to their respective relations and conditions.*[71]

The standard analysis of the *Roberts* case describes Sumner as a hero whose argument presaged the conceptions of racial equality later embodied in the Fourteenth Amendment, and Shaw as a villain whose retrograde views on the nature of equality were to haunt American jurisprudence for one hundred years.[72] But in structure Shaw's opinion simply mirrors the dichotomy between equality of rights and equality of protection, which appears often in antebellum arguments. All men—black or white—are equally entitled to protection of the laws to enforce their legal rights; but unless a particular interest can be classified as a natural right, the legislature may withhold that interest from any class at will. Since public education is not a natural right, the legislature would not violate the principle of limited absolute equality even if blacks were totally excluded.

Ultimately, blacks were successful in desegregating the Boston schools.[73] More frequently, however, Republican efforts were aimed at obtaining education for blacks in a segregated setting. The 1860 debate over the District of Columbia schools is typical. As initially proposed, the bill before the Senate would have simply provided that the city authorities could impose a property tax to benefit the public schools in the District and that the federal government would supply matching funds up to $25,000 per year. Republicans pressed for an amendment to require the city government to use at least part of the funds raised to educate blacks as well as whites. One of the mainstays of the argument for the amendment was that "taxing [blacks] for the exclusive benefit of the white children . . . would be a kind of legal robbery."[74] No mention was made, however, of requiring the schools to be integrated; the object was only to have *some* schools provided for blacks.

Republicans also expressed concern for the education of the freed slaves in the Reconstruction context. For example, in Lincoln's "Proclamation of Amnesty and Reconstruction," he suggested that the ex-Confederate states should "provide for [the] education" of the freed slaves.[75] Similarly, in 1865 the *Springfield Republican* declared that "we can only be secured against future rebellions by the universal education of the people. . . . Let us have an educated common people in the South . . . and we are safe."[76] The antisuffrage *New York Times* also made the education of freedmen a high priority.[77]

Further, Republicans viewed the right to pursue an education as encompassed by the privileges and immunities clause. One of the recurrent Republican criticisms of the Black Codes was that they prohibited the education of the freed slaves.[78] Even before the Civil War, Bingham had included "the right to know" in his list of the privileges and immunities of American citizenship.[79] In the face of such evidence, one simply cannot persuasively argue that the Fourteenth Amendment was not intended to protect a citizen's right to use his or her best efforts to obtain an education.

The existence of such a right, however, does not imply a concomitant right to have the state provide an education. Despite Republican advocacy of free public education, Congress took no action before the Fourteenth Amendment to require the ex-Confederate states to educate freedmen. Thaddeus Stevens and Ignatius Donnelly of Minnesota did seek to have the Freedmen's Bureau assume responsibility for education.[80] But their attempt to change the Freedmen's Bureau Bill was overwhelmingly defeated,[81] and no other education-related measures ever reached the floor. The fate of such causes suggests that Congress was unwilling to interfere with the traditional autonomy of the states in the area of education.

The congressional debates on the Fourteenth Amendment rarely focused specifically on this issue. The most direct discussion is Timothy Howe's well-known speech criticizing the Florida system of segregated schools. Howe noted that both whites and blacks were taxed to support the white schools, while blacks alone provided the funds that financed the black schools. Howe also asserted that the black schools were vastly inferior to their white counterparts; indeed, he seemed to intimate that as a practical matter, education for blacks was almost nonexistent. The maintenance of a system like that in Florida, Howe argued, was inconsistent with section one.[82]

Howe emphasized the privileges and immunities clause in making his case. Although he also decried the failure of some states to provide ''all classes of its citizens the protection of equal laws,'' he seemed to regard the right to protection as one of the privileges and immunities of citizenship. Thus, his statement was undoubtedly an allusion to the generally accepted principle of limited absolute equality, rather than an attempt to describe an additional group of interests covered by the equal protection clause itself.

If one views Howe's argument as resting on an abstract right to equal education, his avowed reliance on the privileges and immunities clause appears somewhat anomalous. The privileges and immunities of citizenship were not typically seen as including the right to have the government provide *any* particular service, save perhaps those necessary to ensure that the citizen would receive protection of the law. Public education as a service was no different in this regard, as the actions of the first session of the Thirty-ninth Congress on education-specific bills demonstrates. The problem thus becomes reconciling Howe's argument—that the Florida system violated section one—with this basically conservative view.

The answer lies in the recognition that Howe linked the issue of education with that of taxation. Before the Civil War, state case-law had posited a right to be free from unequal taxation; this right was often connected not only to explicit state constitutional provisions but also to the more general right to protection from government and immunity from seizure without compensation.[83] The same right was held to imply that taxpayers were entitled to equal access to facilities financed by their tax dollars.[84] Republicans had relied on an analogous argument in the 1860 debate over education for blacks in the District of Columbia. The term *legal robbery* was a clear reference to the just-compensation concepts so prominent in the state taxation cases.[85] Indeed, Republican Daniel Clark stated that he would accept a prohibition on education of blacks so long as they were exempted from the property tax and their pro rata share of the federal contribution was withheld.[86]

Howe's 1866 argument fits comfortably within the same rubric. If the white and black Florida school systems were considered separately, then the taxing of blacks for the education of whites would constitute the taking of property without just compensation. Even if the two systems were considered as integral parts of the same system, the imposition of a separate, additional tax on blacks to support it would be a violation of the more general right to protection from government. In either case, well-established antebellum concepts of the privileges and immunities of citizenship would provide strong support.

Of course, the same argument has important implications for other government services. Presumably, whenever blacks were taxed at the same rate as whites, the state governments would be under an obligation to provide equal services. It should be noted, however, that in this context "equality" is a concept of relatively limited scope, referring only to equal allocation of resources. Intangible concerns such as those cited by Chief Justice Warren in *Brown v. Board of Education*[87] have no place in the taxation/just-compensation argument. Thus, although section one may well have been intended to impose a requirement that blacks be provided with *equal* schools, there is no evidence that the framers of the Fourteenth Amendment intended to address the problem of segregation.

The Bill of Rights

In the ongoing debate over the relevance of the Bill of Rights to the interpretation of the privileges and immunities clause, at least four distinct positions have emerged. One group, led by the late Justice Black, has argued that the clause was intended to incorporate *only* the first eight amendments to the Constitution.[88] At the other extreme, Raoul Berger contends that the first eight amendments are irrelevant to the interpretation of the privileges and immunities clause.[89] In between are those who argue that the privileges and immunities clause incorporates either some or all of the Bill of Rights *in addition* to other rights.[90]

Of the four positions, Justice Black's is the most easily refuted. Throughout the debates, proponents of section one referred to the rights embodied in the Civil Rights Act. Further, none of the speakers who cited the Bill of Rights suggested that it was the exclusive source of privileges and immunities. Thus, to hold that the framers intended reference only to the Bill of Rights seems insupportable.

One can construct a plausible case for each of the other positions. The argument for total incorporation rests heavily on remarks by Howard and Bingham. In his presentation of the Joint Committee proposal to the Senate, Howard explicitly stated that the privileges and immunities clause made applicable to the states the proscriptions of the first eight amendments.[91] In his 1866 speech on the Fourteenth Amendment itself, Bingham made no such assertion. However, in the course of defending his initial proposal, he did state that his amendment would arm Congress with power to enforce the "bill of rights."[92] Also, during the debate over the Civil Rights Bill of 1871, Bingham noted that "the privileges and immunities of citizens of the United States . . . are chiefly defined in the first eight amendments to the Constitution of the United States," and he then read the amendments verbatim.[93]

These statements illuminate a common thread running through Republican arguments dating back to well before the Civil War. In the antebellum era, Republicans viewed themselves as the protectors of the freedoms embodied in the Bill of Rights, and the slave power as the enemy of those freedoms.[94] For example, the Republican platform of 1856 alleges that antislavery advocates in Kansas were denied rights guaranteed by the First, Second, Fourth, Fifth, and Sixth Amendments.[95] Similarly, Republican condemnations of southern governments during the early Reconstruction era are replete with references to violations of the guarantees of the Bill of Rights. Indictments of postwar southern mistreatment of the freed slaves are also liberally sprinkled with discussions of Bill of Rights' provisions.[96] Given the prominence of the first eight amendments in contemporary political discourse, an attempt to apply the Bill of Rights to the states would not be surprising.

Nonincorporationists first face the problem of explaining the statements of Howard and Bingham. Howard is typically discredited as an unreliable witness—a radical on a moderate-dominated committee who actually opposed the replacement of the original Owen-plan "civil rights" language with the ultimate tripartite formulation of section one. Howard's role as Senate spokesman for the Joint Committee is dismissed as a happenstance resulting from the illness of William Pitt Fessenden, the moderate chairman of the committee.[97]

The Bingham references to the Bill of Rights are attacked on several fronts. First, Bingham himself is often described as a muddled thinker with no clear conception of what rights would be constitutionalized by his own proposals.[98] Second, his 1871 reference to the Bill of Rights is rejected as not authoritative. It is characterized as simply a post-hoc comment made in support of an expansive civil rights measure and generated by a political climate quite different from that in 1866.[99] Bingham's 1866 citations of the Bill of Rights, on the other hand, are construed as referring not to the first eight amendments but to "the list of men's natural rights" embodied in the privileges and immunities clause.[100]

On their interpretation of Howard's position, the nonincorporationist arguments are unpersuasive. The fact that Howard was more radical than most of the members of the Joint Committee might plausibly explain why he would deliberately misread section one to establish an open-ended federal authority to protect civil rights generally. But a reference to the Bill of Rights *specifically* would not have accomplished such an objective; indeed, the reference came in the context of a speech that also emphasized the limitation of the privileges and immunities clause to those rights that are "fundamental." Thus there is no reason to doubt Howard's veracity when he expressed his belief that the first eight amendments were incorporated by the clause.

The nonincorporationist explanation of Bingham's statements is even less convincing. First, the disparagement of Bingham's thought processes is considerably overstated. Although his speeches were often pompous and flowery, they enunciated clearly a consistent theme: The comity clause guarantees certain rights to all American citizens, but the prewar Constitution left Congress powerless to enforce those rights. Second, Bingham's February 28, 1866, speech defending his original proposal unequivocally discloses his belief that the protections of the first eight amendments were incorporated in the comity clause. The speech refers to the Bill of Rights three times. Two of those references could be taken as signifying a natural-law bill of rights. At one point, however, he states:

A gentleman on the other side . . . wanted to know if I could cite a decision showing that the power of the Federal Government to enforce in the United States courts the *bill of rights under the articles of amendment to the Constitution* has been denied. I answered that I was prepared to introduce such decisions and that is exactly what makes plain the necessity of adopting this amendment.

Bingham then cited *Barron v. City of Baltimore* and *Lessee of Livingston v. Moore*—two cases that held the Bill of Rights inapplicable to the states—and quoted the following passage in which the Court disposed of the jury trial claim in *Moore*:

As to the amendments of the Constitution of the United States, they must be put out of the case, since it is now settled that those amendments do not extend to the States; and this observation disposes of the next exception, which relies on the seventh article of those amendments.

Noting that these decisions established the principle that "the existing amendments are not applicable and do not bind the states," Bingham then asserted that his proposal would arm Congress with the power to force state governments to respect these "injunctions and prohibitions."[101] There could hardly be any clearer indication that Bingham saw the Bill of Rights as included within the concept of privileges and immunities.

In short, one cannot plausibly argue that Howard and Bingham did not believe the Bill of Rights to be fully incorporated in the privileges and immunities clause. Yet this conclusion does not necessarily imply that their view was generally held in 1866. Nonincorporationists rely on negative inference from the debates over ratification and the read-mission of the various ex-Confederate states. Charles Fairman in par-ticular seeks to capitalize on the fact that the Bill of Rights per se was almost never mentioned in either of these contexts.

Fairman also relies on the evidence that a number of states had con-stitutional provisions inconsistent with the federal Bill of Rights. Surely, he suggests, opponents of ratification would have been quick to note the inconsistency and to make the most of it. Since they did not, he concludes that the only logical reason is that full incorporation was not intended.[102] Fairman's argument on this point would be extremely strong if the incorporationist position depended on the claim that na-tionalization of the Bill of Rights was the sole or primary goal of the drafters of the Fourteenth Amendment. But in fact, it is enough to show that incorporation was simply *an* intended effect of the privileges and immunities clause. And in this context, the force of Fairman's ar-gument is weakened considerably.

The ratification debates over section one were very similar to the con-gressional discussions. Two types of opposition arguments emerged. One was that the proposed privileges and immunities clause would grant blacks too many rights—specifically, the right to vote. A second, subsidiary argument was that the clause would upset the balance of federalism by granting the national government open-ended authority to define and enforce the rights to be enjoyed by the citizenry. Opposi-tion to the application of the Bill of Rights to the states would have been a species of the argument against centralization. Yet the major differences between contemporary state constitutions and the Bill of Rights involved technical matters of criminal procedure—particularly the requirement that prosecutions be based on indictments returned by grand juries.[103] The prospect that states would now have to provide for grand juries was unlikely to stir the emotions of those who were unde-cided about ratification. Moreover, in order to take even the slightest advantage of this inconsistency, opponents of the proposed amendment would in effect have had to declare themselves against the Bill of Rights. To assume such a posture would have been neither comfortable nor politically astute. Thus, there are no inferences to be drawn from the failure of the opposition to discuss the incorporation theory.

Analogous considerations might well explain the lack of discussion of the Bill of Rights in the debate over the admission of Nebraska and readmission of the various southern states. Once again the most com-mon disparity between state constitutions and the Bill of Rights in-volved grand juries; there is also one clear violation of the jury trial provision of the Seventh Amendment and a provision arguably incon-sistent with the Sixth Amendment. As Charles Crosskey has pointed out, the great political issues raised by these requests for admission

mission would have rendered minor discrepancies with the Bill of Rights irrelevant to the debate. In the case of Nebraska, the issue was black suffrage; with respect to the erstwhile Confederate states, the whole concept of Reconstruction was at stake.[104] In the face of the overwhelming significance of the other questions involved, it is not surprising that Congress failed to focus on relatively technical matters of criminal procedure.

The most puzzling anomaly for incorporationists is the failure of proponents of the amendment to make explicit reference to the Bill of Rights as a whole during the ratification campaign. Admittedly, Republicans were principally concerned with deflecting Democratic attacks on their proposal, and the observation that section one secured the first eight amendments *in addition* to other interests would not necessarily have worked in their favor. At the same time, however, Republicans were not shy in pointing to the Civil Rights Act as a primary source for section one; presumably, an added appeal to the Bill of Rights would have had an even stronger, visceral impact. Thus, despite Howard's and Bingham's clear statements on the issue, the full incorporation theory, though not refuted, must be classified as not proven beyond a reasonable doubt.

It should be emphasized, however, that there can be little doubt that the privileges and immunities clause was intended to incorporate *some* of the Bill of Rights. Republicans had constantly complained that slave-state governments had denied opponents of slavery freedom of speech, and both Bingham and Gov. Jacob Cox of Ohio referred directly to these concerns during arguments over ratification.[105] Bingham also mentioned the right to teach the Bible—a clear appeal to the religion clauses.[106] Thus, the evidence impressively demonstrates that the basic guarantees of the First Amendment were understood to be included in the concept of privileges and immunities.

Other values from the Bill of Rights also figured prominently in the Reconstruction-era debates. Those deliberating over section one could hardly have ignored Bingham's repeated, specific assertions that his original proposal was needed to combat the problem of state confiscation statutes—which certainly referred to the Fifth Amendment's just-compensation and due process provisions.[107] One of the persistent criticisms of the southern states was that they denied the freed slaves the right to keep and bear arms;[108] another was that the codes subjected blacks and loyalists to cruel and unusual punishments. The right of blacks to be free from such punishments was recognized even by the archconservative Edgar Cowan.[109] There are also references to problems of search and seizure.[110] In short, one can only conclude that contemporaries must have understood the privileges and immunities clause to embody most of the Bill of Rights, and they probably viewed the first eight amendments as incorporated in their entirety.

Yet the importance of this conclusion should not be overstated. There is no evidence that the framers meant to embrace the seemingly open-ended Ninth Amendment, and they apparently regarded the first eight amendments as defining a relatively narrow, fixed set of rights. Thus from their perspective, the Fourteenth Amendment would not have sanctioned modern decisions requiring state adoption of the exclusionary rule or *Miranda* warnings, nor would it have supported the expansive First Amendment decisions of the Warren era. Instead, as the framers repeatedly stressed, section one was intended to give the federal government only the authority to enforce a catalogue of rights that were in substance largely uncontroversial.

The Right to Vote

Even if there were no direct evidence on the subject, contextual factors would point strongly to the conclusion that the privileges and immunities clause was not supposed to either affect the right to vote generally or grant Congress authority to regulate voting rights. First, the issue of black suffrage was the main stumbling block to the adoption of any constitutional amendment. Second, on the climactic final day of drafting in the Joint Committee, a proposal dealing directly with the issue of suffrage was replaced with one that only offered an adjustment to the basis of representation. Finally, the primary support for substituting Bingham's section one for the Owen plan's came from a coalition of Democrats and moderate Republicans—the same coalition that had blocked black-suffrage proposals throughout the session of Congress. All of these factors indicate persuasively that the proposed Fourteenth Amendment was not intended to affect state control over suffrage.

The conclusion is strongly reinforced by the discussions of section one. Both in and out of Congress, opponents of the proposal charged again and again that it was meant to allow Congress to mandate black suffrage.[111] Supporters, however, emphatically denied the allegation. For example, implicitly rejecting contrary *Corfield* language as an aberration, Jacob Howard stated that

> the first section of the proposed amendment does not give to [any class] the right of voting. The right of suffrage is not, in law, one of the privileges or immunities thus secured by the Constitution. It is merely the creature of law. It has always been regarded in this country as the result of positive local law, not regarded as one of

those fundamental rights lying at the basis of all society and without which a people cannot exist except as slaves, subject to a despotism.[112]

Similarly, John Bingham asserted that "the second section excludes the conclusion that by the first section suffrage is subjected to congressional law" except in cases where the guaranty clause is violated.[113]

The Report of the Joint Committee was even more emphatic on this point. Here the discussion of voting came in the context of the analysis of section two, which altered the basis of representation. Although noting the unfairness of race-based suffrage requirements, the committee continued:

> Doubts were entertained whether Congress had power . . . to prescribe the qualifications of voters in a State, or could act directly on the subject. It was doubtful in the opinion of your committee, whether the States would consent to surrender a power they had always exercised and to which they were attached. As the best if not the only method of surmounting the difficulty, and as eminently just and proper in itself, your committee came to the conclusion that political power should be possessed in all the States exactly in proportion as the right of suffrage should be granted, without distinction of color or race. This it was thought would leave the whole question with the people of each State, holding out to all the advantage of increased political power as an inducement to allow all to participate in its exercise.[114]

One can hardly imagine a clearer statement of an intent to leave state control over suffrage untouched.

This viewpoint is also reflected in the editorial stances of Republicans both for and against the proposed amendment. For example, terming the Joint Committee plan "entirely reasonable,"[115] *Harper's Weekly* noted that "Congress has chosen . . . wisely to leave the regulation of suffrage to the State"[116] because to do otherwise "would have been widely regarded as a radical blow at the most sacred of states rights, and a consummation of centralization."[117] By contrast, the *National Anti-Slavery Standard* cited the lack of provision for black suffrage as a reason for opposing the congressional plan, calling it "inconsistent with itself, wholly inadequate to its professed purpose, unjust to the negro and disgraceful to the nation."[118]

In short, Republicans in 1866 generally believed that the proposed Fourteenth Amendment would not give the federal government new power over suffrage.[119] This conclusion must be placed in context, however. The statements of the Joint Committee and Bingham and Howard individually merely indicate that the Fourteenth Amendment was not intended to disturb prior law on suffrage issues. Republicans who believed that the antebellum Constitution granted Congress authority to regulate voting rights continued to hold that view. Moreover, even those Republicans who denied federal power were typically in favor of black suffrage. Indeed, the extension of suffrage became an even more central issue when Congress reconvened in 1867.

8

Interregnum: Congress and the Right to Vote between the Fourteenth and Fifteenth Amendments

The decision not to pursue black suffrage directly in the Fourteenth Amendment set the tone for congressional action on voting rights for the remainder of the first session of the Thirty-ninth Congress. As late as May 15, the House of Representatives had voted overwhelmingly to enfranchise blacks in the territories;[1] later efforts, however, were doomed by the Republican determination not to come before the voters as the party of black suffrage. The proceedings on the District of Columbia and Tennessee are typical.

On January 10, 1866, the Senate Committee on the District of Columbia had reported its own universal suffrage bill, which had originally been introduced by Benjamin Wade of Ohio.[2] The bill was debated briefly on January 16 and then set aside for discussions of the Freedmen's Bureau Bill.[3] The suffrage bill subsequently disappeared for a time—perhaps for political reasons. Although the House suffrage bill was reported favorably to the Senate on February 21,[4] it was not immediately discussed because "there were several other measures considered of such importance . . . as to justify their consideration at that time, which necessarily excluded the consideration of [the suffrage] bill."[5] The political sensitivity of the suffrage issue may have contributed to this judgment.[6] On April 13, however, Lot M. Morrill of Maine—the chairman of the Senate District of Columbia Committee—promised to call up the House bill "at an early date."[7]

The "early date" proved to be June 27—*after* the Senate had adopted the Fourteenth Amendment. It was the Senate rather than the House bill that came before the full Senate for consideration.[8] Morrill immediately moved to impose an English literacy requirement for enfranchisement.[9] The amendment was defeated by a vote of 19 to 15; the margin of defeat, however, was provided by three Democrats who voted to retain universal suffrage, presumably in the hope of defeating the entire bill.[10] Moreover, Republicans Samuel C. Pomeroy and James W. Grimes opposed the amendment, not because it would disfranchise blacks, but because many naturalized citizens were literate only in their native tongues.[11] Thus it seems fair to conclude that in 1866 a near-majority of Republican senators preferred to pass only an impartial-suffrage bill, which would have outlawed discrimination only on the basis of race. Waitman T. Willey of West Virginia offered an amendment that would have altered the proposal in this respect.[12] Before it could be acted upon, however, the bill lost its place on the calendar because Morrill became ill.[13] The District of Columbia suffrage issue did not reemerge until the second session of Congress, after the elections. A Democratic commentator may well have been accurate in asserting that advocates of the District of Columbia bill were "afraid to take responsibility for its passage [because] [t]hey are every day more in doubt of the expediency of going before the people on a negro suffrage platform."[14]

The Tennessee issue also came to a head after the Republican party had committed itself to the Fourteenth Amendment as the basis for Reconstruction. Once the Tennessee legislature ratified the amendment, the imposition of new conditions on the state might have been viewed as a breach of faith by both the northern electorate and the unreconstructed states of the defeated Confederacy. Thus the overwhelming vote in both houses to readmit Tennessee without the black suffrage requirement[15] was not a rejection of the basic concept of black suffrage but rather a reaffirmation of the moderate Republican policy already adopted.[16] Related considerations doomed similar efforts to make black suffrage the prerequisite for admitting the territories of Nebraska and Colorado to the Union.[17]

THE FOURTEENTH AMENDMENT AND BLACK SUFFRAGE
IN THE ELECTIONS OF 1866

Despite the readmission of Tennessee, the status of the proposed Fourteenth Amendment as a final solution to the problem of Reconstruction was uncertain. Moderate Republicans clearly hoped that no further conditions would be imposed. Although lamenting the failure of Congress to mandate impartial suffrage, the *Nation* conceded, "that restoration has been, in effect offered to any state which would ratify the constitutional amendment is a fact that cannot be doubted."[18] Similarly, while reaffirming its support for the adoption of impartial suffrage throughout the Union, *Harper's Weekly* concluded that it was "advisable that each suspended state should be restored upon its individual acceptance of the amendment."[19]

More radical forces, however, refused to accept this conclusion. The *National Anti-Slavery Standard* reiterated its unremitting hostility to the amendment, describing it as "fundamentally wrong."[20] The *New York Independent* took slightly more temperate ground, describing the proposal as "an equitable measure—one which we hope to be adopted for its own sake, but not for the sake of making its adoption the final condition of restoration."[21] John W. Forney embraced a similar position, supporting the amendment but contending that states should not be reconstructed without impartial suffrage.[22]

The theory that ratification of the Fourteenth Amendment would bring immediate readmission was never tested, for Tennessee was the only ex-Confederate state to ratify.[23] Initially, leaders of the southern states thought that the forces led by President Johnson would win in the elections of 1866; such a victory would result in their immediate readmission without further preconditions. Johnson first made efforts to organize a new party composed of Democrats and conservative Republicans, culminating in the National Union Convention held in Philadelphia in August 1866.[24] It soon became clear, however, that Republicans in large numbers would not be drawn to the new party; thus the Democrats became the hope of both Johnson and the majority of southern whites. During the campaign, Democrats repeatedly sought to portray the Republicans as the party of black suffrage.[25] Republicans in turn consistently denied that the Fourteenth Amendment deprived any state of authority over suffrage.[26] When the votes were counted, the Republicans were the clear victors in the fall elections, maintaining a greater than two-thirds majority in both houses of Congress.

Despite the defeat of their northern allies, the southern states unanimously refused to ratify the constitutional amendment. Southern strategists split into two camps. Some advocated "masterly inactivity": "accepting nothing, rejecting nothing, recognizing no right of the North to exact from us more than has already been conceded, performing no act that might be construed into an assent to Northern dominion, and quietly abide [sic] our time."[27] Proponents of this strategy were heartened by the decision in *Ex parte Milligan*,[28] which seemed to strike at the entire concept of military rule in the South. Other southerners sought compromise; the most prominent effort became known as the North Carolina plan, which was based on a watered-down version of the proposed Fourteenth Amendment together with state constitutional amendments that recognized qualified black suffrage.[29]

The victorious Republicans were in no mood to retreat. The election results had strengthened the position of the radical wing of the party. Moreover, new instances of mistreatment of southern freedmen highlighted the continuing need to provide for their protection. The most visible demonstrations were the race riots in Memphis and New Orleans;[30] but Republican periodicals also regularly reported more prosaic examples of the insecure position of the newly freed slaves.[31]

THE RIGHT TO VOTE IN THE SECOND SESSION
OF THE THIRTY-NINTH CONGRESS

The elections of 1866 yielded a dramatic, sweeping victory for the Republican party. Despite the fact that during the campaign the Republicans had strenuously tried to avoid being labeled the party of black suffrage, the magnitude of their victory radically changed the political dynamic governing the issue. With firm Republican control of the national legislature, fears of an antiblack backlash from white voters receded (at least temporarily). Moreover, the events of 1866 had recast the party itself; the most conservative leaders who had hitherto identified themselves as Republicans had sided with Andrew Johnson and alienated themselves from the remainder of the party. Thus cabinet members such as Montgomery Blair and Gideon Welles and senators such as James Doolittle of Wisconsin and James Dixon of Connecticut were no longer factors in the formulation of Republican policy. Admittedly, some conservatives retained their status as Republicans by abandoning Johnson and supporting the Fourteenth Amendment as a solution to the Reconstruction problem; Cong. Henry Raymond of New York is a prime example. Nonetheless, the party as a whole was clearly more radical than it had been at the beginning of the Thirty-ninth Congress. It is therefore not surprising that in 1867 Republicans intensified their efforts to achieve reforms that would grant blacks the right to vote.

When the Thirty-ninth Congress met for its second, lame-duck session early in 1867, the change in atmosphere wrought by the election results immediately became apparent. The upper house moved quickly on the District of Columbia suffrage bill, brushing aside with little debate both Willey's amendment[32] and a proposal by James Dixon to engraft a requirement that all new voters demonstrate an ability to read and write.[33] Among mainstream Republicans, only Willey's West Virginia colleague Peter Van Winkle and Connecticut's La Fayette S. Foster ultimately opposed passage of the suffrage measure.[34] Similarly, the House action granting blacks the right to vote in the territories also passed the Senate with little discussion; on this issue, Van Winkle was the lone Republican dissenter.[35] Johnson's veto of the District of Columbia bill was easily overridden.[36]

The shift in position on the issue of the admission of Nebraska and Colorado was even more dramatic. In 1866 measures requiring black suffrage in both nascent states as a condition for admission had been easily defeated.[37] However, Andrew Johnson did not wish to have Republican strength in Congress increased, so despite their lack of black-suffrage requirements, he vetoed both the Nebraska and Colorado bills. When the subject was taken up again in 1867, the elections of 1866 had changed the situation in two ways. First, the magnitude of the Republican victory had in general left party members with a greater determination to pursue ideological goals. Second, from a Republican perspective the victory had reduced the urgency of admission of the two states. As Henry Wilson of Massachusetts noted, it had appeared before the election that the votes of the Republican senators who would represent Nebraska and Colorado might well be critical in the Reconstruction struggle; thus, the principle of black suffrage might be sacrificed in order to speedily secure those ballots. After the election of 1866, however, it appeared that the mainstream Republicans had captured a clear two-thirds majority in both houses of Congress. Since the potential votes were no longer necessary, the suffrage issue could be directly confronted on its merits without fear of the consequences of delay.[38]

Given this background, it is logical that proposals to force Nebraska and Colorado to implement black suffrage would now attract substantial support. The issue of Nebraska was considered first and thus generated most of the debate on the suffrage question. In the Senate, three different black-suffrage proposals were introduced, each designed to remedy the fact that as drafted, the state constitution limited suffrage to whites. All three proposals required as a "fundamental condition" of admission that the new state be perpetually forbidden from using race as a qualification for voters. They differed, however, in their respective provisions for implementation. B. Gratz Brown of Missouri would have delayed admission until the voters themselves had ratified the suffrage condition;[39] Henry Wilson would have placed the ratification responsibility with the territorial legislatures;[40] and George T. Edmunds of Vermont would have admitted the states immediately and simply imposed the condition by congressional fiat.[41] All three of these provisions mandated impartial (rather than universal) suffrage; thus it is not surprising that among Republicans there was no dissent from the premise that blacks should be allowed to vote in both Nebraska and Colorado. The desirability and constitutionality of *congressional* action were, by contrast, issues that generated substantial controversy.

Advocates of the suffrage requirement deployed a variety of arguments in support of their position. As in all suffrage cases, some cited the guarantee clause as the fountainhead of congressional power over the issue.[42] They also noted that the Constitution granted Congress plenary authority over the admission of territories.[43] The sponsors of these provisions, supported by other radicals such as A. J. Creswell of Maryland and Charles Sumner, argued that these constitutional sources provided ample authority for the imposition of the suffrage requirement as a condition of admission.

Opponents of the suffrage stipulation also relied on several points. Some of their contentions were directed only to the specific problems presented by imposing such requirements in the particular cases being considered. For example, Benjamin F. Wade of Ohio and Samuel J. Kirkwood of Iowa stressed the need to add still further to Republican strength without unnecessary delay.[44] Wade also believed that the imposition of the fundamental condition was unfair in a nation where many other states prohibited blacks from voting.[45] Taking another tack, John Sherman of Ohio and Samuel Pomeroy of Kansas noted that the 1864 statute authorizing the constitutional convention had not required black suffrage and argued that imposing a new requirement in 1867 would constitute a breach of faith with the people of Nebraska.[46]

Other arguments, however, addressed the basic issues of federalism raised by the imposition of suffrage requirements by the federal government. Opponents stressed that the suffrage condition was intended to bind Nebraska *after* it had been admitted on an "equal footing" with existing states, and they denied that Congress had the power to regulate the suffrage in any state.[47] The strongest attacks were leveled at the Edmunds proposal, which sought to obligate permanently the nascent state without any participation in the decision by its inhabitants or their representatives. Jacob Howard asserted that the theory underlying the proposal "denies to the people of the States almost all . . . of those original and immemorial rights which have been exercised by the people of the States since [the Revolutionary War]."[48] Samuel Kirkwood questioned the enforceability of the provision in the event the people of the state of Nebraska refused to remove the offending language from their state constitution;[49] similar concerns were expressed by James Grimes and William Pitt Fessenden, both of whom were generally in favor of the concept of fundamental conditions.[50] Edmunds suggested that this eventuality would lead to the expulsion of the state's congressional delegation, but this hardly seemed a practical solution.[51]

The Edmunds proposal did, however, have one advantage: Unlike the Brown and Wilson formulations, it allowed for the immediate admission of Nebraska. In the Senate, this factor ultimately proved decisive. After the other two versions of implementation were rejected,[52] the Edmunds language was adopted. Its margin of victory was razor-thin; after initially being rejected on a tie vote,[53] the congressionally imposed fundamental condition was added to the Nebraska bill by a vote of 20 to 18.[54] Not only did seven Republicans join the opposition to the proposal, but the final tally overstated the depth of party support for the concept. Wade, for example, ultimately voted in favor of fundamental conditions despite his doubts about their constitutionality; he reasoned that adoption of the Edmunds amendment would tend to "harmonize all the friends" of universal suffrage,[55] thus ensuring passage of the Nebraska bill itself. Sherman was even more explicit on this point, arguing that unilateral congressional implementation of fundamental conditions was "unwise policy," "entirely nugatory," and unconstitutional.[56] Nonetheless, like Wade he voted for the amendment because of his belief that it would facilitate the admission of Nebraska. Other senators no doubt harbored similar sentiments.

Thus amended, the Nebraska admission bill passed the Senate by a 24 to 15 margin, with only four Republicans dissenting.[57] In the House, however, the Edmunds amendment was once more subjected to a storm of criticism. Moderates such as James G. Blaine of Maine and Henry L. Dawes of Massachusetts joined radicals James Wilson of Iowa and George Boutwell of Massachusetts in pressing for a requirement that the fundamental condition be ratified by a Nebraska authority;[58] John Bingham and Christopher Delano of Ohio, by contrast, attacked the entire concept of fundamental conditions.[59] The critical vote came on a proposal by Boutwell to make approval of the fundamental condition by the Nebraska legislature a prerequisite of admission. Moderates split, and the Boutwell amendment passed by a vote of 87 to 70, with twenty-four Republicans in opposition.[60] The Nebraska bill then passed the House on an almost straight party-line vote, 103 to 55.[61] With little further discussion, the Senate concurred in the House amendment by a vote of 28 to 14.[62] After a similar sequence of events, the bill to admit Colorado passed with a similar proviso by a vote of 27 to 12.[63]

Andrew Johnson vetoed the admission of both territories, but the ultimate fate of the two bills was different. While both houses voted resoundingly to override the Nebraska veto,[64] the Senate's override vote on Colorado was only 29 to 19—three votes short of the necessary two-thirds majority.[65] Although a variety of factors may have influenced this outcome,[66] some senators seem to have been motivated by a fear that the Colorado legislature would not adopt a black-suffrage measure.[67]

The protracted debate over the conditions under which Nebraska was to be admitted reflects a number of the recurring themes of the Reconstruction era. One is the continued commitment of the Republican party to the basic principle that race per se should not be a qualification for suffrage. A second is the pervasiveness of the belief that this commitment would have to be tempered by respect for principles of federalism. Although radicals were generally less concerned about issues of federalism when black suffrage was at stake, both themes cut across factional differences within the party. For example, Jacob Howard—one of the most radical men in the Senate—was also one of the most persistent critics of the idea that Congress could set suffrage-related conditions for admission to statehood that would bind erstwhile territories after the admission process was completed.[68] Finally, like the debate over the District of Columbia bill, the maneuvering over the precise form of the fundamental condition for the admission of Nebraska revealed not only the variety of opinions within the party on suffrage-

128 CHAPTER EIGHT

related issues but also the complexities inherent in efforts to mediate among them.

When Republicans turned to the most important question facing the second session of the Thirty-ninth Congress—Reconstruction—their consideration of the suffrage problem would be affected by the same concerns. However, the context in which the suffrage issue was debated would dramatically alter the political dynamic surrounding the issue. The resulting action would not only set the course for the states of the defeated Confederacy, it would also have important consequences for the voting rights of blacks throughout the nation.

As in the first session of the Thirty-ninth Congress, the eventual decision on black suffrage was intimately related to more general Reconstruction issues. Actions taken in 1866 set the parameters for debate within the Republican party. At one end of the spectrum were conservatives and moderates who followed John Bingham in urging that the adoption of the proposed Fourteenth Amendment should be the sole standard for restoration of congressional representation.[69] At the other end were radicals such as George Julian of Indiana, who argued that the defeated states should be treated as territories and that Congress should make no commitments regarding restoration.[70] Black suffrage provided a compromise solution.

Thaddeus Stevens began the 1867 debate over the terms of Reconstruction by proposing a substitute to the measure reported by the Joint Committee on Reconstruction in 1866. The Stevens bill would have required the former Confederate states (with the exception of Tennessee) to hold new constitutional conventions, with the delegates to the conventions to be selected by universal manhood suffrage. Many adherents to the Confederate cause would, however, have been disfranchised. The bill also required that the new constitutions and all laws passed under their authority not discriminate on the basis of race, language, or previous condition of servitude. Any deviation from this principle— even after readmission—would result in the loss of representation in Congress.[71]

The suffrage provisions of the Stevens bill came under attack from both radical and conservative elements of the Republican party. The radical *National Anti-Slavery Standard* complained because the bill did not require universal suffrage in the state constitutions.[72] By contrast, more conservative Republicans such as Jehu Baker of Illinois and John Bingham blasted the entire theory of attaching fundamental conditions that would continue to limit state control of suffrage even after Congress had approved readmission.[73]

Yet suffrage was something of a side issue in the January 1867 debate over the Stevens proposal. The key question was whether Congress would adhere to the policy that ratification of the Fourteenth Amendment alone would guarantee readmission or would instead add new conditions that the southern states would be forced to satisfy. When the vote was taken, Republicans who were against new conditions, led by Bingham, won a signal victory; by a margin of 88 to 65, the Stevens bill was referred to the Joint Committee on Reconstruction.[74]

It soon became clear, however, that the southern state governments established under the auspices of Andrew Johnson were not going to ratify the Fourteenth Amendment. This realization spurred Republicans to impose additional requirements. Throughout, Bingham battled to limit these stipulations as much as possible. In the Joint Committee itself he proposed that the ex-Confederate states only be required to provide for impartial suffrage in addition to ratifying the Fourteenth Amendment.[75] But after a good deal of wrangling, the committee reported a bill that listed no conditions for readmission; instead, the bill simply placed the defeated states under military rule.[76]

Dissatisfied with the Joint Committee's solution, Bingham and his allies pressed for a congressional commitment to specific conditions under which the southern states would be restored to equal status in the Union. He first attempted to have the Joint Committee report the original Stevens bill as well as its military-government proposal.[77] When this effort failed, both Bingham and James G. Blaine offered amendments on the House floor to establish firm criteria for restoration.[78] Each used the ratification of the Fourteenth Amendment as a starting point for readmission; each in addition required the affected states to modify their constitutions to allow blacks to vote. On the suffrage issue, however, the two proposals differed in one important respect. While Bingham would have required that the states confer ''equal and impartial suffrage to *the* male citizens of the United States without distinction of race or color,'' the Blaine language mandated that the state constitutions should provide that ''the elective franchise shall be enjoyed equally and impartially by *all* male citizens of the United States . . . without regard to race, color or previous condition of servitude,'' except those disfranchised for participation in the rebellion. Thus the Bingham amendment would have forced only impartial suffrage on the states subject to Reconstruction; Blaine would have prescribed universal suffrage—a position he had argued for earlier in the session.[79] Blaine later made this point even clearer by dropping the words ''equally and impartially'' from his proposal so that the state constitutions would be required to allow ''all male citizens'' to vote, with the exception of those the amendment specifically excluded.[80] It was Blaine's language that ultimately formed the basis of the moderate position on Reconstruction.

Republican radicals, however, did not wish Congress to commit to readmitting the southern states under any circumstances. As a result the

House was presented with the unusual spectacle of moderates pressing for stringent suffrage requirements and radicals opposing them. Democrats were torn; some joined the moderates because their proposal set clear conditions for the full restoration of the prerogatives of the southern states, but others voted with the radicals in hopes of deadlocking the Republicans and preventing the passage of any bill at all. On a key preliminary procedural motion, the Blaine/Bingham forces won a narrow victory.[81] A dramatic speech by Thaddeus Stevens in favor of the unamended Joint Committee bill, however, changed enough minds that on the merits of the moderate approach the House rejected a motion to recommit the bill with instructions to add the Blaine amendment.[82] House Republicans then united to pass the original military-government bill without the suffrage amendment.[83]

The situation was further complicated by House passage of a separate Reconstruction measure applicable only to Louisiana.[84] Generally more radical than the Military Reconstruction Bill, the Louisiana bill required that delegates to a state constitutional convention be elected by universal suffrage (some former Confederates excepted) but that the state constitution itself provide only for impartial suffrage.[85] The suffrage issues were not addressed during the consideration of the bill.

When the Senate took up the Military Reconstruction Bill, the course of the suffrage debate illustrated the complexity of the political concerns surrounding the measure. Although George Williams of Oregon initially planned to introduce a proposal identical to the Blaine amendment, that step was ultimately taken by Reverdy Johnson—a *Democrat*.[86] Democrat Thomas A. Hendricks of Indiana moved to alter the Johnson amendment to require only impartial suffrage.[87] Radicals Henry S. Lane of Indiana and B. Gratz Brown of Missouri attacked the Hendricks suggestion, fearing that blacks could be disfranchised by indirection.[88] Conservative Waitman Willey of West Virginia supported Hendricks "with some reluctance."[89] Hendricks withdrew his motion before a formal test of strength ensued.[90] On the other hand, John Henderson of Missouri, concerned that as written the Johnson proposal guaranteed only impartial suffrage,[91] achieved his goal of incorporating language in the Johnson amendment that eliminated all doubt as to its intention to require universal suffrage.[92] Most believed, however, that the Henderson modification did not materially change the Johnson amendment but simply rendered it "more explicit, and . . . more easily understood."[93]

By this point, it had become clear that Senate Republicans were so deeply divided on the overall issue of Reconstruction that resolution of their differences on the floor would be extremely difficult, if not impossible. At a party caucus the entire matter was referred to a seven-member committee. The group recommended modifying the military bill to obligate southerners to hold new constitutional conventions, with delegates selected by universal suffrage (excluding some former rebels). The committee plan did not, however, mandate that the new state constitutions themselves provide for even impartial suffrage.[94]

In the full caucus, Charles Sumner and Henry Wilson of Massachusetts led the fight to overturn the latter omission. Initially the caucus split evenly on a proposal to require universal suffrage in the constitutions, but on a second vote, Sumner and Wilson prevailed by a narrow 15 to 13 margin.[95] After more wrangling over matters not related to the suffrage issue, both the House and Senate adopted a further-altered version of the military bill.[96] Andrew Johnson applied his veto, but it was countered by a predictable override in both houses of Congress.[97] Universal suffrage thus became a cornerstone of Republican Reconstruction policy.

THE AFTERMATH OF THE RECONSTRUCTION BILL

The decision to force color-blind suffrage on the South by federal action created substantial tensions with the Republican policy that left the matter to the discretion of the loyal states. Unlike the District of Columbia and Nebraska measures, the military bill confronted the most prominent political issue of the day—Reconstruction. In its proffered solution to the problem, Republicans had clearly committed themselves to federal control of suffrage. Moreover, whatever justification was given for congressional authority over Reconstruction, Americans in general were accustomed to regarding the governmental entities that had adhered to the Confederate cause as states within the Union. Indeed, the insistence upon this status was the foundation of the political theory upon which the Union effort in the Civil War had been based. Thus, federal action on black suffrage in the South had substantially different implications than similar action dealing with the District of Columbia (an area perpetually under federal control) or Nebraska (a territory asking to be admitted).

Some Republicans believed that the problem could be resolved by the emergence of a national consensus on the black-suffrage issue. Their hopes were fed by a suggestion from the Democratic *Chicago Times* that the opposition party accept and embrace the inevitability of at least impartial suffrage; there was also the fact that the House Democrats had not attacked the suffrage features of the Louisiana Reconstruction Bill.[98] It soon became clear, however, that the *Times* did not speak for most Democrats and that failure to deal effectively with the seeming inconsistency in Republican policy would have adverse political consequences.

These problems were particularly acute for Republicans in the ex-Confederate states—a region in which the party hoped to develop and maintain substantial political power. White southern Democrats could claim that their region was being singled out for unduly oppressive federal action; they could also contend that the absence of black-suffrage requirements in the North demonstrated that Republicans were not really concerned about the welfare of freedmen but were simply using them as pawns to further Republican political goals. Both of these arguments were effective ammunition for attacks on Republican organizing efforts.[99]

Republicans used several lines of reasoning to try to deflect these accusations. In theory, the situation in the ex-Confederate states could be distinguished from that in the North; federal power over suffrage in the former could be justified by reference even to the relatively conservative grasp of war doctrine, not to mention more radical conceptualizations of the position of the rebellious states. Moreover, Republicans consistently stressed the need for black suffrage to create a loyal counterweight to the potential political power of the rebellious whites—a need that obviously did not exist in the states that had adhered to the Union cause. Finally, Republicans also argued that the social and legal climate in the erstwhile slave states placed blacks at particular risk; hence, granting freedmen the ballot was the best and least intrusive means of protecting them from the predations of their former masters.[100]

However sound in the abstract, these arguments did not dissolve the tension created by the universal-suffrage requirement in the Reconstruction plan, and Republicans turned to other avenues to resolve their difficulties. At first, they continued to press for state constitutional reform which would guarantee impartial suffrage in the loyal states; in 1867 Republican-controlled state legislatures succeeded in placing the issue on the ballot for fall elections in Kansas, Minnesota, and Ohio. But state-by-state reform would of necessity be a gradual, drawn-out process, and it would not address the federalism issues generated by the imposition of suffrage on the ex-Confederate states. The possibility of nationwide federal action became more real.

Radicals pressed their demand for a statute that would guarantee impartial suffrage throughout the nation. They argued that Congress possessed the requisite authority by virtue of the guarantee clause and/or the enforcement provision of the Thirteenth Amendment.[101] The most persistent and vociferous proponents of the radical position on this point were Charles Sumner and Henry Wilson, each of whom sponsored national impartial-suffrage bills that were introduced during the first session of the Fortieth Congress.[102]

Even from within the Republican party, the constitutional arguments of the radicals generated strong dissent. George Edmunds stated that while Sumner's proposal had "supreme moral merit . . . I am a little afraid . . . that there is a higher law [i.e., the Constitution] that will bind us not to pass [the Sumner bill] for want of power."[103] As early as 1867, some had suggested that ratification of the Fourteenth Amendment would give Congress the necessary authority.[104] Others, however, took an opposing view.

Conservative Republicans were particularly alarmed by the general implications of Sumner's theory that the guarantee clause was a "sleeping giant" that "gives to Congress . . . supreme power over the states."[105] Lyman Trumbull's counterargument received the widest circulation. While noting his support for the basic concept of impartial suffrage and state constitutional amendments establishing that principle, Trumbull asserted that "even to do a right thing in a wrong way is often fraught with greater danger than to leave the thing undone, and is never justifiable when there is a right way by which it may be accomplished." He warned against constitutional theories that granted Congress unlimited discretion, asserting that "to allow [Congress] to exercise powers not granted would be to make [the legislators] masters instead of the servants of the people, and such a representative government would be little better than despotism." Addressing the guarantee-clause claim specifically, Trumbull suggested that permitting Congress to control the conditions of suffrage in the loyal states would be "a sacrifice of the obvious meaning and spirit of the [Constitution]." Thus, the passage of a black-suffrage statute "would be the subversion instead of the guarantee of the republican form of government and would necessarily abrogate all existing state governments."[106]

The *Springfield Republican* and *New York Times* voiced similar concerns. Responding to a *Washington Chronicle* editorial embracing the radical view of the guarantee clause, the *Times* argued that under the radical theory

Congress . . . is henceforward to have absolute charge over local as well as national concerns.

For this authority that "must compel the States to have republican forms of government" would, if permitted, soon push its pretensions far beyond the suffrage. Mr. Sumner contends that certain educational plans are an essential feature of republicanism; and the power which asserts its right to regulate the suffrage in all the States will not hesitate to assume the direction of the school systems of the country, or to any subjects, now local in character, which . . . radicalism might desire to manipulate for its special advantage.[107]

After initially flirting with the idea of supporting a national suffrage bill,[108] the *Republican* took a similar stance, arguing that the radical theory denied "that there is a constitutional and sound theory of state rights, not to be trampled out, but sacredly maintained and preserved, as the true guarantee of both individual liberty and national unity."[109] The same commentator also noted the grave political dangers inherent in the radical position, asserting that it "would strand the party . . . hopelessly beyond the reach of any future tide of popular favor."[110]

The key test of strength came during the short session of July 1867. In apparent contravention of a resolution limiting the business of the session to Reconstruction matters, Sumner attempted to bring his universal suffrage bill to the floor for consideration. On the question of whether the motion to consider the bill was in order, Sumner was able to muster only twelve radical supporters; fifteen Republicans joined seven Democrats in refusing to consider the bill.[111]

Condemnation of statutory regulation of suffrage should not be taken as evidence that moderate and conservative Republicans opposed a national guarantee of impartial suffrage in principle. Indeed, by mid–1867 a consensus in favor of such regulation seems to have emerged among Republican leaders. For moderate and conservative Republicans, adherence to this position required some doctrinal adjustments; since these Republicans generally did not view the right to vote as either a natural right or a necessary concomitant of citizenship, they could not defend national regulation as a vindication of the concept of limited absolute equality. Nonetheless, most Republicans believed that circumstances warranted some federal action on the suffrage question. The crucial difference was that moderates and conservatives believed that the goal could only be reached through the adoption of a constitutional amendment.

Even before the passage of the Reconstruction Act of 1867, important moderate organs such as the *Republican* and the *Chicago Tribune* (which had substantially tempered its politics since 1866) advocated such an amendment as a simple, final solution to the problem of Reconstruction generally.[112] After the imposition of universal suffrage on the ex-Confederate states, the anomaly between the treatment of North and South added momentum to the movement for a constitutional amendment. The *Republican* asserted that for the northern states to demand universal suffrage as a precondition for readmission without recognizing the right of their own blacks to vote was "contemptible."[113] Other moderate and conservative journals took the same position. The *Nation* joined the campaign for a suffrage amendment— as did J. B. McCullough, the conservative Washington correspondent of the *Cincinnati Commercial* who had opposed even the Civil Rights Act of 1866.[114] Similarly, in the same editorial in which it attacked the radical plan to impose universal suffrage by statute, the *Times* argued that it was necessary to "strengthen [the principle of impartial suffrage] with constitutional forms [so] that no single state shall have the power to disturb it."[115]

For moderate and conservative Republicans, support for a constitutional amendment provided a means of balancing the perceived need to impose impartial suffrage nationwide with their basically conservative constitutional philosophy. The open-ended theory of federal power espoused by Sumner and like-minded Republicans remained anathema to men such as Lyman Trumbull. A constitutional amendment dealing with suffrage would admittedly be an infringement on states' rights, but, at the same time, it could be a narrowly defined federal encroachment that would leave the balance of power between the state and federal governments otherwise unaltered. It is thus understandable that moderates and conservatives endorsed this approach.

On March 7, 1867, John Henderson reintroduced his proposal for a constitutional amendment prohibiting racial discrimination in voting rights.[116] Moderates did not press hard for this proposal, however, perhaps reasoning that the short sessions of the Fortieth Congress in March and July 1867 were ill suited to the adoption of new constitutional amendments. These sessions were concerned primarily with improving the basic Reconstruction acts that had been passed in the second session of the Thirty-ninth Congress. Initially, prospects for the long session scheduled for early 1868 seemed brighter;[117] but in the interim, the elections of 1867 intervened and changed the political situation dramatically.

These elections did not generally involve the selection of national officers; rather, voters were to choose the officials to serve in the state governments. Nonetheless, issues of national scope had a strong influence on the campaigns. The Reconstruction policy of the Republican party was understood to be one of these issues; black suffrage was another. In three states—Kansas, Minnesota, and Ohio—state constitutional amendments enfranchising blacks were on the ballot. Ohio was generally considered the most important test in this regard; the *Commercial* asserted that in that state, "if the [suffrage] amendment does not prevail, the Republican party will be substantially defeated" even if party members carried all other state offices.[118]

When the votes were tallied, the result was a stunning Republican defeat. The suffrage amendment in Ohio not only lost by thirty-eight thousand votes but also proved to be a formidable drag on the remainder of the ticket. Republicans barely retained the governorship, and Democrats gained control of the state legislature. The news was no better elsewhere: Suffrage amendments were also defeated in both Kansas and Minnesota, and Republicans lost ground in virtually every state contested, including California, New York, and Pennsylvania.[119] Although a range of issues no doubt affected the elections, many viewed the Republican advocacy of black suffrage as the most significant factor in the defeat. The *Republican* aptly summed up the views of the party membership when it described the result as "a disgrace and humiliation to the republican party."[120]

The responses of the different elements of the party to the "disgrace and humiliation" varied widely. Radical Republicans blamed the defeat on the moderate wing of the party[121] and urged Congress to "rise above party considerations" and take radical action.[122] The *National Anti-Slavery Standard* advocated immediate passage of a national impartial-suffrage bill,[123] and J. W. Forney argued that "by planting ourselves upon the great doctrine of Universal Manhood Suffrage, we shall recall the wanderers and consolidate the whole Republican Party . . . thus giving us complete and lasting command of the political situation."[124] Faced with such belligerency, the Washington correspondent of the *Republican* asserted that there was "no doubt" radicals would press for an equal-suffrage bill when Congress reassembled, and he feared that the resulting controversy would split the party.[125]

Yet despite their defiant rhetoric, radicals were clearly disheartened by the election results. The Washington correspondent of the *New York Independent*, who before the New York election had given a positive assessment of the prospects for a national suffrage bill,[126] conceded after the elections that there was virtually no chance that such a bill would pass in the Fortieth Congress.[127] Even the normally indefatigable Sumner was forced to recognize that "times haven't been propitious" for black-suffrage legislation.[128]

Nonetheless, in March 1868, John H. Broomall of Pennsylvania brought such legislation to the floor of the House of Representatives for debate.[129] Rufus P. Spalding of Ohio attacked the bill as unconstitutional and also declared that passage at that time would be the "death knell of our hopes . . . in the approaching presidential canvass."[130] Spalding was simply echoing the fears of the *Republican*, which had stated that adoption of a national suffrage law would "give [almost] every state in the Union to the Democrats."[131] The bill never even came to a vote; by March 19 it was reported that no Republican had "the slightest idea" that any such measure would be voted on (let alone adopted) during that session of Congress.[132]

The defeat in Ohio also severely damaged the moderate/conservative drive for a constitutional amendment dealing with suffrage. Some moderates remained committed to such a proposal. The *Republican*, for example, continued to assert that a constitutional amendment should be made a "leading issue" by Republicans in the presidential campaign of 1868, arguing that the party must stand for equal suffrage everywhere or "confess that it has no basis at all on which to stand."[133] The *Commercial* disagreed, arguing that the elections of 1867 had settled the point, and Republicans should not press the suffrage question in the upcoming campaign.[134] It was reported that some Republicans were even willing to abandon the requirement that the ex-Confederate states guarantee impartial suffrage as a condition for readmission.[135]

Under the circumstances, the spring elections of 1868 took on special importance. A smashing Republican success in the New Hampshire canvass gave the prosuffrage element a significant boost in March. Their hopes were dashed, however, by the results of the April elections in Connecticut, which were inconclusive, and by those in Michigan, where the inclusion of a black-suffrage provision led to the defeat of a proposed new state constitution. As the *Times* noted, these elections proved that the Republican party "has no strength to throw away, and that it has good reason for behaving itself just as well as it can."[136] The *Commercial* concurred, reiterating its position that the "Party cannot risk success this fall by a conspicuous recognition of the doctrine . . . of negro suffrage in the North."[137] Even the *Republican* was forced to retreat, conceding bitterly that the Connecticut and Michigan results

> indicate beyond a doubt that the rank and file of the republican party . . . are yet so far from being unanimous in favor of black suffrage, that the more immediate interests of reconstruction might be jeopardized by forcing the issue at this juncture, and it is therefore certain that the party leaders and party press will only be too ready to ignore or postpone it.[138]

In any event, the suffrage issue was not foremost in the minds of congressional Republicans in early 1868. Instead, the impeachment and trial of Andrew Johnson took center stage.[139] After earlier radical efforts to oust the president had failed in the House of Representatives, Johnson's attempt to remove Edwin M. Stanton as secretary of war united House Republicans and resulted in a Bill of Impeachment. Conviction was initially expected in the Senate, but when the critical vote was taken on May 16, Johnson survived by a single ballot. The Senate action demonstrated once more the pivotal position of the more conservative moderates during the early Reconstruction era; the defection of a mere seven of the Senate's forty-three mainstream Republicans was enough to prevent the conviction of the president.

The same wing of the party dominated proceedings when the Republican National Convention met in Chicago on May 19 and 20. By the time the convention opened, the presidential aspirations of Benjamin Wade and Chief Justice Salmon P. Chase—men prominently associated with the radical prosuffrage position—had evaporated. Instead, the nomination of Ulysses S. Grant, the favorite of the conservative and moderate elements of the party, was a foregone conclusion. Wade was also shunted aside for the vice presidency in favor of the less ideologically committed Speaker of the House, Schuyler Colfax of Indiana.[140] Finally, ignoring the radicals' demands that the party irrevocably bind itself to at least impartial suffrage,[141] the convention deliberately evaded that key issue. While supporting the power of Congress to require universal suffrage in the South, the party platform also declared that "the question of suffrage in all the loyal States properly belongs to the people of those States."[142]

Radicals were enraged. Wendell Phillips decried the plank on suffrage as "in bad faith and . . . a practical surrender of the whole question as a national issue."[143] In the *Boston Commonwealth*, another radical organ, a writer argued that the suffrage plank "is affirming and consenting to a doctrine which springs from the corrupt blood of States rights; which is refuted by the constitution itself, by the writings of our most eminent publicists, and by the whole spirit of our institutions."[144]

But the convention had captured the mood of the majority of party members, which the *Republican* summarized perfectly: Expressing regret that the Republican party could not bring the country to accept impartial suffrage, the paper nevertheless concluded that "since it has been distinctly proved that it can not, there is no reason why it should go so far ahead as to lose the nation, in a vain attempt to achieve an impossible good."[145] Individually, Republicans would continue to express support for the concept of black suffrage throughout the campaign of 1868; but they would also seek to eliminate it as a party issue.[146]

From the beginning, the Republican attempt to remove the black-suffrage issue from the presidential campaign faced grave difficulties. The platform plank could not erase the forceful position that party candidates had espoused in 1867. Moreover, the platform language failed to deal effectively with the tension between Republican policy toward the ex-Confederate states and its policy toward the loyal states. This strain was exacerbated after the Republican convention as Congress prepared to readmit many of the southern states.

Actually, the first concerted effort in this direction had taken place as early as March, when the House Reconstruction Committee reported a bill recognizing the restoration of Alabama. Responding to concerns that once restored to full status the state would fall under the control of unreconstructed rebels, the committee bill revived the concept of the "fundamental condition" and stipulated that the state constitution could never be amended to restrict the suffrage of those currently enfranchised or to enfranchise any person disqualified from holding office under the Fourteenth Amendment.[147] The result was a replay of the

Nebraska/Colorado debate, with a twist: The foes of fundamental conditions included some radicals who opposed restoration under any circumstances. Thus, when John Bingham declared that the "basis of the whole American system is the right of the people to alter and amend their constitutions of government at leisure, subject [only to] restrictions of the Constitution of the United States,"[148] he received backing from radical Benjamin F. Loan of Missouri, who insisted that the imposition of fundamental conditions would violate the principle that all states be on an "equal footing."[149] Bolstered by support from this unlikely quarter, Bingham succeeded in having the fundamental conditions removed from the bill by a vote of 71 to 39.[150] Without the conditions, many Republicans were unwilling to vote for restoration. Consequently, on the motion of Rufus Spalding of Ohio, the bill was altered to recognize the new Alabama government as provisional only.[151]

With the success of the impeachment of Andrew Johnson increasingly in doubt and the presidential election looming closer, the drive to readmit the southern states gained momentum in May. On May 7, the case of Arkansas was taken up by the House of Representatives through a bill that stipulated a guarantee of universal suffrage. Unlike the Alabama bill, however, no enforcement provision was included.[152] Most House moderates were now willing to acquiesce in the imposition of fundamental conditions in order to ensure the passage of the readmission legislation. James G. Blaine caught the prevailing sentiment: "If there is any subject which has been talked to death in this country, it is the subject of reconstruction. What is needed now is action."[153] With minimal debate, the Arkansas bill passed with the fundamental condition intact.[154]

In the Senate, the issue was much more fully discussed. Charles D. Drake of Missouri offered an amendment to require as a precondition of readmission that the Arkansas legislature ratify the fundamental condition; without such ratification, he asserted, the condition might be unenforceable.[155] Just as they had in the Thirty-ninth Congress, other influential senators expressed reservations about the whole concept of fundamental conditions. Although he declined to express an opinion regarding their constitutionality, Lyman Trumbull stated, "I have very little faith in these provisions."[156] Oliver Morton objected more strongly, arguing that "this Government has no right, and it has no power, to impose a fundamental condition on any State by which that State parts with any right which it has under the Constitution of the United States"; included in those rights, said Morton, were the right to regulate suffrage and the right to amend the state constitution at will.[157]

The key votes came on two attempts by Orrin S. Ferry of Connecticut

to delete the entire concept of fundamental conditions from the Reconstruction bill. Despite support from thirteen mainstream Republicans,
his proposals failed by votes of 21 to 20 and 22 to 18.[158] One of the crucial ballots was cast by John Sherman, who had expressed doubts about
the idea of fundamental conditions in 1867 but nonetheless opposed
Ferry in the hope of speeding the Reconstruction process.[159] Drake then
modified his Arkansas proposal to protect only impartial suffrage; thus
sweetened to gain moderate support, it passed 26 to 14.[160] In conference, however, the basic premise of the House version was restored, and
universal suffrage became a fundamental condition for the readmission
of Arkansas.[161] The Arkansas bill in turn became a model for the rapid
readmission of six other states—North Carolina, South Carolina, Louisiana, Georgia, Alabama, and Florida—in June 1868.[162]

The debate over fundamental conditions highlighted the constitutional issues involved in congressional regulation of the suffrage; at the
same time, it provided the Democrats with a new weapon in the presidential campaign. After an extremely contentious convention and a
dalliance with the idea of nominating Salmon P. Chase on an
impartial-suffrage platform, the Democrats chose Horatio Seymour of
New York as their standard-bearer and Francis A. Blair, Jr., of Missouri
as his running mate.[163] Though not attacking black suffrage outright,
the party platform condemned attempts by Congress to regulate suffrage as "a flagrant usurpation of power which can find no warrant in
the Constitution."[164]

In the presidential campaign of 1868, Republicans generally tried to
ignore the suffrage issue while Democrats attacked hard on several
suffrage-related fronts. A distaste for the very notion of black suffrage
was at the core of the Democratic barrage. Reminding voters of the
1867 campaign, Democrats characterized the Republican party as the
champion of voting rights for blacks, and the platform plank on this issue as a "cowardly . . . evasive dodge," which covered the true Republican position with "the thin veil of expediency."[165] The *Philadelphia
Age* urged voters to dismiss the disclaimers in the Republican platform
for two reasons. First, the *Age* noted that in the campaign of 1866, Republicans had promised not to impose black suffrage on the South and
then promptly broken that promise after the election.[166] Second, the
imposition of fundamental conditions on the readmitted states was a
demonstration that the platform was a "humbug."[167] Democrats also
sought to focus attention on the dichotomy in the Republican position
that was inherent in the suffrage plank. Many suggested that the plank
showed a Republican propensity for political hypocrisy and cowardice.[168] Others argued that requiring fundamental conditions for readmission was a violation of the principle that all states were equal under
the Constitution.[169]

Despite the Democratic attacks on the suffrage question and other issues, the personal popularity of Grant and the Republican pledge to bring a speedy end to the Reconstruction process were too much to overcome. Republicans swept to victory in the elections of 1868— albeit with a somewhat decreased majority in the House of Representatives.[170]

Grant's election did not heal the divisions in the Republican party over suffrage. Although virtually all Republicans remained committed to black suffrage in principle, they continued to differ sharply on the scope of protection that was appropriate and the constitutional theory (if any) that would justify federal intervention on its behalf. Moderates had been forced to placate their more radical colleagues on the suffrage question in order to secure the admission of Nebraska and the readmission of the ex-Confederate states. At the same time, however, moderates remained adamantly opposed to a general, open-ended reading of the Constitution that would allow federal control of suffrage in existing states that had adhered to the Union. Further, the platform struggle had demonstrated that a majority of party members were willing to limit action on black suffrage for reasons of political expediency. All of these issues were to come to a head in the debate over the Fifteenth Amendment.

9
The Coming of
the Fifteenth Amendment

Within weeks of the election, representatives from a variety of viewpoints within the Republican party renewed the call for a constitutional amendment to finally settle the suffrage issue.[1] Several factors influenced the new sense of purpose with which this goal was sought. First, the election itself had reduced the political problems involved in aggressively pursuing the suffrage issue. The presidency was Republican for four years, and the Senate and House of Representatives, for at least two years. Of course, advocacy of black suffrage still could cost the Republicans votes in local elections, but this problem would always remain. Nevertheless, in early 1869 the dangers consequent to party advocacy of impartial or universal suffrage were at their nadir.

In addition, the results of the election had engendered within Republican ranks a sense that the Fortieth Congress might be the last opportunity to pass a suffrage amendment. In the lame-duck third session, the party would have a clear two-thirds majority in both houses of Congress. Indeed, Republican strength had been enhanced with the arrival of the senators and congressmen from the newly readmitted states. By contrast, some Republicans feared that in the Forty-first Congress, which would convene in March, the requisite majority would not exist in the House of Representatives (although this was not entirely certain).[2] Others expressed the concern that the party would soon lose control of some state legislatures whose approval would be necessary for ratification.[3]

In short, the elections of 1868 had created an ideal climate for the Republican party to relieve at last the tension that had existed in its suffrage policy since early 1867. There can be little doubt that Republicans felt this tension acutely. Southern Republicans were particularly uncomfortable; Frederick A. Sawyer, the senator from the recently reconstructed state of South Carolina, complained that ''we have for two years been subject to the charge . . . that the Republican party of the northern States put the negro on one platform in the loyal States and upon another platform in the lately disloyal States.''[4] But the general opinion went beyond sectional discontent. James G. Blaine later recalled that it was ''obviously unfair and unmanly'' to impose impartial suffrage upon the South without requiring similar action from the

142

North and that most party members "became heartily ashamed of [the platform position on the suffrage issue] long before the political canvas had closed." Thus there was a "desire and common purpose among Republicans to correct the unfortunate position in which the party had been placed by the National Convention" by action on a national suffrage measure.[5]

Other considerations also influenced the near-unanimous belief among Republican congressmen that a constitutional amendment was needed. Examining the words and deeds of Republicans from 1866 through 1868, one cannot help but conclude that most party members agreed with the sentiments of Edmund G. Ross of Kansas: "The first great and sufficient reason why the negro should be admitted to the right of suffrage in all the States is that it is right."[6] Admittedly, the party had at times been forced to mute its support of impartial suffrage for reasons of political expediency, but when political conditions permitted, Republican advocacy of color-blind voting had been consistent and forceful. Indeed, Republicans had sometimes pursued the cause of black suffrage even when the issue presented substantial political dangers.[7]

By proceeding through the medium of a constitutional amendment, Republicans could avoid the problems that had thwarted their efforts to enfranchise blacks on a state-by-state basis. The individual states would still have to ratify any amendment proposed by Congress, but this ratification could be accomplished solely by action of the state legislatures—bodies in which Republicans had had great success in achieving their suffrage goals. In the North, state constitutional amendments had failed in the referenda necessary to ratify the legislative actions; a federal constitutional amendment would not have to face such tests. Democrats were clearly cognizant of this point. In the Senate, they pressed for a requirement that the suffrage amendment be ratified by specially called state conventions, rather than by the state legislatures. Republicans easily defeated such proposals.[8]

States that had not yet enfranchised blacks in 1869 were not the only Republican concern. Many Republicans also viewed the position of blacks as unsafe in the ex-Confederate states, despite the mandate that those states provide for black suffrage in their state constitutions. Even before the elections of 1868, the *Nation* had expressed fears that when the southern states were restored to their full status, whites would seize control of the governing process and disfranchise blacks.[9] The imposition of fundamental conditions was intended to eliminate this danger. As already noted, however, many Republicans had doubts regarding the constitutionality and enforceability of such conditions.

Events of late 1868 had done nothing to ease Republican anxieties on this point. In Louisiana, attempts by blacks to vote for Republican candidates had been met with violence and intimidation. In Georgia, the state legislature had refused to seat duly elected black members. Incidents such as these fueled the apprehensions of Republicans who saw the need for a continuing federal commitment to protect the voting rights of freedmen.[10]

In addition, some Republicans saw potential long-term political gains in the loyal states from federal enfranchisement of blacks. Their calculations on this issue were obviously complicated, for the elections of 1867 had clearly demonstrated the unpopularity of black suffrage among members of a critical sector of the electorate. Moreover, there was no real indication that the situation had changed in 1868 and 1869; the radical *Philadelphia Press*, for example, predicted that the adoption of a black-suffrage amendment by a Republican Congress would cost the party control of the Pennsylvania state government in the next election.[11] The more moderate *Philadelphia North American* also recognized that vigorous advocacy of a black-suffrage amendment would mean the loss of some white votes.[12]

But throughout the two-year debate over this question, prosuffrage Republicans argued that the newly enfranchised blacks would vote for party candidates in sufficient numbers to offset any defection of white support.[13] In the loyal former slave states of Kentucky, Delaware, and Maryland, votes from large numbers of freedmen were regarded as the best hope for overcoming the power of the state Democratic parties. Although in the free states the number of potential black voters was much smaller, the totals needed to place Republicans firmly in control were also smaller. Thus, some argued that granting the vote to blacks would have a salutary impact on the political situation in those states as well.[14]

Finally, by dealing conclusively with black suffrage, Republicans hoped to remove two volatile issues from the national political scene. The first of these was the issue of race itself. For years, Democrats had capitalized on the Republican position on the race question by appealing to a racist populace. Through an irrevocable grant of suffrage to blacks, Republicans hoped to put this issue to rest. Oliver Morton of Indiana made this point very clearly:

> The Democratic party for more than twenty years has lived upon the negro question. It has been its daily food, and if the negro question shall now be withdrawn from politics the Democracy, as a party, will literally starve to death. . . . This constitutional amendment . . . will forever withdraw the subject from politics, and will strike down that prejudice to which the Democratic party has appealed for years.[15]

Second, by adopting a constitutional provision guaranteeing blacks the right to suffrage, Republicans also aspired to put Reconstruction behind them. The party theme in the presidential campaign had been "let us have peace." Unfortunately, as already noted, events in the newly reconstructed states during the election campaign did not augur well for a peaceful resolution to the race problem in the South. William Stewart of Nevada later recalled that the adoption of a suffrage amendment was seen as a way to avoid the need for a permanent federal presence in that region. Granting the suffrage to the freed slave irrevocably, Stewart argued, would "save him from peon laws and obtain powerful friends who would prevent his reenslavement."[16] When introducing the suffrage amendment in the Senate, he stated the point more eloquently: "Let [impartial suffrage] be made the immutable law of the land; let it be fixed; and then we shall have peace. Until then there is no peace."[17]

Taken together, these factors created a consensus in the Republican party regarding the desirability of congressional action on the suffrage issue in the third session of the Fortieth Congress. Not surprisingly, Democrats vigorously opposed all efforts to pass a voting rights amendment. They argued first that granting suffrage to blacks was not a good idea under any circumstances;[18] second, that any congressional action on the issue was inconsistent with the basic structure of American federalism;[19] and third, that for Republicans to advocate such action was inconsistent with the party platform and thus constituted a breach of faith.[20] Given the numerical weakness of the Democrats, however, such objections could not possibly prevail against a cohesive Republican front.

The major problem was to unite the party on a single formulation. Although Republicans unanimously endorsed the basic concept of federal action on suffrage, they continued to be deeply divided over what form that intervention should take. These divisions were sharpened by the realization that far more than mere policy considerations was at stake; in the words of John Sherman, the action on the suffrage issue was also "to lay the foundation for a political creed" for the Republican party of the future.[21]

The primary responsibility for finding a workable formulation fell to two quite different personalities. In the House of Representatives, the floor manager of the black-suffrage proposals was George S. Boutwell of Massachusetts, well known as a doctrinaire radical. Boutwell's Senate counterpart was the more moderate William M. Stewart of Nevada.[22]

THE DRAFTING OF THE FIFTEENTH AMENDMENT

Despite being somewhat difficult to follow at times, the deliberations that generated the ultimate language of the Fifteenth Amendment reveal an unusually complete picture of the entire range of Republican views on the suffrage issue. Unlike the debates over section one of the Fourteenth Amendment, the congressional discussions of the Fifteenth Amendment included proposals to substitute a wide variety of alternative formulations. The implications of many of these proposals were discussed in detail, particularly in the Senate, where almost unlimited debate was allowed. A close examination of key portions of these debates thus illuminates rather clearly both the forces that produced the final suffrage amendment and the Republican understanding of what that amendment would and would not accomplish.

Constitutional versus Statutory Change

Unlike earlier congressional deliberations, the debate over black suffrage in the third session of the Fortieth Congress was dominated by proposals for constitutional change. As the *New York Times* pointed out, this shift reflected "a decided gain on the part of more moderate Republicans."[23] Radicals, however, did not easily abandon their hopes for a statutory solution to the problem. In the House of Representatives, George Boutwell led the fight for an impartial-suffrage statute; in the Senate, Charles Sumner pressed the issue with typical vigor.

The radicals presented two arguments in favor of proceeding by statute. The first of these rested on the complexity of the process by which a constitutional amendment must be adopted. A statute would go into "instant operation," but any proposed amendment would have to await "the uncertain concurrence of State Legislatures."[24] Thus at best the effective date of a proposed amendment would be delayed; at worst, the amendment would never become operative.

The second radical argument reflected concerns about constitutional theory. Some radicals contended that by resorting only to a constitutional amendment, Republicans would be conceding that absent an amendment, Congress possessed no authority to regulate suffrage. This interpretation was abhorrent to the radicals; indeed, Sumner was so fearful of this possibility that he opposed any attempt to amend the Constitution in such a way that race-based suffrage restrictions would be struck down. He also suggested that the struggle over ratification of any proposed amendment would allow the Democratic party to use the issue "as the pudding-stick with which to stir the bubbling mass."[25] Most radicals, however, shared the view of Boutwell, who believed that passage of a constitutional amendment in addition to a statute was desirable in order to make the principle of impartial suffrage as secure as possible.[26]

In offering their proposal, advocates of the suffrage statute faced the perennial problem of finding constitutional authority for Congress to

take the relevant action. Sumner took the most extreme ground, asserting that *"anything for Human Rights is constitutional"* and that
"there can be no State Rights against Human Rights."[27] More temperate radicals relied on the now-standard foundations of the guarantee
clause[28] and the Thirteenth Amendment.[29] But they also pursued a new
line of attack; seizing on the ratification of the Fourteenth Amendment
in 1868, proponents of a suffrage statute claimed that Congress derived
the necessary authority from the privileges and immunities clause of
section one and the section five enforcement power.[30]

Radicals found little support for their claims, however. Both Democrats and more moderate Republicans rose to challenge the assertion
that Congress had authority to regulate suffrage without a constitutional amendment.[31] In refuting the new argument based on the Fourteenth Amendment, they focused on the repeated denials by Republicans in 1866 that the privileges and immunities clause covered the
right to vote.[32] It soon became clear that a suffrage statute could not
pass. Sumner only garnered nine votes in support of his position in the
Senate;[33] in the House of Representatives, Boutwell's proposal never
even came to a vote. Any national action to guarantee the right of
blacks to vote would take the form of a constitutional amendment.

Universal Suffrage and the Right to Hold Office

The issues of universal suffrage and the right to hold office were the
two questions that most sharply divided Republicans during the debate
over the Fifteenth Amendment. In choosing among the available options, party members were forced to consider not only principle but
also expediency. Thus it is not surprising that the pattern of results
generated by the two houses in their separate deliberations was often
confusing and at times seemed contradictory.

In the House of Representatives, Boutwell began the legislative process by introducing a proposed constitutional amendment on January
11, 1869. It provided simply that "the right of any citizen of the United
States to vote shall not be denied or abridged by the United States or
any State by reason of race, color, or previous condition of slavery."[34]
Boutwell's proposal was immediately challenged by Republicans who
wanted more expansive constitutional protection. As Samuel Shellabarger pointed out, a mere requirement of impartial suffrage could be
easily circumvented; imposition of race-neutral criteria such as property or education could effectively disfranchise most blacks, particularly in the former slave states.[35] To meet this danger, Shellabarger proposed a constitutional mandate of universal suffrage, subject only to a
proviso that states might disfranchise onetime rebels.[36] John Bingham

advocated extending the franchise even further; in essence his proposal adopted the "universal suffrage and universal amnesty" philosophy which had gained increasing support among more conservative moderates.[37]

When the votes were taken, Boutwell prevailed rather easily. Shellabarger's proposal was considered first and defeated by a margin of 126 to 61.[38] In the next ballot, Bingham was able to garner only twenty-four votes in support of his amendment.[39] In a fit of pique, Bingham then opposed Boutwell's proposal as well; only three other Republicans dissented, however, as the Boutwell language carried by a vote of 150 to 42.[40]

Even before the House had completed work on its version, the Senate began debate on a suffrage proposal. The version reported from the Senate Judiciary Committee was managed by William Stewart. Cognizant of what had happened in Georgia, the Stewart language protected the right to hold office as well as the right to vote; like the Boutwell formulation, however, the original Senate proposal was limited to prohibiting discrimination based on race, color, or previous condition of servitude.[41] In the speech introducing his proposal on January 28, Stewart pressed for quick action. He noted that "every person in the country has discussed it; it has been discussed in every local paper, by every local speaker; [and] it has been discussed by the firesides." Thus, he declared, "I cannot add to the many eloquent speeches that have [already] been made on this great question. . . . I want a vote . . . I hope we shall soon have a vote on the question."[42]

Yet the liberal Senate rules left Stewart powerless to attain his wish. The Judiciary Committee proposal was the subject of seemingly unending debate, and a plethora of amendments was offered. The key votes came on a proposal by Henry Wilson to constitutionalize the concept of universal suffrage. In seeking this goal, Wilson took a slightly different tack than did Shellabarger in the House. Rather than including sweeping language that abolished by its terms virtually all limitations on the right to vote, Wilson suggested that the proposed amendment prohibit specifically discrimination based on race, color, nativity, property, education, or creed.[43] John Sherman summarized the arguments in favor of Wilson's proposal:

Why should we protect the African in the enjoyment of suffrage when in certain States of the Union even naturalized citizens cannot vote? Why should we protect the descendant of the African, when in certain States of the Union a man who has the misfortune not to be able to read and write cannot vote? Why should we apply this supreme remedy of the Constitution only in favor of this particular class of citizens? Senators must see at once that to rest this constitutional amendment on so narrow a ground is not defensible.[44]

Opponents of the Wilson formulation raised two different objections. First, some suggested that an educational stipulation was in fact a desirable prerequisite for exercise of the franchise. As Roscoe Conkling of New York put it, such a stipulation limited suffrage to those who possessed "a standard of intelligence above the most groveling and besotted ignorance."[45] Others were concerned with the impact of the Wilson proposal on states' rights; for example, Jacob Howard complained that its adoption would "overthrow and uproot the very foundations of the State constitutions."[46]

On February 9, two roll-call votes were taken on the issue of universal suffrage. Initially, the Wilson language was defeated on a 24 to 19 vote;[47] in a later vote, however, the same proposal passed by a 31 to 27 margin.[48] Obviously, a number of Republican senators who were absent for the first vote ultimately supported Wilson. Moreover, he could not have achieved victory without the votes of three Republicans (Joseph C. Abbott of North Carolina, Thomas Robertson of South Carolina, and Waitman T. Willey of West Virginia) who switched sides and one Democrat (Thomas A. Hendricks of Indiana) who no doubt hoped to kill the entire project by making the amendment unacceptably broad.

Before the final Senate vote on passage, the waters were muddied still more by the addition of a provision that would have changed the method by which presidential electors were chosen.[49] Faced with accepting this entire package or abandoning totally even an impartial-suffrage amendment, only five mainstream Republicans demurred. When the final vote was taken on February 9, the margin of victory was 39 to 16.[50] By only three votes, the amendment process remained alive.

The struggle over the ultimate shape of the Fifteenth Amendment was far from over, however. The Senate had adopted its measure as a substitute for the House-passed version. Thus House members seriously considered only two alternatives: They would either accept the Senate language or request a committee of conference. On February 15, Boutwell took the floor to argue against simply agreeing to the changes wrought by the Senate;[51] John Bingham, on the other hand, led the battle for concurrence.[52]

Boutwell focused on what he saw as "two fatal objections" to the Senate proposal, declining to enumerate "many others of great magnitude." One of those objections concerned the provision to alter the constitutional allocation of power over the selection of electors. He argued that the Senate provision reforming presidential elections was sloppily drafted and could not be severed from the Wilson formulation establishing universal suffrage.[53] The Speaker of the House removed this obstacle by ruling that the electoral college provision could be voted upon separately from the universal suffrage proposal.[54]

The other objection, however, was potentially devastating. Boutwell noted that despite his obvious intent to constitutionalize universal suffrage, Wilson had neglected to prohibit discrimination based on previous condition of servitude. Thus, Boutwell reasoned, the ex-Confederate states could disfranchise almost all blacks by the easy expedient of denying the right to vote to all former slaves.[55] Bingham vigorously attacked Boutwell's argument on this point,[56] but the mere possibility that Boutwell was right was sufficient to convince even some advocates of universal suffrage of the desirability of proceeding to a conference. Moreover, because of the parliamentary situation, adoption of a simple amendment to remedy this flaw would only have sent the measure back to the Senate for further consideration. Bingham's motion to concur in the Wilson proposal received only thirty-seven votes,[57] and a conference with the Senate was therefore requested.

When notice of the action by the House reached the Senate on February 27, Stewart boldly attempted to avoid additional delay by moving that the Senate accept the original Boutwell version of the suffrage amendment.[58] This motion set off a bitter debate between Stewart and proponents of the Wilson formulation. Wilson accused Stewart of abandoning the Georgia blacks who had been excluded from the state legislature;[59] Stewart responded by charging that if Wilson himself had not insisted on attaching universal suffrage to protection for black officeholders, the latter measure would have had a much better chance for passage. He also noted that "some of our leading Republican journals in the country have objected to [the protection of the right to hold office]" and asserted that "the only hope for getting anything is to vote for [the House] proposition."[60] Frederick A. Sawyer of South Carolina responded, "I would rather have nothing than to have this."[61]

When the votes were counted, it became clear that Stewart had stepped into a parliamentary trap of his own creation. In order for his proposal to pass, the Senate would have to agree in separate votes to take two steps. First, a simple majority vote would be necessary for the Senate to recede from its own version of the suffrage amendment. Second, two-thirds of those voting would have to concur in the Boutwell amendment. The motion to recede carried by a 33 to 24 margin.[62] In the final vote on passage, however, Stewart was able to convince only four additional Republicans to join him—James Harlan of Iowa, John Pool of North Carolina, John Sherman of Ohio, and Benjamin F. Wade of Ohio. Moreover, this gain was more than offset by four defections—George F. Edmunds of Vermont, Alexander McDonald of Arkansas, Samuel C. Pomeroy of Kansas, and Adonijah S. Welch of Florida—and by opposition from some senators who had refused to vote on the motion to recede. The margin in favor of concurring with the original Boutwell amendment was thus only 31 to 27—far short of what was needed for passage.[63] Stewart's maneuver had resulted in near catastrophe; the process of drafting a constitutional amendment had returned to square one.

The Senate then took up once again Stewart's original proposition to bar racial discrimination with respect to the right to vote and the right to hold office. As an exhausted Senate remained in session for twelve hours, tempers became increasingly frayed. James W. Nye of Nevada summed up the mood of the Senate when he exclaimed, "I am sick of hearing [this discussion]. It has become painful to listen to it."[64] In a war of attrition, Stewart eventually prevailed; the Senate sent his proposal to the House by a vote of 35 to 11. Not a single mainstream Republican dissented.[65]

The position of the Stewart amendment was quite different from that which the Wilson proposal had occupied. From the parliamentary perspective of the House of Representatives, the Senate had passed an entirely new bill. Therefore, before any request for a conference could be acted upon, the House would have to adopt some resolution of its own by the requisite two-thirds majority. In this context, amendments to the Stewart version were far more likely. In fact, Bingham, Shellabarger, and John A. Logan of Illinois all pressed for changes in the Senate language.[66]

The first of two crucial votes was triggered by Logan's proposal to delete the protection for the right to hold office. Logan relied primarily on a federalism-based argument as his defense. In essence, Stewart's formulation placed the federal government in the position of determining who should make key governmental decisions for the states. This power, Logan argued, "has been properly left [to the states themselves] by the Constitution." Logan also believed that direct constitutional protection for the right to hold office was unnecessary; once granted the right to vote, he contended, "[blacks] will take care of the right to hold office [for themselves]."[67] Lurking beneath the surface were more explicitly race-based concerns. To allow blacks to vote was one thing; to be ruled by them was something else entirely.[68] Logan could persuade only thirty-seven Republicans to support his position. His amendment was therefore defeated by a vote of 95 to 70.[69] It seemed that a large majority of the party was committed to protecting the right of blacks to hold office.

The House then took action on John Bingham's proposal to extend the prohibition on discrimination to include not only race, color, and previous condition of servitude but also nativity, property, and creed. Benjamin F. Butler of Massachusetts pleaded with the House to accept the Senate version of the suffrage amendment without change in order to ensure that some proposal would be submitted to the state legislatures for ratification.[70] However, Bingham was able to carry a majority of both the Republican representatives and the House as a whole, and his amendment passed by a vote of 92 to 70.[71] The two houses of Congress had, in the words of William Gillette, performed a "legislative somersault";[72] the House of Representatives rather than the Senate was now proposing the more radical amendment.

A comparison of the voting on Bingham's language with that on the Shellabarger universal suffrage proposal only three weeks earlier provides insight into the complexities of the forces that ultimately shaped the Fifteenth Amendment. Fifty-one congressmen who had opposed Shellabarger—thirty-one Republicans and twenty Democrats—voted in favor of the Bingham proposal. Conversely, eighteen Republicans who had supported Shellabarger opposed Bingham. A number of factors combined to generate this seeming contradiction.

What is most easily explained is the switch by the twenty Democrats who supported the Bingham measure. For the Democratic party, the best chance to stop the submission of a suffrage amendment lay in the possibility that Republicans would reach an impasse on the form the amendment would take. If the language of the amendment was radicalized, some Democrats believed that a substantial number of moderates could be persuaded to oppose it, thus creating the desired stalemate.[73]

There were very different motives behind the movement of Republicans toward Bingham's proposal. First, the vote on January 30 on the original Shellabarger formulation undoubtedly understated the depth of Republican support for the basic concept of universal suffrage. Shellabarger had not drafted his proposal carefully; as some critics pointed out, the language might well have been interpreted to invalidate even laws that required potential voters to be registered in order to exercise their right of suffrage.[74] Concerns regarding this problem may have discouraged some Republicans from mobilizing behind Shellabarger's version.

Moreover, the parliamentary situation had resulted in a split between the friends of universal suffrage. Shellabarger's language had been characterized as a *substitute* for the "universal suffrage and universal amnesty" language that had yet to be voted upon. Thus, a Republican congressman who favored amnesty could not vote with Shellabarger—even if the same congressman also favored universal suffrage generally. And indeed, most Republicans who had backed universal amnesty on January 30 (notably Bingham himself) would become staunch supporters of broad voting rights guarantees at later stages of the debate.[75]

Finally, on February 20 Bingham did not in fact propose to constitutionalize universal suffrage. Instead, his language was something of a compromise, allowing states to continue to disfranchise citizens on the basis of educational qualifications. The change from the Wilson language was deliberately calculated to win approval not only in Congress but also in the ratification process.[76] It is not surprising that such a measure would gain support from some moderates who would oppose a true universal suffrage alternative.

The decision of some of Shellabarger's supporters to vote against Bingham is more puzzling. Although not a true universal suffrage measure, Bingham's proposal was clearly more radical than the Stewart formulation. Yet the group that had supported Shellabarger and voted against Bingham included some of the most radical members of the House of Representatives—men such as Broomall and Kelley of Pennsylvania and Hamilton Ward of New York. Two conflicting considerations may have influenced the votes of this group.

One possibility is that these men were moved by Boutwell's and Butler's pleas that even a narrow amendment was better than nothing and that an amendment containing only a prohibition against racial discrimination had the best chance to be ratified by the states. Moreover, simple concurrence with the Senate proposal would avoid the need for further congressional action, with its attendant danger of deadlock. By February 20, this position had gained increasing strength among radical Republicans, and on that day, it won the explicit endorsement of the *National Anti-Slavery Standard*—the single most reliable barometer of radical Republican thought.[77]

A second factor that almost certainly produced some negative votes was the pendency of a third alternative to the Stewart proposal—a revised universal suffrage amendment authored by Shellabarger himself. The new Shellabarger language was designed to obviate the possibility that his amendment would be interpreted to bar the use of state registration laws to control the exercise of the suffrage.[78] As Shellabarger recognized, previous votes demonstrated that at best universal suffrage would carry by a narrow margin. Moreover, the best chance for adoption of his language lay in having it presented as the only alternative to the Stewart measure; some moderates might prefer Shellabarger's universal suffrage proposal to Stewart's simple prohibition on discrimination on the basis of race, but they would vote for the more specific Bingham language in preference to both. Thus, defeating the Bingham proposal seemed to be the first step in a strategy to place universal suffrage before the House.

Shellabarger's actions clearly reflected this understanding. He first voted against Bingham's amendment; after the amendment had passed, he withdrew the universal suffrage measure "in view of the result of the last vote and in order not to waste the time of the House."[79] Other radicals who opposed Bingham might well have been proceeding on a similar theory.

In any event, once Bingham's amendment had received majority approval, Republicans united to send it to the Senate by a vote of 140 to 37.[80] The new language would not have provided truly effective federal protection for the rights of southern blacks; since most former slaves were illiterate, they could still have been excluded from the suffrage by the adoption of a literacy test. Even so, while less radical than the Wilson proposal, the Bingham language was plainly more expansive than that advocated by either Boutwell or Stewart.

When the action of the House was reported to the Senate, Stewart did not repeat his earlier tactical error. Instead, he moved to request a conference; with little discussion, the motion carried by a 32 to 17 margin on February 22.[81] Six southern Republicans—Abbott and Pool of North Carolina, William P. Kellogg of Louisiana, Rice of Arkansas, Sawyer of South Carolina, and Willard Warner of Alabama—joined the Democrats in opposing this motion, because they feared that a conference would eliminate the protection for the right to hold office.[82] Stewart, Conkling, and Edmunds were appointed to represent the Senate in conference. The following day the House reciprocated and designated Bingham, Boutwell, and Logan to act on behalf of its interests.[83]

The report that emerged from the conference confirmed the worst fears of the southern senators. The conferees decided not only to delete the right to hold office from the text but also to limit the amendment to racial discrimination. The moving forces behind the decision were Bingham and Logan, both of whom had opposed the officeholding provision in the House. They were able to convince Stewart and Conkling to join them.[84] The choice was not based on a philosophical opposition to protecting the right to hold office; instead, the problem was a "fear . . . that [the] people will not be satisfied to give the negro the right to run against themselves for some office, but they are willing to confer upon him the boon of voting for them."[85]

On February 25, the House of Representatives adopted the committee report without debate by a vote of 144 to 44.[86] In the Senate the situation was different; led by Edmunds, who refused to sign the report, radicals launched a furious attack. Pomeroy of Kansas assailed the action of the conference committee as "unparliamentary and almost unprecedented."[87] Pointing to the example of Georgia, others noted the impossibility of arguing credibly that the right to vote automatically carries with it the right to hold office.[88]

Moderates were unmoved by these arguments. Although most favored the officeholding provision in principle, they were willing to sacrifice it in order to secure the passage of a suffrage amendment. They asserted that once blacks were securely enfranchised, the officeholding problem would eventually take care of itself.[89] Speaking earlier, George Nye had expressed this position in colorful language:

> Give me the majority of the ballots, and I will fix who shall hold offices in a State. [Blacks] will fix it; and they are not so black or so stupid that they will not fix it in opposition, if need be, to the Senators who represent them up on this floor.[90]

In the end, the radicals were helpless. With the session drawing to a close, it was obvious that the choice was between the conference committee report and nothing at all. Henry Wilson summed up their dilemma as well as the conclusion reached by most Republican senators:

> I have asked always for what was right and taken on all occasions what I could get. I have acted upon the idea that one step taken in the right direction made the next step easier to be taken. I suppose . . . I must act upon that idea now.[91]

When the vote was taken on February 26, the proposed amendment was passed by a vote of 39 to 13.[92] A number of radicals abstained, but only one mainstream Republican—Pool of North Carolina—was sufficiently incensed to vote against the committee proposal. Thus, congressional action on the Fifteenth Amendment was complete.

The process that generated the final form of the Fifteenth Amendment reflects the dynamic governing early congressional Reconstruction actions generally. A majority of Republicans would no doubt have preferred a more radical measure; in order to garner the necessary votes for passage, however, they were forced to placate their more conservative colleagues. Moved by considerations of federalism and political expediency, conservative Republicans forced more radical party members to accept a very narrow formulation of the suffrage amendment. Further, in rejecting the Boutwell/Sumner call for a federal statute to settle the suffrage question, Congress firmly repudiated the opened-ended view of federal power that was the cornerstone of the radicals' constitutional theory. In short, the ultimate result clearly reflected the dominance of more conservative Republicans in shaping congressional action on civil rights.

THE INTENT OF THE DRAFTERS
OF THE FIFTEENTH AMENDMENT

Unlike the debates over the passage of the Thirteenth and Fourteenth Amendments, congressional discussions of the Fifteenth Amendment provide a clear picture of the general understanding of its scope. The main objection to the Boutwell/Stewart proposal was that it would allow states to discriminate on any basis other than race per se, so long as the qualifications for voting were applied to all races equally. As both supporters and opponents of the ultimately adopted language recognized, states would still be allowed to deliberately disfranchise the "vast, overwhelming mass" of black voters simply by adopting race-blind suffrage qualifications based upon education or property ownership.[93] This understanding was one of the prime motivations for those who advocated language such as that proposed by Shellabarger and Wilson.[94]

Given this background, the only plausible conclusion is that the protections provided by the Fifteenth Amendment were understood to be even narrower than the most conservative modern justices have believed. Not only did the drafters intend to leave untouched those qualifications that have a racially disproportionate *impact*; even those qualifications that are *intended* to disfranchise blacks were purposefully left intact. The drafters understood that the only new requirement they were adding was that any qualification for voting has to be applied equally to all races. Such a requirement might have little practical impact; it was, however, all that was attainable at the time.

10
Conclusion

The early years of the Reconstruction era witnessed an unprecedented expansion of the role of the federal government in protecting the rights of citizens—particularly those of the freed slaves. At the same time, the pace of this expansion was slowed by the necessity of obtaining the acquiescence of the more conservative members of the Republican party. These Republicans fought hard and usually successfully against measures that they viewed as threatening an undue increase of federal power. The result was a series of enactments that reflected the ideology of conservative Republicans rather than their more radical compatriots.

Two elements of this ideology stand out. First, on race relations issues, conservative Republicans embraced the concept of limited absolute equality rather than total racial equality. Ultimately, they were forced to modify this view slightly and accept federal imposition of race-blind suffrage in the Fifteenth Amendment. However, this acceptance was a somewhat reluctant concession to the exigencies of the times and did not signal an alteration in their basic approach to racial issues.

Second, conservative Republicans were even more concerned with maintaining constraints on the scope of federal power generally. They vigorously opposed measures that explicitly provided Congress with sweeping authority over matters that had hitherto been the exclusive province of the state governments or that implicitly suggested that the Constitution was an open-ended grant of power to the federal government to deal with matters that might appear to be of national concern. This opposition forced the alteration of the Civil Rights Act of 1866, section one of the Fourteenth Amendment, and the Fifteenth Amendment.

This background is particularly important to a proper understanding of the seemingly open-ended language of the Fourteenth Amendment. It is inconceivable that conservative Republicans would have supported a general grant of authority to the federal government to guarantee equality; indeed, fears that the original Bingham amendment was just such a grant led to its demise. Admittedly, section one was intended to go beyond prohibition of racial discrimination, but it was understood to be circumscribed by the theory of limited absolute equality, which in turn was based on a relatively narrow, fixed conception of both natural rights and the privileges and immunities of citizenship. This was the conception that the framers understood to be embodied in the Fourteenth Amendment; to interpret it otherwise is to read into the Constitution ideas that were utterly foreign to their world view.

Notes

PREFACE

1. Earl M. Maltz, "The Failure of Attacks on Originalist Theory," *Constitutional Commentary* 4 (1987): 43; Earl M. Maltz, "Some New Thoughts on an Old Problem: The Role of the Intent of the Framers in Constitutional Theory," *Boston University Law Review* 63 (1983): 811.

2. For differing perspectives, see Raoul Berger, *Government by Judiciary: The Transformation of the Fourteenth Amendment* (Cambridge, Mass., 1977); Michael Kent Curtis, *No State Shall Abridge: The Fourteenth Amendment and the Bill of Rights* (Durham, N.C., 1986); William E. Nelson, *The Fourteenth Amendment: From Political Principle to Judicial Doctrine* (Cambridge, Mass., 1988); Alexander M. Bickel, "The Original Understanding and the Segregation Decision," *Harvard Law Review* 69 (1955): 1; Robert J. Kaczorowski, "Revolutionary Constitutionalism in the Era of Civil War and Reconstruction," *New York University Law Review* 61 (1986): 863.

3. Jacobus tenBroek, *The Antislavery Origins of the Fourteenth Amendment* (Berkeley, 1951); Harold M. Hyman and William M. Wiecek, *Equal Justice under Law: Constitutional Development 1835–1875* (New York, 1982), ch. 11.

4. Eric McKitrick, *Andrew Johnson and Reconstruction* (Chicago, 1960); Michael Les Benedict, *A Compromise of Principle: Congressional Republicans and Reconstruction 1863–1869* (New York, 1974).

5. LaWanda Cox and John H. Cox, *Politics, Principle and Prejudice 1865–1866* (London, 1963).

6. Harold M. Hyman, *A More Perfect Union: The Impact of the Civil War and Reconstruction on the Constitution* (New York, 1973).

7. Hyman and Wiecek, *Equal Justice under Law*, chs. 11–12.

CHAPTER 1. REPUBLICANS AND BLACK RIGHTS
PRIOR TO RECONSTRUCTION

1. Extended discussions of the debates include Don E. Fehrenbacher, *Prelude to Greatness: Lincoln in the 1850s* (Stanford, 1962), and Harry V. Jaffa, *Crisis of the House Divided: An Analysis of the Lincoln-Douglas Debates* (Garden City, N.Y., 1959).

2. 60 U.S. (19 How.) 393 (1857). For discussions of the holding and impact of the *Dred Scott* decision, see Don E. Fehrenbacher, *The Dred Scott Case: Its Significance in American Law and Politics* (New York, 1978), and Paul Finkelman, *An Imperfect Union: Slavery, Comity and Federalism* (Chapel Hill, 1981), chs. 8–10.

3. Robert W. Johannsen, ed., *The Lincoln-Douglas Debates of 1858* (New York, 1965), 45–46.

4. In-depth treatments of the views of the more advanced antislavery forces

include Dwight L. Dumond, *Antislavery: The Crusade for Freedom* (Ann Arbor, 1961), and William M. Wiecek, *The Sources of Anti-Slavery Constitutionalism in America, 1760–1848* (Ithaca, 1977).

5. See, e.g., *Congressional Globe*, 35th Cong., 2d Sess., 982–85 (1859) (Congressman Bingham); and 974–75 (Congressman Dawes).

6. Leon F. Litwack, *North of Slavery: The Negro in the Free States, 1790–1860* (Chicago, 1961), and Paul Finkelman, "Prelude to the Fourteenth Amendment: Black Legal Rights in the Antebellum North," *Rutgers Law Journal* 17 (1986): 415, survey the legal position of blacks in the free states before the Civil War.

7. Eugene Berwanger, *The Frontier against Slavery: Western Anti-Negro Prejudice and the Slavery Extension Controversy* (Chicago, 1967), and Eric Foner, *Free Soil, Free Labor, Free Men* (New York, 1970), 265–67, discuss the influence of racism on the development of the Republican position.

8. Johannsen, *Lincoln-Douglas Debates*, 51.

9. Ibid., 162.

10. Ibid., 196.

11. Thomas D. Morris, *Free Men All: The Personal Liberty Laws of the North, 1780–1861* (Baltimore, 1974), provides an overview of the disputes that centered around the personal liberty laws.

12. 62 U.S. (21 How.) 506 (1859).

13. *In re* Sherman Booth, 3 Wis. 1 (1854).

14. *In re* Sherman M. Booth, 3 Wis. 67 (1854); *In re* Booth and Rycraft, 3 Wis. 144 (1855).

15. Ableman v. Booth, 62 U.S. (21 How.) 506 (1859).

16. Johannsen, *Lincoln-Douglas Debates*, 19.

17. Ibid., 198.

18. Ibid., 19 (emphasis in original).

19. Foner, *Free Soil, Free Labor, Free Men*, 288–90; Johannsen, *Lincoln-Douglas Debates*, 52–53.

20. See, e.g., *In re* Booth, 3 Wis. 13, 46–47 (1858); "Freedom National, Slavery Sectional," in Charles Sumner, *His Complete Works*, vol. 3 (Boston, 1870–83), 257, 329.

21. *Congressional Globe*, 35th Cong., 1st Sess., 1967 (1858) (Senator Wilson); *Debates and Proceedings of the Oregon Constitutional Convention of 1857*, 358.

22. Pa. Const., art. IX, sec. 1, reprinted in William F. Swindler, ed., *Sources and Documents of United States Constitutions*, vol. 8 (Dobbs Ferry, N.Y., 1979), 265–67; see also, e.g., Oreg. Const., art. I, sec. 1, reprinted in ibid., 2050; Va. Const., art. I, sec. 1, reprinted in ibid., vol. 10, 68.

23. Morton J. Horwitz, *The Transformation of American Law, 1780–1860* (Cambridge, Mass., 1977), ch. 1.

24. 36 U.S. (11 Pet.) 419, 539 (1837).

25. White v. White, 5 Barb. 474, 484 (N.Y. 1849). See also, e.g., Riggs v. Martin, 5 Ark. 506 (1844); Parham v. The Justices, 9 Ga. 341 (1851); Billings v. Hill, 7 Cal. 1 (1857); Harold M. Hyman and William M. Wiecek, *Equal Justice under Law: Constitutional Development 1835–1875* (New York, 1982), 20–23; Rodney L. Mott, *Due Process of Law: A Historical and Analytical Treatise of the Principles and Methods Followed by the Courts in the Application of the Concept of the "Law of the Land"* (Indianapolis, 1926), 200–202.

26. 6 Ind. 515 (1855).

27. Oliver Wendell Holmes, ed., *Kent's Commentaries*, vol. 2 (Boston,

1896), 1. See Hoke v. Henderson, 15 N.C. (4 Dev.) 1 (1833); Hathorn v. Lyon, 2 Mich. 97 (1851). Even Kent's formulation may have been unduly broad. For example, the property rights of aliens were often deemed properly limited by the states. See *Congressional Globe*, 39th Cong., 1st Sess., 505 (1866) (Senator Johnson).

28. V. Jacque Voegeli, *Free But Not Equal: The Midwest and the Negro during the Civil War Era* (Chicago, 1967), ch. 1.

29. Ibid., ch. 4.

30. Arthur C. Cole, *Centennial History of Illinois: The Era of the Civil War 1848-1870*, vol. 3 (Springfield, Ill., 1919), 271; J. Cornelius, *A History of Constitution-Making in Illinois* (Urbana, 1969).

31. *Congressional Globe*, 37th Cong., 2d Sess., 356-57, 361 (1863).

32. Herman Belz, *A New Birth of Freedom: The Republican Party and Freedmen's Rights, 1861-1866* (Westport, Conn., 1976), 143-44.

33. Voegeli, *Free but Not Equal*, ch. 8.

34. Ibid., 99-125. See also Belz, *A New Birth of Freedom*, ch. 2.

35. Voegeli, *Free but Not Equal*, 166.

36. *Congressional Globe*, 38th Cong., 1st Sess., 3263 (1864).

37. Ibid., 2253.

38. *Congressional Globe*, 38th Cong., 2d Sess., 63 (1864), 1418 (1865).

39. *Congressional Globe*, 38th Cong., 1st Sess., 3261, 3402 (1864).

40. Ibid., 1161, 3127, and app. 142 (1864); *Congressional Globe*, 38th Cong., 2d Sess., 604, 1334 (1865); Belz, *A New Birth of Freedom*, 147-48; Earl M. Maltz, " 'Separate but Equal' and the Law of Common Carriers in the Era of the Fourteenth Amendment," *Rutgers Law Journal* 17 (1986): 553, 558-67.

41. *Opinions of the Attorneys General of the United States*, 1:506 (1821); Dred Scott v. Sandford, 60 U.S. (19 How.) 393, 399-454 (1857).

42. E.g., Douglass v. Stephens, 1 Del. Ch. 465, 470 (1821).

43. Amy v. Smith, 1 Litt. 327, 334-335 (Ky. 1822); *Opinions of the Attorneys General of the United States*, 1:508 (1821).

44. James H. Kettner, *The Development of American Citizenship, 1808-1870* (Chapel Hill, 1978), 322.

45. Johannsen, *Lincoln-Douglas Debates*, 34.

46. State v. Hunt, 2 Hill 1, 102-3 (S.C. 1834) (argument of Attorney General Smith); ibid., 257 (Harper, J., dissenting).

47. *Opinions of the Attorneys General of the United States*, 10:382 (1862).

48. Ibid., 388.

49. Ibid., 412.

50. Ibid., 408.

51. Ibid., 398.

52. Ibid.

53. Ibid., 388.

54. Ibid., 398-99, 407-8.

55. *Congressional Globe*, 38th Cong., 1st Sess., 1459-65 (1864) (Senator Henderson); and 1780-81 (Senator Van Winkle).

56. Ibid., 1346.

57. Ibid.

58. Ibid.

59. Ibid., 1362-63.

60. Ibid.

61. Ibid., 1361.

62. Ibid., 1364.

63. Ibid., 1362 (Senator Saulsbury).
64. Ibid., 1651.
65. Ibid., 1652.
66. Ibid.
67. Ibid., 2351.
68. Ibid., 2511.
69. Ibid., 2512.
70. Ibid., 2543.
71. Ibid., 2545.
72. Ibid., 1706.
73. *New York Times*, May 18, 1864, p. 4.
74. *Congressional Globe*, 38th Cong., 1st Sess., 2512 (1864) (Senator Morrill); and 2543 (Senator Grimes).
75. The account that follows is taken largely from Herman Belz, *Reconstructing the Union: Theory and Policy during the Civil War* (Westport, Conn., 1979), chs. 7 and 8.
76. *Congressional Globe*, 38th Cong., 1st Sess., 3449 (1864).
77. Ibid.
78. Mary Berry, *Military Necessity and Civil Rights Policy: Black Citizenship and the Constitution, 1861–1868* (Fort Washington, Pa., 1977).
79. William Gillette, *The Right to Vote: Politics and the Passage of the Fifteenth Amendment* (Baltimore, 1965), 25–26.

CHAPTER 2. THE COMING OF
THE THIRTEENTH AMENDMENT

1. The following discussion of antislavery action before the Thirteenth Amendment is taken from Herman Belz, *A New Birth of Freedom: The Republican Party and Freedmen's Rights, 1861–1866* (Westport, Conn., 1976), passim.
2. *Congressional Globe*, 36th Cong., 2d Sess., 1264 (1861).
3. V. Jacque Voegeli, *Free but Not Equal: The Midwest and the Negro during the Civil War Era* (Chicago, 1967).
4. *Congressional Globe*, 38th Cong., 1st Sess., 20 (1864).
5. Ibid., 1096 (bill of Congressman Arnold).
6. Ibid., 1314.
7. Ibid., 1460.
8. Ibid., 19.
9. Ibid., 21.
10. Ibid., 1314
11. Ibid., 521.
12. *Congressional Globe*, 38th Cong., 2d Sess., 138 (1865) (emphasis in original).
13. *Congressional Globe*, 38th Cong., 1st Sess., 2989 (1864) (emphasis in original).
14. Ibid., 522.
15. Ibid., 1313.
16. Ibid., 1322.
17. The impact of the concept of the slave power on the development of Republican ideology is discussed in Eric Foner, *Free Soil, Free Labor, Free Men* (New York, 1970), ch. 3; Michael Holt, *Slavery, Republicanism and the Repub-*

lican Party (New York, 1978), ch. 7; and William E. Gienapp, "The Republican Party and the Slave Power," in Robert H. Abzug and Stephen E. Maizlish, eds., *New Perspectives on Race and Slavery in America: Essays in Honor of Kenneth M. Stampp* (Lexington, Ky., 1986).

18. *Congressional Globe,* 38th Cong., 1st Sess., 2984 (1864).

19. Ibid., 1369.

20. For an in-depth examination of the factional disputes within the Democratic party, see Joel H. Silbey, *A Respectable Minority: The Democratic Party in the Civil War Era, 1860-1868* (New York, 1977).

21. Ibid., 2952 (Congressman Coffroth); *Congressional Globe,* 38th Cong., 2d Sess., 153 (1865) (Congressman Rogers).

22. *Congressional Globe,* 38th Cong., 2d Sess., 181 (1865).

23. Ibid., 195.

24. *Congressional Globe,* 38th Cong., 1st Sess., 2980 (1864).

25. Ibid., 2986-87.

26. Ibid., 2962.

27. *Congressional Globe,* 38th Cong., 2d Sess., 242 (1865).

28. Ibid., 214.

29. Ibid., 223.

30. *Congressional Globe,* 38th Cong., 1st Sess., 2962 (1864).

31. Ibid., 2981.

32. Ibid., 1490.

33. Ibid., 2995.

34. *Congressional Globe,* 38th Cong., 2d Sess., 525 (1865).

35. These efforts are chronicled in detail in LaWanda Cox and John H. Cox, *Politics, Principle and Prejudice 1865-1866* (London, 1963), ch. 1.

36. *Congressional Globe,* 39th Cong., 1st Sess., 1123 (1866).

37. John G. Nicolay and John Hay, *Abraham Lincoln: A History,* vol. 10 (New York, 1890), 84-85. For a detailed examination of the dispute over the Camden and Amboy, see David F. Trask, "Charles Sumner and the New Jersey Railroad Monopoly during the Civil War," *New Jersey Historical Society Proceedings* 75 (1957): 259.

38. *Congressional Globe,* 38th Cong., 2d Sess., 531 (1865).

39. For varying perspectives on these issues, see Belz, *A New Birth of Freedom,* ch. 7; G. Sidney Buchanan, *The Quest for Freedom: A Legal History of the Thirteenth Amendment* (Houston, 1976); Charles Fairman, *Reconstruction and Reunion 1864-88, Part 1* (New York, 1971), ch. 19; Harold M. Hyman and William M. Wiecek, *Equal Justice under Law: Constitutional Development 1835-1875* (New York, 1982), ch. 11; Jacobus tenBroek, *The Antislavery Origins of the Fourteenth Amendment* (Berkeley, 1951); Michael P. Zuckert, "Completing the Constitution: The Thirteenth Amendment," *Constitutional Commentary* 4 (1987): 259.

40. *Congressional Globe,* 38th Cong., 1st Sess., 1488 (1864). See also Howard K. Beale, ed., *The Diary of Edward Bates* (Washington, D.C., 1933), 330.

41. Oreg. Const. of 1857, in William F. Swindler, ed., *Sources and Documents of United States Constitutions,* vol. 8 (Dobbs Ferry, N.Y., 1979), 219.

42. Nelson v. The People, 33 Ill. 390 (1864).

43. 14 Ga. 185, 198 (1853)

44. Thomas R. R. Cobb, *An Inquiry into the Law of Negro Slavery in the United States* (N.p. , 1858; reprint, New York, 1968) ch. 22.

45. The emancipation of slaves in the North is discussed in Arthur Zilver-

smit, *The First Emancipation: The Abolition of Slavery in the North* (Chicago, 1967).

46. William M. Wiecek, *The Sources of Anti-slavery Constitutionalism in America, 1760-1848* (Ithaca, 1977), 210. The relationship between the Northwest Ordinance and slavery was in fact more complex. See Peter Onuf, *Statehood and Union: A History of the Northwest Ordinance* (Bloomington, 1987); Paul Finkelman, ''Slavery and the Northwest Ordinance: A Study in Ambiguity,'' *Journal of the Early Republic* 6 (1986): 343.

47. *Congressional Globe*, 38th Cong., 1st Sess., 1489 (1864).

48. Ibid., 1482-83. For the reaction of one conservative Republican, see Beale, *Diary of Edward Bates*, 407.

49. *Congressional Globe*, 38th Cong., 2d Sess., 170-71 (1865).

50. *Congressional Globe*, 38th Cong., 1st Sess., 1780-81 (1864).

51. Ibid., 1465.

52. *Congressional Globe*, 38th Cong., 2d Sess., 138 (1865).

53. *Congressional Globe*, 38th Cong., 1st Sess., 1439-40 (1864).

54. Ibid., 2990.

55. See Emma Lou Thornbrough, *Indiana in the Civil War Era, 1850-1880* (Indianapolis, 1965), 227, 231.

56. *Journal of Missouri Constitutional Convention of 1863*, 229.

57. Ibid., 296-97, 315.

58. *Debates of the Constitutional Convention of the State of Maryland* (1864), 1:235.

59. Ibid., 235-36, 238.

60. Ibid., 237-38.

61. Ibid., 237.

62. See *Congressional Globe*, 39th Cong., 1st Sess., 39-42, 110-11 (1866).

63. Ibid., 499-500, 1291-92.

CHAPTER 3. THE RECONSTRUCTION DYNAMIC

1. *Harper's Weekly*, February 11, 1865, p. 83.

2. *National Anti-Slavery Standard*, June 3, 1865, p. 3.

3. *Harper's Weekly*, October 14, 1865, p. 642.

4. *Harper's Weekly*, May 20, 1865, p. 300. See also *Springfield Republican*, July 11, 1865, p. 2.

5. *Harper's Weekly*, June 24, 1865, p. 386.

6. *Congressional Globe*, 37th Cong., 3d Sess., 735 (1863).

7. Jacobus tenBroek, *The Antislavery Origins of the Fourteenth Amendment* (Berkeley, 1951), passim.

8. Robert J. Kaczorowski, *The Politics of Judicial Interpretation: The Federal Courts, Department of Justice and Civil Rights, 1866-1876* (New York, 1985).

9. For a lucid description of the various congressional theories of the Reconstruction problem, see Eric McKitrick, *Andrew Johnson and Reconstruction* (Chicago, 1960), ch. 5.

10. Phillip S. Paludan, *A Covenant with Death: The Constitution, Law, and Equality in the Civil War Era* (Urbana, 1975).

11. Among the more lucid contemporary discussions of the theory of state sovereignty are the arguments of counsel in State v. Hunt, 2 Hill 1, 1-210 (S.C. 1834) and Calhoun's famous Fort Hill Address, reprinted in Clyde N. Wilson, ed., *Papers of John C. Calhoun*, vol. 11 (Columbia, S.C., 1978) 413-40. Percep-

tive modern summaries and analyses include William W. Freehling, *Prelude to Civil War: The Nullification Controversy in South Carolina* (New York, 1966), ch. 5, and Albert Bestor, "State Sovereignty and Slavery: A Reinterpretation of Proslavery Constitutional Doctrine 1846–1860," *Journal of the Illinois State Historical Society* 54 (1961): 148.

12. See Bestor, "State Sovereignty and Slavery."

13. *Congressional Globe*, 36th Cong., 2d Sess., 156 (1861). See also, e.g., ibid., app. 63 (Congressman Ashley) and app. 84 (Congressman Lovejoy).

14. See *Congressional Globe*, 35th Cong., 2d Sess., 984 (1859) (Congressman Bingham).

15. *Congressional Globe*, 39th Cong., 1st Sess., 157–58, 1064, 1292 (1866).

16. *National Anti-Slavery Standard*, May 15, 1865, p. 2.

17. *Nation*, July 13, 1865, p. 39.

18. *Congressional Globe*, 39th Cong., 1st Sess., 2446 (1866). See also, e.g., *Harper's Weekly*, November 10, 1866, p. 706; "Open Letter from Carl Schurz to William Fessenden," *Cincinnati Commercial*, May 18, 1866, p. 2; *Springfield Republican*, April 5, 1866, p. 4; Eric Foner, *Reconstruction: America's Unfinished Revolution, 1863–1877* (New York, 1988), 257–58; Harold M. Hyman, *A More Perfect Union: The Impact of the Civil War and Reconstruction on the Constitution* (New York, 1973), 300–301, 393–96; William E. Nelson, *The Fourteenth Amendment: From Political Principle to Judicial Doctrine* (Cambridge, Mass., 1988).

19. *Reports to the General Assembly of Illinois, 24th Session*, 1:28; see also p. 42 (inaugural address of Gov. Richard J. Oglesby).

20. *National Anti-Slavery Standard*, July 22, 1865, p. 2.

21. *Congressional Globe*, 39th Cong., 1st Sess., 1265–66 (1866). See also Paludan, *A Covenant with Death*, 34–35.

22. See, e.g., *Harper's Weekly*, January 21, 1865, p. 34.

23. *Springfield Republican*, November 17, 1865, p. 2.

24. *Congressional Globe*, 40th Cong., 2d Sess., 2742 (1869). See also, e.g., *Harper's Weekly*, July 1, 1865, p. 402.

25. Herman Belz, *Reconstructing the Union: Theory and Policy during the Civil War* (Westport, Conn., 1969), chs. 3–4; McKitrick, *Andrew Johnson and Reconstruction*, 99–120

26. Belz, *Reconstructing the Union*, ch. 4.

27. *Springfield Republican*, July 11, 1865, p. 2 (emphasis added). See also "Letter to Andrew Johnson," ibid., August 22, 1865, p. 2; Valedictory Address of John Andrew, reprinted in Albert G. Browne, Jr., *Sketch of the Official Life of John A. Andrew as Governor of Massachusetts* (New York, 1868), 171–72 (by implication).

28. *National Anti-Slavery Standard*, May 27, 1865, p. 2.

29. Similar premises underlie the discussion in *Harper's Weekly*, May 27, 1865, p. 322, and the widely circulated plan outlined by outgoing governor John A. Andrew of Massachusetts, in Browne, *Sketch of the Official Life of John A. Andrew*, 171–72.

30. *National Anti-Slavery Standard*, February 18, 1865, p. 2.

31. *New York Tribune*, May 27, 1865, p. 4.

32. *Harper's Weekly*, May 20, 1865, p. 200.

33. *Nation*, July 6, 1865, p. 4.

34. *Germantown Telegraph*, July 3, 1865, p. 3.

35. *Springfield Republican*, July 11, 1865, p. 2.

36. *Harper's Weekly*, October 14, 1865, p. 842.

37. See U.S. Const., Art. I, sec. 2, par. 3.

38. *Germantown Telegraph*, July 3, 1865, p. 3; *Nation*, July 6, 1865, p. 4.

39. See "Oberlin Letter," reprinted in *Cincinnati Commercial*, July 1, 1865, p. 1.

40. *New York Times*, June 3, 1865, p. 4.

41. *Philadelphia Press*, May 30, 1865, p. 2; July 3, 1865, p. 2 ("Occasional"). See also *Cincinnati Commercial*, September 30, 1865, p. 2 (speech of Oliver H. P. T. Morton); *Springfield Republican*, July 28, 1865, p. 2.

42. *Nation*, July 6, 1865, p. 4; *New York Tribune*, May 27, 1865, p. 4.

43. *Harper's Weekly*, May 13, 1865, p. 290.

44. *Springfield Republican*, July 26, 1865, p. 2.

45. See *Harper's Weekly*, October 21, 1865, p. 658.

46. *Senate Executive Document No. 2*, 39th Cong., 1st Sess., 21 (December 19, 1865).

47. Ibid., 9.

48. The most comprehensive study of the Black Codes is by Theodore B. Wilson, *The Black Codes of the South* (University, Ala., 1965). In addition, see Eric Foner, *Nothing but Freedom: Emancipation and Its Legacy* (Baton Rouge, 1983), ch. 2.

49. See, e.g., *Harper's Weekly*, June 10, 1865, p. 355; *New York Tribune*, May 20, 1865, p. 4.

50. *Cincinnati Commercial*, October 13, 1865, p. 4.

51. *Harper's Weekly*, June 10, 1865, p. 355. See also *Nation*, August 17, 1865, p. 202.

52. *Harper's Weekly*, December 2, 1865, p. 754. See also *Philadelphia North American and United States Gazette*, July 11, 1865, p. 4.

53. See, e.g., *Congressional Globe*, 39th Cong., 1st Sess., 1115–19 (1866) (Congressman Wilson); and 1832–37 (Congressman Lawrence).

54. For a lucid explanation of the theoretical basis for this position, see *Congressional Globe*, 37th Cong., 2d Sess., 1614–15 (1862) (Congressman Thomas).

55. *Congressional Globe*, 39th Cong., 1st Sess., 1293–94 (1866).

56. Ibid., app. 293–94.

57. This point is explored in chapter 4.

58. This point is explored in David Donald, *The Politics of Reconstruction* (Baton Rouge, 1965).

59. More detailed information on Johnson's life and career can be found in Michael Les Benedict, *The Impeachment and Trial of Andrew Johnson* (New York, 1973); Albert Castel, *The Presidency of Andrew Johnson* (Lawrence, Kans., 1979); Eric McKitrick, ed., *Andrew Johnson: A Profile* (New York, 1969); Hans L. Trefousse, *Impeachment of a President: Andrew Johnson, the Blacks, and Reconstruction* (Knoxville, 1975).

60. *Springfield Republican*, April 17, 1865, p. 4.

61. Quoted in McKitrick, *Andrew Johnson and Reconstruction*, 91.

62. *National Anti-Slavery Standard*, May 6, 1865, p. 3 ("Avon").

63. McKitrick, *Andrew Johnson and Reconstruction*, 89.

64. LaWanda Cox and John H. Cox, *Politics, Principle and Prejudice 1865–1866* (London, 1963).

65. Summaries of the change in view include Larry G. Kincaid, "Victims of Circumstance: An Interpretation of Changing Attitudes toward Republican Policy Makers and Reconstruction," *Journal of American History* 57 (1970): 48,

and Bernard Weisberger, ''The Dark and Bloody Battle Ground of Reconstruction Historiography,'' *Journal of Southern History* 25 (1957): 427.

66. Influential studies adopting this position include Howard K. Beale, *The Critical Year: A Study of Andrew Johnson and Reconstruction* (New York, 1930); Claude Bowers, *The Tragic Era: The Revolution after Lincoln* (Cambridge, Mass., 1929); John W. Burgess, *Reconstruction and the Constitution, 1866-1876* (New York, 1902); and William A. Dunning, *Essays on the Civil War and Reconstruction, and Related Topics* (New York, 1898).

67. E.g., Michael Les Benedict, *A Compromise of Principle: Congressional Republicans and Reconstruction 1863-1869* (New York, 1974); William R. Brock, *An American Crisis: Congress and Reconstruction 1865-1867* (New York, 1963); Cox and Cox, *Politics, Principle and Prejudice*; John Hope Franklin, *Reconstruction: After the Civil War* (Chicago, 1961); Hyman, *A More Perfect Union*; McKitrick, *Andrew Johnson and Reconstruction*; James M. McPherson, *The Struggle for Equality: The Abolitionists and the Negro in the Civil War and Reconstruction* (Princeton, 1964); Kenneth M. Stampp, *The Era of Reconstruction, 1865-1877* (New York, 1965); Hans L. Trefousse, *The Radical Republicans: Lincoln's Vanguard for Racial Justice* (New York, 1969).

68. For a detailed study of these interactions, see Benedict, *A Compromise of Principle*.

CHAPTER 4. PRELIMINARY SKIRMISHING

1. *Congressional Globe*, 39th Cong., 1st Sess., 39 (1865).
2. Ibid., 43.
3. Ibid., 42.
4. *New York Times*, January 6, 1866, p. 4; February 25, 1866, p. 4.
5. *Cincinnati Commercial*, January 20, 1866, p. 4.
6. *Congressional Globe*, 39th Cong., 1st Sess., 173-74 (1866) (Congressman Wilson); 255 (Congressman Julian); and 309 (Congressman Boutwell).
7. Ibid., 279-81 (Congressman Hale); *New York Times*, February 13, 1866, p. 4.
8. *Congressional Globe*, 39th Cong., 1st Sess., 235-41 (1866) (Congressman Kasson); and 278-79 (Congressman Darling).
9. N.Y. Const. of 1846, art. II, sec. 1, reprinted in Benjamin Poore, ed., *The Federal and State Constitutions, Colonial Charters and Other Organic Laws of the United States*, vol. 2 (Washington, D.C., 1877), 1353.
10. *New York Times*, January 16, 1866, p. 4.
11. *Congressional Globe*, 39th Cong., 1st Sess., 173 (1866).
12. Ibid., 173-75 (Congressman Wilson); and 255-59 (Congressman Julian).
13. Ibid., 239.
14. Ibid., 239-40.
15. Ibid., 279.
16. Ibid., 279-81.
17. Ibid., 311.
18. Ibid., 310.
19. Ibid.
20. Ibid.
21. *New York Times*, January 8, 1867, p. 4.

22. Much of this account is taken from Michael Les Benedict, *A Compromise of Principle: Congressional Republicans and Reconstruction 1863–1869* (New York, 1974), 147–50.

23. See, e.g., *Congressional Globe*, 39th Cong., 1st Sess., 318–19 (1866) (Senator Hendricks); 372–73 (Senator Johnson); and 623 (Congressman Kerr).

24. See, e.g., ibid., 365 (Senator Fessenden).

25. Ibid., 322–23 (Senator Trumbull); and 339–40 (Senator Wilson).

26. Ibid., 421.

27. Ibid., 688.

28. See Benedict, *A Compromise of Principle*, 155–56.

29. *Congressional Globe*, 39th Cong., 1st Sess., 943 (1866). The seven included Doolittle, Stewart, James Dixon of Connecticut, Edwin D. Morgan of New York, Daniel S. Norton of Minnesota, and Peter Van Winkle and Waitman T. Willey of West Virginia. The list does not include Edgar Cowan of Pennsylvania, who had embraced the Democratic cause even before the veto of the Freedmen's Bureau Bill.

30. Benjamin B. Kendrick, *The Journal of the Joint Committee of Fifteen on Reconstruction, 39th Congress, 1865–1867* (New York, 1914), 51–52.

31. Thaddeus Stevens submitted such a proposal to the Joint Committee. See Kendrick, *Journal of the Joint Committee*, 41.

32. See, e.g., *Congressional Globe*, 39th Cong., 1st Sess., 357 (1866) (Congressman Conkling).

33. See, e.g., ibid.

34. See ibid., 535–36 (Congressman Benjamin).

35. Kendrick, *Journal of the Joint Committee*, 53.

36. See Eric McKitrick, *Andrew Johnson and Reconstruction*, (Chicago, 1960), 339.

37. See, e.g., *Congressional Globe*, 39th Cong., 1st Sess., 405 (1866) (Congressman Shellabarger); and 406–7 (Congressman Eliot).

38. See, e.g., ibid., 483–92 (Congressman Raymond); and 353–56 (Congressman Rogers).

39. See, e.g., ibid., 406 (Congressman Eliot).

40. See, e.g., ibid., 535 (Congressman Schenck).

41. See ibid., 483.

42. *New York Times*, January 29, 1866, p. 5.

43. *Congressional Globe*, 39th Cong., 1st Sess., 508 (1866).

44. Ibid., 538.

45. Ibid.

46. Quoted in *National Anti-Slavery Standard*, February 10, 1866, p. 1.

47. Quoted in ibid.

48. Quoted in ibid., p. 2.

49. Ibid.

50. The definitive work on Sumner is David Donald's two-volume biography, *Charles Sumner and the Coming of the Civil War* (New York, 1960), and *Charles Sumner and the Rights of Man* (New York, 1970).

51. *Congressional Globe*, 39th Cong., 1st Sess., 704 (1866).

52. Ibid., 1227 (emphasis in original).

53. Ibid., 673. Ironically, Sumner's biographer suggests that his opposition to the Joint Committee proposal was based largely on political considerations. Donald, *Charles Sumner and the Rights of Man*, 243–45.

54. *Congressional Globe*, 39th Cong., 1st Sess., 1229, 1321 (1866).

55. Ibid., 1284, 1287, 1288.

56. Ibid., 1289.

57. Benedict, *A Compromise of Principle*, 152–61; Joseph B. James, *The Framing of the Fourteenth Amendment* (Urbana, 1956) 68–74; McKitrick, *Andrew Johnson and Reconstruction*, 337.

58. *Cincinnati Commercial*, March 5, 1868, p. 2 (Mack).

59. *Cincinnati Commercial*, April 17, 1868, p. 2 (Swede). For other assessments of Bingham's role in the Reconstruction process, see Erving E. Beauregard, "John A. Bingham and the Fourteenth Amendment," *Historian* 50 (November, 1987): 67; Donald C. Swift, "John A. Bingham and Reconstruction: The Dilemma of a Moderate," *Ohio History* 77 (1968): 81.

60. *Congressional Globe*, 39th Cong., 1st Sess., 14 (1866).

61. Ibid., 157–158.

62. For other discussions of the Hoar affair see, e.g., George F. Hoar, *Autobiography of Seventy Years*, vol. 1 (New York, 1908), 24–27; Henry Wilson, *History of the Rise and Fall of the Slave Power*, vol. 1 (Boston, 1875–77), 578–82; *Congressional Globe*, 31st Cong., 1st Sess., app. 1663–64 (1850); ibid., 39th Cong., 1st Sess., 42 (1866).

63. *Congressional Globe*, 35th Cong., 2d Sess., 984–85 (1858).

64. See Kendrick, *Journal of the Joint Committee*, 49–51, 56–58, 60–62.

65. Ibid., 62.

66. *Springfield Republican*, January 26, 1866, p. 2.

67. *Congressional Globe*, 39th Cong., 1st Sess., 1095 (1866).

68. See Kendrick, *Journal of the Joint Committee*, 46.

69. Ibid., 57, 61, 62; *Congressional Globe*, 39th Cong., 1st Sess., 1063, 1064 (1866).

70. *Congressional Globe*, 39th Cong., 1st Sess., app. 133–35 (1866).

71. Ibid., 1064, 1082, 1095.

72. Ibid., 1063–64.

73. Ibid., 1064.

74. Ibid.

75. Ibid., 1095.

76. Ibid., 1089.

77. Ibid., 1090.

78. Ibid., 1089–90.

79. See generally Earl M. Maltz, "The Concept of Equal Protection of the Laws—A Historical Inquiry," *San Diego Law Review* 22 (1985): 499.

80. See, e.g., Oliver Wendell Holmes, ed., *Kent's Commentaries*, vol. 2 (Boston, 1896), 331–32, 339.

81. See Jacobus tenBroek, *The Antislavery Origins of the Fourteenth Amendment* (Berkeley, 1951), 145–48, 212–14.

82. *Congressional Globe*, 39th Cong., 1st Sess., 1292 (1866) (emphasis added).

83. See ibid., 1082 (Senator Stewart); 1083, 1087 (Congressman Davis); and 1095 (Congressman Conkling) (by implication).

84. Ibid., 1095.

85. *Springfield Republican*, March 2, 1866, p. 2. The debate over the original Bingham proposal is also discussed in detail in Michael P. Zuckert, "Congressional Power under the Fourteenth Amendment—The Original Understanding of Section Five," *Constitutional Commentary* 3 (1986): 123.

CHAPTER 5. THE CIVIL RIGHTS ACT OF 1866

1. *Congressional Globe*, 39th Cong., 1st Sess., 211 (1866).
2. For a detailed examination of the concept of the right to protection in nineteenth century thought, see Earl M. Maltz, "The Concept of Equal Protection of the Laws—A Historical Inquiry," *San Diego Law Review*, 22 (1985): 499.
3. See *Congressional Globe*, 39th Cong., 1st Sess., app. 158 (1866).
4. Ibid., 474, 1115.
5. For a comprehensive discussion of this point, see James H. Kettner, *The Development of American Citizenship, 1608-1870* (Chapel Hill, 1978), 311–33.
6. 60 U.S. (19 How.) 393 (1857).
7. *Congressional Globe*, 39th Cong., 1st Sess., 475, 499–500, 600 (1866).
8. Ibid., 600.
9. Ibid., 500.
10. Ibid., 606.
11. Ibid., 505.
12. Ibid., 1115.
13. See, e.g., Joseph Story, *Commentaries on the Constitution of the United States*, vol. 3 (Boston, 1833), 674–75; Oliver Wendell Holmes, ed., *Kent's Commentaries*, vol. 2 (Boston, 1896), 71. Wilson may have come to this conclusion as early as 1864. See Michael Kent Curtis, "The Fourteenth Amendment and the Bill of Rights," *Connecticut Law Review* 14 (1982): 237, 243.
14. See *Congressional Globe*, 35th Cong., 2d Sess., 984 (1858).
15. 41 U.S. (16 Pet.) 539 (1842).
16. See, e.g., *Congressional Globe*, 39th Cong., 1st Sess., 1115–19, 1293–94, 1757 (1866).
17. Ibid., 1835.
18. Ibid., app. 156.
19. Ibid., 1118.
20. 41 U.S. (16 Pet.) 629–30 (1842).
21. Ibid., 630.
22. *Congressional Globe*, 39th Cong., 1st Sess., 476 (1866).
23. Ibid., 599.
24. Ibid., 1115 (emphasis added).
25. See *Philadelphia North American and United States Gazette*, April 7, 1866, p. 2.
26. *Congressional Globe*, 39th Cong., 1st Sess., 1294 (1866). See also ibid., 1117–18 (Congressman Wilson); *and* 3034–35 (Senator Henderson).
27. March 28, 1866, in *Civil Rights Scrapbook*, p. 32, Edward McPherson Papers, box 99 (on file, Library of Congress). Robert J. Kaczorowski argues that the Civil Rights Act was intended to mandate a minimum level of rights for all Americans—white or black—rather than simply to prohibit racial discrimination in the enumerated rights. Kaczorowski, "Revolutionary Constitutionalism in the Era of the Civil War and Reconstruction," *New York University Law Review* 61, (1986): 863, 897–98 and n. 153. In a sense this observation is correct; the act did guarantee the *status* of citizenship to whites as well as blacks. See, e.g., *Congressional Globe*, 39th Cong., 1st Sess., 1265 (1866); *Chicago Republican*, March 28, 1866, in *Civil Rights Scrapbook*, p. 37. On the issue of what specific rights were protected, however, the weight of the evidence is against the Kaczorowski position.

For evidence, he relies primarily on newspaper accounts in the *Civil Rights Scrapbook*. Some of those he cites are ambiguous; others, however, plainly describe the act as color-blind in application. See, e.g., *Philadelphia Press*, undated, *Civil Rights Scrapbook*, p. 26; *Philadelphia North American and United States Gazette*, April 7, 1866, *Civil Rights Scrapbook*, p. 78. My own sense of the Republican newspaper accounts—both those collected in the scrapbook and others I have examined—is that such views were the exception rather than the rule; the vast majority either implicitly or explictly take the position that only racial discrimination was prohibited. See, e.g., *Norwich Bulletin*, undated, *Civil Rights Scrapbook*, p. 52; *Boston Journal*, undated, *Civil Rights Scrapbook*, p. 57. Moreover, the latter views are clearly more consistent with the evolution of the statutory language and the expressions of influential Republicans such as Shellabarger and Wilson.

28. *Congressional Globe*, 39th Cong., 1st Sess., 1293–94 (1866) (Congressman Shellabarger); Harold M. Hyman, *A More Perfect Union: The Impact of the Civil War and Reconstruction on the Constitution* (New York, 1973), 401–61 passim.

29. See, e.g., *Congressional Globe*, 39th Cong., 1st Sess., 1116–17, 1266, 1291, 1293, app. 156 (1866); *Opinions of the Attorneys General of the United States*, 10:382 (1862).

30. *Congressional Globe*, 39th Cong., 1st Sess., app. 158 (1866).

31. Ibid., 1291, app. 156–59.

32. Ibid., 1265, 1267, 1291–92.

33. See, e.g., ibid., 1291 (Congressman Bingham); and 1265 (Congressman Davis).

34. See, e.g., *Harrisburg Daily Telegraph*, March 29, 1866, p. 2; *Springfield Republican*, April 14, 1866, p. 4.

35. *Congressional Globe*, 39th Cong., 1st Sess., 1152 (1866).

36. Ibid., 475.

37. Ibid., 1296.

38. Ibid.

39. See Michael Les Benedict, *A Compromise of Principle: Congressional Republicans and Reconstruction 1863–1869* (New York, 1973), 169.

40. *Congressional Globe*, 39th Cong., 1st Sess., 1366–67 (1866).

41. Ibid., 1367.

42. See Benedict, *A Compromise of Principle*, 148–49, 164–65.

43. *National Anti-Slavery Standard*, April 7, 1866, p. 2.

44. *Congressional Globe*, 39th Cong., 1st Sess., 943 (1866).

45. William M. Stewart, *Reminiscences of Senator William M. Stewart of Nevada* (New York, 1908), pp. 199–200.

46. For a more extensive explanation of the Stockton affair, see Eric McKitrick, *Andrew Johnson and Reconstruction* (Chicago, 1960), 319–22.

47. *Congressional Globe*, 39th Cong., 1st Sess., 1564–73, 1589–1602, 1635–48, 1666–79 (1866).

48. For an analysis of Morgan's situation, see LaWanda Cox and John H. Cox, *Politics, Principle and Prejudice 1865–1866* (London, 1963), 199–201. On Lane, see W. H. Stephenson, *The Political Career of James H. Lane* (Topeka, 1930), 154–57, who concludes that the critical issue in Lane's decision was control of Kansas patronage.

49. *Congressional Globe*, 39th Cong., 1st Sess., 1809, 1861 (1866).

50. Ibid., app. 183; see also 1268 (Congressman Kerr).

51. *Germantown Telegraph*, April 4, 1866, p. 3.

52. *Cincinnati Commercial*, March 30, 1866, p. 4; see also April 30, 1866, p. 2 ("Mack").

53. Ibid., April 16, 1866, p. 4; April 21, 1866, p. 4.

54. *Philadelphia North American and United States Gazette*, April 10, 1866, p. 2.

55. See Earl M. Maltz, " 'Separate but Equal' and the Law of Common Carriers in the Era of the Fourteenth Amendment," *Rutgers Law Journal* 17 (1986): 553.

56. 4 Met. 564, 566 (Mass. 1842). See also cases cited in Civil Rights Cases, 109 U.S. 3, 37-39 (1883) (Harlan, J., dissenting); Robert D. Hutchinson, *A Treatise on the Law of Carriers as Administered in the Courts of the United States and England* (Chicago, 1880), 30 n. 1.

57. Jones v. Albert Mayer Co., 392 U.S. 409 (1968); Robert Kohl, "The Civil Rights Act of 1866: Its Hour Come Round at Last: *Jones v. Albert Mayer Co.*," *Virginia Law Review* 55 (1969): 272.

58. See St. George Tucker, ed., *Blackstone's Commentaries*, vol. 1 (Philadelphia, 1803), 63; Charles Fairman, *Reconstruction and Reunion, 1864-1888, Part 1* (New York, 1971), 1238-42.

59. Hursh v. North, 40 Penn St. 241, 243 (1861).

60. Burr & Co. v. Sickles & Co., 17 Ark. 428, 434 (1857).

61. 41 U.S. (16 Pet.) 1, 18 (1842). See also United States v. Arredondo, 31 U.S. (6 Pet.) 691, 714-15 (1832).

62. *Congressional Globe*, 39th Cong., 1st Sess., 1785 (1866).

63. See Jones v. Albert Mayer Co., 392 U.S. 409, 423 n. 30 (1968).

64. See Benedict, *A Compromise of Principle*, 419 n. 53.

65. *Congressional Globe*, 39th Cong., 1st Sess., 475 (1866).

66. Ibid., 1785.

67. See Robert J. Kaczorowski, *The Politics of Judicial Interpretation: The Federal Courts, Department of Justice and Civil Rights, 1866-1876* (New York, 1985), ch. 3.

68. *Congressional Globe*, 39th Cong., 1st Sess., 1680-81 (1866).

69. Ibid., 1759 (emphasis added).

70. Jones v. Albert Mayer Co., 392 U.S. 409, 427-28 (1968); Kohl, "The Civil Rights Act of 1866."

71. See, e.g., *Report of the Joint Committee on Reconstruction*, 39th Cong., 1st Sess., 17 (1866).

72. See, e.g., *Cincinnati Commercial*, March 30, 1866, p. 4.

73. See, e.g., *Congressional Globe*, 39th Cong., 1st Sess., 1159-60 (1866) (Congressman Windom); *New York Tribune*, May 16, 1866, p. 4.

74. See, e.g., *Congressional Globe*, 39th Cong., 1st Sess., 1160 (1866)(Congressman Windom); and 504 (Senator Howard).

75. V. Jacque Voegeli, *Free but Not Equal: The Midwest and the Negro during the Civil War Era* (Chicago, 1967), 172.

76. *Congressional Globe*, 39th Cong., 1st Sess., 541 (1866) (Congressman Dawson); and 1121-22 (Congressman Rogers).

77. Ibid., 505.

78. Ibid., 505-6.

79. Ibid., 505.

80. Ibid., 600.

81. Ibid., 632-33.

82. See ibid., app. 293-94.

83. Shellabarger to Trumbull, April 7, 1866, Trumbull Papers, Library of Congress.

84. *Congressional Globe*, 39th Cong., 1st Sess., 1785 (1866).

85. *Philadelphia Press*, April 9, 1866, p. 4 (letter from "Occasional") (J. W. Forney). See also ibid., March 28, 1866, p. 4 (letter from "Occasional"); *Springfield Republican*, January 6, 1866, p. 4; *Washington Chronicle*, March 28, 1866, p. 2.

86. *Congressional Globe*, 39th Cong., 1st Sess., 1759 (1866).

87. See "Letter from Jacob Cox to Andrew Johnson," *Philadelphia Press*, February 27, 1866, p. 1.

CHAPTER 6. THE DRAFTING OF
THE FOURTEENTH AMENDMENT

1. Benjamin B. Kendrick, *The Journal of the Joint Committee of Fifteen on Reconstruction, 39th Congress, 1865-1867* (New York, 1914), 292-93; Eric McKitrick, *Andrew Johnson and Reconstruction* (Chicago, 1960), 344-45.

2. See Kendrick, *Journal of the Joint Committee*, 83-85.

3. See *Report of the Joint Committee on Reconstruction*, 39th Cong., 1st Sess., 16-18; McKitrick, *Andrew Johnson and Reconstruction*, 21-42.

4. Kendrick, *Journal of the Joint Committee*, 37-129.

5. Ibid., 85.

6. Ibid.

7. Ibid.

8. See, e.g., *Congressional Globe*, 39th Cong., 1st Sess., 1093 (1866).

9. Kendrick, *Journal of the Joint Committee*, 87-88.

10. Ibid., 98-99.

11. Ibid., 99.

12. See ibid., 86-87.

13. See, e.g., ibid., 302; McKitrick, *Andrew Johnson and Reconstruction*, 347.

14. Johnson, who had voted with Bingham on April 21, voted against him on April 25. The explanation for his change of heart may have been distaste for the privileges and immunities clause, which was not included in Bingham's original April 21 proposal. See *Congressional Globe*, 39th Cong., 1st Sess., 3041 (1866) (motion on Senate floor to remove privileges and immunities clause). Morrill voted against Bingham on April 21 but with him on April 25. There are no clues to Morrill's motives.

15. Kendrick, *Journal of the Joint Committee*, 99.

16. See sources cited at n. 13, above.

17. Morrill and Washburne did not vote.

18. Kendrick, *Journal of the Joint Committee*, 100.

19. See ibid., 101.

20. Ibid.

21. Ibid., 102.

22. See ibid., 104.

23. See ibid., 105.

24. See ibid., 105-6.

25. Ibid., 106-7.

26. See ibid., 87, 98, 99.

CHAPTER 7. THE INTENTIONS OF
THE DRAFTERS OF SECTION ONE

1. *Congressional Globe*, 39th Cong., 1st Sess., 2459 (1866).
2. Ibid., 2541.
3. See, e.g., ibid., 2462-63, 2543-45; Joseph B. James, *The Ratification of the Fourteenth Amendment* (Macon, Ga. 1984), 91; Benjamin B. Kendrick, *The Journal of the Joint Committee of Fifteen on Reconstruction, 39th Congress, 1865-1867* (New York, 1914), 349-52.
4. *Congressional Globe*, 39th Cong., 1st Sess., 2542 (1866).
5. Ibid., 2500.
6. Ibid., 2451.
7. Ibid., 2538; see also 2467 (Congressman Boyer).
8. See, e.g., ibid., 2463 (Congressman Garfield); and 2537 (Congressman Beaman).
9. See ibid., 2890-91 (Senator Cowan); and 2397-98 (Congressman Phelps).
10. *Congressional Record*, 43 Cong., 2d Sess., 3:979-80 (1875).
11. See *Springfield Republican*, April 30, 1866, p. 2; May 1, 1866, p. 2; May 8, 1866, p. 2; May 26, 1866, p. 4; June 1, 1866, p. 2.
12. *Congressional Globe*, 39th Cong., 1st Sess., 2467 (1866). See also ibid., 3147 (Congressman Harding); *Pennsylvania Legislative Record*, app. 41 (1867) (Congressman Jenks); *Charleston Courier*, November 1, 1866, p. 2.
13. *Congressional Globe*, 39th Cong., 1st Sess., 2549 (1866). See also ibid., 2539 (Congressman Farnsworth); *Cincinnati Commercial*, October 25, 1866, p. 2 (Zachariah Chandler); and September 6, 1866, p. 2 (William M. Dickson).
14. *Report of the Joint Committee on Reconstruction*, 39th Cong., 1st Sess., 17 (1866) (emphasis added).
15. *Congressional Globe*, 39th Cong., 1st Sess., 2765-66 (1866) (Senator Howard); and 157-58 (Congressman Bingham).
16. Raoul Berger, *Government by Judiciary: The Transformation of the Fourteenth Amendment* (Cambridge, Mass., 1977), 216-19.
17. *Congressional Globe*, 39th Cong., 1st Sess., 359 (1866).
18. Ibid., 1292.
19. Ibid., 2765.
20. See, e.g., Plyler v. Doe, 457 U.S. 202 (1982); Graham v. Richardson, 403 U.S. 365 (1971).
21. *Congressional Globe*, 39th Cong., 1st Sess., 2765-66 (1866). See also speech of Oliver Morton, *Cincinnati Commercial*, September 24, 1866, p. 2; speech of William Dickson, ibid., September 9, 1866, p. 2.
22. St. George Tucker, ed., *Blackstone's Commentaries*, vol. 1 (Philadelphia, 1803), 44.
23. 2 Tex. 250, 251-52 (1852). See also Trustees of Dartmouth College v. Woodward, 17 U.S. (4 Wheat.) 518, 581-82 (1819) (argument of Daniel Webster); Thomas M. Cooley, *A Treatise on the Constitutional Limitations Which Rest upon the Legislative Power of the States of the Union* (Boston, 1867), 351-59; Rodney L. Mott, *Due Process of Law: A Historical and Analytical Treatise of the Principles and Methods Followed by the Courts in the Application of the Concept of the "Law of the Land"* (Indianapolis, 1926), 259-74.
24. Ervine's Appeal, 16 Pa. 256, 268 (1851).
25. Barnet v. Barnet, 15 Serg. & R. 72 (Pa. 1826); Cooley, *A Treatise on the Constitutional Limitations*, 393-97; Mott, *Due Process of Law*, 259-74.
26. *Congressional Globe*, 39th Cong., 1st Sess., 2766 (1866).

27. Ibid., 3036 (emphasis added).
28. Kendrick, *Journal of the Joint Committee on Reconstruction*, 85.
29. *Congressional Globe*, 39th Cong., 1st Sess., 3041 (1866).
30. Ibid., 2891; see also 2919 (Senator Davis).
31. Walter Fleming, *Documentary History of Reconstruction*, vol. 2 (Cleveland, 1906), 215.
32. *New York Times*, October 24, 1966, p. 1; (letter of Orville Browning); *North Carolina Senate Reports*, p. 96 (1866), quoted in Charles Fairman, "Does the Fourteenth Amendment Incorporate the Bill of Rights," *Stanford Law Review* 2 (1949): 5, 93–94; *Pennsylvania Legislative Record*, app. 12 (1867) (Senator Wallace); letter from George Weston, *National Intelligencer*, July 10, 1866, p. 2. But see *Philadelphia Public Ledger*, October 1, 1866, p. 2; *Fourteenth Amendment Scrapbook*, p. 24, in Edward McPherson Papers (on file, Library of Congress).
33. Herman Belz, *A New Birth of Freedom: The Republican Party and Freedmen's Rights, 1861–1866* (Westport, Conn., 1976), 173–74.
34. *Congressional Globe*, 42d Cong., 1st Sess., app. 153 (1871)(Congressman Garfield); and 579–80 (Senator Trumbull).
35. See, e.g., *Congressional Record*, 43d Cong., 2d Sess., 3:979–80 (1875)(Congressman Hale); *Congressional Globe*, 42d Cong., 1st Sess., app. 251–52 (1871)(Senator Morton); 604 (Senator Pool).
36. See *Congressional Globe*, 42d Cong., 1st Sess., app. 231 (Senator Blair); *Congressional Globe*, 42d Cong., 2d Sess., app. 3 (1872)(Senator Morrill).
37. Judith A. Baer, *Equality under the Constitution: Reclaiming the Fourteenth Amendment* (Ithaca, 1983), 75; Alfred Avins, "The Civil Rights Act of 1875: Some Reflected Light on the Fourteenth Amendment and Public Accommodations," *Columbia Law Review* 66 (1966): 873; Donald Ziegler, "Reassessment of the *Younger* Doctrine in Light of the Legislative History of Reconstruction," *Duke Law Journal* (1983): 987.
38. *Congressional Globe*, 42d Cong., 1st Sess., app. 81–86 (1871).
39. Ibid., app. 150–51.
40. Ibid., app. 83 (emphasis added); see also app. 69 (Congressman Shellabarger); and 608 (Senator Pool).
41. Michael Les Benedict, *A Compromise of Principle: Congressional Republicans and Reconstruction 1863–1869* (New York, 1974), chs. 16–17.
42. See *Congressional Globe*, 42d Cong., 1st Sess., 196–97 (1871) (Senator Ames); and 154–60 (Senator Sherman).
43. See Patrick Riddleberger, "The Break in the Radical Ranks: Radicals vs. Stalwarts in the Election of 1872," *Journal of Negro History* 44 (1959): 136.
44. *Congressional Globe*, 42d Cong., 2d Sess., app. 3 (1872) (Senator Morrill); *Congressional Globe*. 41st Cong., 2d Sess., 687 (1870) (Schurz).
45. *Congressional Record*, 43d Cong., 2d Sess., 3:979–80 (1875).
46. *Congressional Globe*, 39th Cong., 1st Sess., 1089–90 (1866).
47. Ohio Executive Document, pt. 1, no. 282 (1867), quoted in Fairman, "Does the Fourteenth Amendment Incorporate the Bill of Rights," 96; Benedict, *A Compromise of Principle*, 170.
48. J. Bingham to Ross, Washington, D.C., January 10, 1866, quoted in Erving E. Beauregard, "John A. Bingham and the Fourteenth Amendment," *Historian* 50 (November 1987):67, 73 (emphasis added).
49. *Congressional Globe*, 39th Cong., 1st Sess., 1759 (1866).
50. Joseph Story, *Commentaries on the Constitution of the United States*, vol. 2 (Boston, 1833), 53.

51. Oliver Wendell Holmes, ed., *Kent's Commentaries*, vol. 2 (Boston, 1896), 72.

52. 6 Fed. Cases 546, 551-52 (No. 3230) (C.C.E.D. Pa. 1823).

53. 23 Mass. (6 Pick.) 89, 92 (1827).

54. 3 H & McH. 535, 554 (Md. 1797).

55. See, e.g., *Congressional Globe*, 39th Cong., 1st Sess. 1835-38 (1866) (Congressman Lawrence); ibid., 474-75 (Senator Trumbull).

56. E.g., Abbott v. Bayley, 23 Mass.(6 Pick.) 89, 92 (1827); Campbell v. Morris, 3 H. & McH. 535, 554 (Md. 1797).

57. 6 Fed. Cases 546, 551-52 (No. 3230) (C.C.E.D. Pa. 1823).

58. 60 U.S. (19 How.) 393, 416-17 (1857).

59. Kendrick, *Journal of the Joint Committee of Reconstruction*, 85.

60. *Congressional Globe*, 39th Cong., 1st Sess., 3041 (1866).

61. Ibid., 2538. See also ibid., 2397-98 (Congressman Phelps); *Pennsylvania Legislative Record*, app. 73 (Congressman Deise); letter from James Orr, *New York Times*, December 2, 1866, p. 5; speech of George H. Pendleton, *Cincinnati Commercial*, July 23, 1866, p. 2; *Raleigh Sentinel*, October 9, 1866, p. 2.

62. *Congressional Globe*, 39th Cong., 1st Sess., 1064, 1082, 1095 (1866).

63. Ibid., 1095.

64. Ibid., 2765.

65. George Boutwell, *Reminiscences of Sixty Years in Public Affairs*, vol. 2 (New York, 1902), 42.

66. *Congressional Globe*, 39th Cong., 1st Sess., 2766 (1866).

67. See, e.g., *Congressional Globe*, 39th Cong., 1st Sess., 474-75, 1117-18, 2459 (1866); *Cincinnati Commercial*, August 3, 1866, p. 1 (speech of Lyman Trumbull); *New York Times*, October 24, 1866, p. 4.

68. See Paul Finkelman, "Prelude to the Fourteenth Amendment: Black Legal Rights in the Antebellum North," *Rutgers Law Journal* 17 (1986): 415, 463-75.

69. 59 Mass. (5 Cush.) 198 (1849).

70. Charles Sumner, *His Complete Works*, vol. 3 (Boston, 1870- 83), 55-56, 70-81.

71. 59 Mass. at 206.

72. Baer, *Equality under the Constitution*, 77; Harold M. Hyman and William M. Wiecek, *Equal Justice under Law: Constitutional Development 1835-1875* (New York, 1982), 95-96; Leonard Levy, *The Law of the Commonwealth and Chief Justice Shaw* (Cambridge, Mass., 1957), 108-17.

73. See Finkelman, "Prelude to the Fourteenth Amendment," 467; J. Morgan Kousser, " 'The Supremacy of Equal Rights': The Struggle against Racial Discrimination in Antebellum Massachusetts and the Foundation of the Fourteenth Amendment," *Northwestern University Law Review*, 82 (1988), 941.

74. *Congressional Globe*, 36th Cong., 1st Sess., 1681 (1860).

75. Roy P. Basler, ed., *The Collected Works of Abraham Lincoln*, vol. 7 (New Brunswick, N.J., 1953-55), 55.

76. *Springfield Republican*, July 7, 1865, p. 2.

77. *New York Times*, May 5, 1865, p. 4.

78. See, e.g., *Congressional Globe*, 39th Cong., 1st Sess., 474 (Senator Trumbull), 3034 (Senator Henderson) (1866).

79. *Congressional Globe*, 35th Cong., 2d Sess., 985 (1858).

80. *Congressional Globe*, 39th Cong., 1st Sess., 585-90, 655 (1866).

81. Ibid., 688.

82. Ibid., app. 219-20.

83. See, e.g., Sanborn v. Commissioners of Rice County, 9 Minn. 273, 277 (1864); Sharpless v. Mayor of Philadelphia, 21 Penn. St. 147, 168 (1853).

84. Cooley, *A Treatise on the Constitutional Limitations*, 495.

85. *Congressional Globe*, 36th Cong., 1st Sess., 1681 (1860).

86. Ibid., 1680.

87. 347 U.S. 483 (1954).

88. Adamson v. California, 332 U.S. 46, 68–92 (1946) (Black, J., dissenting).

89. Berger, *Government by Judiciary*, ch. 8; Jacobus tenBroek, *The Antislavery Origins of the Fourteenth Amendment* (Berkeley, 1951), 213–14; Fairman, "Does the Fourteenth Amendment Incorporate the Bill of Rights."

90. The most comprehensive defense of this position is Michael Kent Curtis, *No State Shall Abridge: The Fourteenth Amendment and the Bill of Rights* (Durham, N.C., 1986). In addition, see Hyman and Wiecek, *Equal Justice under Law*, ch. 11; Adamson v. California, 332 U.S. 46, 123–25 (1946).

91. *Congressional Globe*, 39th Cong., 1st Sess., 2765 (1866).

92. Ibid., 1089–90.

93. *Congressional Globe*, 42d Cong., 1st Sess., app. 84 (1871).

94. See Russell B. Nye, *Fettered Freedom* (East Lansing, 1949), passim.

95. Donald B. Johnson, ed., *National Party Platforms*, vol. 1 (Urbana, 1978), 27. See also Hyman and Wiecek, *Equal Justice under Law*, 404.

96. See, e.g., *Congressional Globe*, 39th Cong., 1st Sess., 1621–22, 1629, 1838 (1866).

97. Berger, *Government by Judiciary*, 147.

98. Ibid., 145; Fairman, "Does the Fourteenth Amendment Incorporate the Bill of Rights," 24–26, 30–37.

99. Fairman, "Does the Fourteenth Amendment Incorporate the Bill of Rights," 136–37.

100. Ibid., 33–34; tenBroek, *Antislavery Origins of the Fourteenth Amendment*, 213–14.

101. *Congressional Globe*, 39th Cong., 1st Sess., 1089–91 (1866).

102. Fairman, "Does the Fourteenth Amendment Incorporate the Bill of Rights," 81–134.

103. Ibid.

104. Charles Crosskey, "Charles Fairman, 'Legislative History' and the Constitutional Limitations on State Authority," *University of Chicago Law Review* 22 (1954): 1, 85–88; Benedict, *A Compromise of Principle*, ch. 16.

105. *Ironton Register*, September 13, 1866, p. 1 (Congressman Bingham); *Ohio Executive Document*, pt. 1, 282 (1867) (Cox), quoted in Fairman, "Does the Fourteenth Amendment Incorporate the Bill of Rights," 96.

106. *Ironton Register*, September 13, 1866, p. 1.

107. *Congressional Globe*, 39th Cong., 1st Sess., 1065, 1090–91 (1866).

108. Ibid., 1629, 1838.

109. Ibid., 500; see also 2542 (Congressman Bingham).

110. Ibid., 1629 (search and seizure).

111. See, e.g., ibid., 2397, 2538; *Pennsylvania Legislative Record*, app. 72, 73, 80 (1867).

112. *Congressional Globe*, 39th Cong., 1st Sess., 2766 (1866).

113. Ibid., 2542.

114. *Report of the Joint Committee on Reconstruction*, 39th Cong., 1st Sess., 12.

115. *Harper's Weekly*, May 12, 1866, p. 290.

116. Ibid., May 26, 1866, p. 323.

117. Ibid., May 12, 1866, p. 290.
118. *National Anti-Slavery Standard*, May 26, 1866, p. 2.
119. For forceful presentations of opposing views, see William E. Nelson, *The Fourteenth Amendment: From Political Principle to Judicial Doctrine* (Cambridge, Mass., 1988), 127–32; William Van Alstyne, "The Fourteenth Amendment, the 'Right' to Vote, and the Understanding of the Thirty-Ninth Congress," in Philip B. Kurland, ed., *1965 Supreme Court Review* (Chicago, 1965).

CHAPTER 8. INTERREGNUM:
CONGRESS AND THE RIGHT TO VOTE BETWEEN
THE FOURTEENTH AND FIFTEENTH AMENDMENTS

1. *Congressional Globe*, 39th Cong., 1st Sess., 2602–03 (1866).
2. Ibid., 162.
3. Ibid., 245–51.
4. Ibid., 952.
5. Ibid., 1934.
6. Michael Les Benedict, *A Compromise of Principle: Congressional Republicans and Reconstruction 1863–1869* (New York, 1974), 146.
7. *Congressional Globe*, 39th Cong., 1st Sess., 1934 (1866).
8. Ibid., 3432.
9. Ibid.
10. Ibid., 3434.
11. Ibid., 3433.
12. Ibid., 3434.
13. Ibid., 3453.
14. *National Intelligencer*, July 4, 1866, p. 2 ("Observer").
15. *Congressional Globe*, 39th Cong., 1st Sess., 3980–81, 4000, 4007 (1866).
16. Benedict, *A Compromise of Principle*, 196–97.
17. *Congressional Globe*, 39th Cong., 1st Sess., 2180, 2373, 4222 (1866).
18. *Nation*, July 26, 1866, p. 70.
19. *Harper's Weekly*, June 23, 1866, p. 386.
20. *National Anti-Slavery Standard*, September 22, 1866, p. 2.
21. Quoted in ibid.
22. *Philadelphia Press*, June 25, 1866, p. 2.
23. For detailed accounts of the southern attitude toward the Fourteenth Amendment during this time period, see Joseph B. James, *The Ratification of the Fourteenth Amendment* (Macon, Ga., 1984), chs. 7–9; Michael Perman, *Reunion without Compromise: The South and Reconstruction* (Cambridge, England, 1973), 235–65.
24. The National Union Convention is discussed in Benedict, *A Compromise of Principle*, 192–201.
25. *Philadelphia Age*, August 6, 1866, p. 2; August 24, 1866, p. 2.
26. Speech of John P. Logan, *Philadelphia Press*, July 23, 1866, p. 2; ibid., September 8, 1866, p. 4.
27. Editorial of *Jackson Clarion*, quoted in Perman, *Reunion without Compromise*, 249.
28. 71 U.S. (4 Wall.) 2 (1866).

29. See Benedict, *A Compromise of Principle*, 221–22; Perman, *Reunion without Compromise*, 260–65.

30. *Harper's Weekly*, June 2, 1866, p. 339; August 18, 1866, p. 514; *Nation*, May 15, 1866, p. 616.

31. *Nation*, May 11, 1866, p. 594; August 30, 1866, p. 202.

32. *Congressional Globe*, 39th Cong., 2d Sess., 46 (1867).

33. Ibid., 107.

34. Ibid., 109.

35. Ibid., 382.

36. Ibid., 313, 344.

37. *Congressional Globe*, 39th Cong., 1st Sess., 2180, 2373, 4222 (1866).

38. *Congressional Globe*, 39th Cong., 2d Sess., 191 (1867).

39. Ibid., 125.

40. Ibid., 190.

41. Ibid., 329.

42. Ibid., 329–30, app. 57–58. The definitive study of the guarantee clause is William M. Wiecek, *The Guarantee Clause of the U.S. Constitution* (Ithaca, 1972).

43. *Congressional Globe*, 39th Cong., 2d Sess., 162 (Senator Sumner), 215 (Senator Edmunds) (1867).

44. Ibid., 334 (Senator Kirkwood), 335 (Senator Wade).

45. Ibid., 164.

46. Ibid., 127–28 (Senator Sherman), 199 (Senator Pomeroy).

47. Ibid., 126 (Senator Wade), 333 (Senator Howard).

48. Ibid., 219.

49. Ibid., 220.

50. Ibid., 332 (Senator Grimes), 337 (Senator Fessenden).

51. Ibid., 337–38.

52. Ibid., 328, 359.

53. Ibid., 359.

54. Ibid., 360.

55. Ibid., 357

56. Ibid., 360.

57. Ibid.

58. Ibid., 399 (Congressman Wilson), 449 (Congressman Blaine), 452–53 (Congressman Dawes), 472 (Congressman Boutwell).

59. Ibid., 449–50 (Congressman Bingham), 473–74 (Congressman Delano).

60. Ibid., 481.

61. Ibid.

62. Ibid., 487.

63. Ibid., 364, 481, 487.

64. Ibid., 1096, 1121.

65. Ibid., 1928.

66. James G. Blaine, *Twenty Years of Congress: From Lincoln to Garfield with a Review of the Events Which Led to the Political Revolution of 1860*, vol. 2 (Norwich, Conn., 1884–86), 279–89.

67. *Philadelphia North American and United States Gazette*, December 28, 1867, p. 2; *Springfield Republican*, March 4, 1867, p. 2.

68. *Congressional Globe*, 39th Cong., 2d Sess., 185, 219, 333 (1867).

69. Ibid., 500.

70. Ibid., app. 78–80.

71. Ibid., 250.

72. *National Anti-Slavery Standard*, January 12, 1867, p. 1.
73. *Congressional Globe*, 39th Cong., 2d Sess., 504 (Congressman Bingham), app. 77 (Congressman Baker) (1867).
74. Ibid., 817.
75. Benjamin B. Kendrick, *The Journal of the Joint Committee of Fifteen on Reconstruction, 39th Congress, 1865–1867* (New York, 1914), 123.
76. Ibid., 129.
77. Ibid.
78. *Congressional Globe*, 39th Cong., 2d Sess., 1176–77 (Congressman Bingham), 1182 (Congressman Blaine) (1867).
79. Ibid., 53.
80. Ibid., 1213.
81. Ibid.
82. Ibid., 1215.
83. Ibid.
84. Ibid., 1175.
85. Ibid., 1128–29.
86. Ibid., 1360–61.
87. Ibid., 1374.
88. Ibid., 1378.
89. Ibid.
90. Ibid., 1379.
91. Ibid., 1384, 1391.
92. Ibid., 1392.
93. Ibid., 1391–92; *New York Times*, February 16, 1867, p. 2 (Blaine amendment in original form guarantees universal suffrage).
94. Benedict, *A Compromise of Principle*, 234–35.
95. *National Anti-Slavery Standard*, June 13, 1868, p. 1; Benedict, *A Compromise of Principle*, 236.
96. *Congressional Globe*, 39th Cong., 2d Sess., 1400 (1867); and 1645.
97. Ibid., 1733, 1976.
98. Ibid., 1365 (Congressman Wilson); *Cincinnati Commercial*, January 2, 1867, p. 2; *Philadelphia Press*, January 6, 1867, p. 1.
99. *Congressional Globe*, 39th Cong., 2d Sess., 1372 (1867) (Senator Henderson); speech of Beverly Nash, *Cincinnati Commercial*, March 27, 1867, p. 4; *Harper's Weekly*, April 27, 1867, p. 258; *Nation*, April 11, 1867, p. 295; letter from Herschel Johnson, *New York Tribune*, August 12, 1868, p. 4.
100. *Cincinnati Commercial*, April 27, 1867, p. 2 (Mack); *Philadelphia North American and United States Gazette*, March 25, 1867, p. 2.
101. *National Anti-Slavery Standard*, May 11, 1867, p. 1; letter from Charles Sumner, ibid., April 20, 1867, p. 2.
102. *Congressional Globe*, 40th Cong., 1st Sess., 292 (1867) (Senator Wilson); and 345 (Senator Sumner).
103. Ibid., 614–15. See also *Chicago Tribune*, April 3, 1867, p. 2.
104. *Germantown Telegraph*, July 17, 1867, p. 3; *Philadelphia North American and United States Gazette*, March 29, 1867, p. 2.
105. *Congressional Globe*, 40th Cong., 1st Sess., 614 (1867).
106. *New York Times*, September 2, 1867, p. 2.
107. Ibid., July 5, 1867, p. 4.
108. *Springfield Republican*, March 25, 1867, p. 2.
109. Ibid., November 14, 1867, p. 2.
110. Ibid., August 3, 1867, p. 2.

111. *Congressional Globe*, 40th Cong., 1st Sess., 615 (1867).

112. *Springfield Republican*, January 1, 1867, p. 2; *Chicago Tribune*, February 17, 1867, p. 2.

113. *Springfield Republican*, March 13, 1867, p. 4.

114. *Nation*, April 11, 1867, p. 295; *Cincinnati Commercial*, February 4, 1867, p. 2; April 27, 1867, p. 2 (Mack).

115. *New York Times*, July 5, 1867, p. 4.

116. *Congressional Globe*, 40th Cong., 1st Sess., 13 (1867).

117. *Cincinnati Commercial*, July 17, 1867, p. 1.

118. Ibid., September 18, 1867, p. 4. See also *National Anti-Slavery Standard*, October 5, 1867, p. 3; *New York Tribune*, August 15, 1867, p. 4.

119. Benedict, *A Compromise of Principle*, 272–73.

120. *Springfield Republican*, October 10, 1867, p. 2.

121. *Cincinnati Commercial*, October 2, 1867, p. 2; *National Anti-Slavery Standard*, November 9, 1867, p. 4; *New York Tribune*, November 6, 1867, p. 4.

122. *National Anti-Slavery Standard*, November 9, 1867, p. 4.

123. Ibid., January 23, 1868, p. 2.

124. *Philadelphia Press*, October 16, 1867, p. 4 ("Occasional").

125. *Springfield Republican*, November 2, 1867, p. 2.

126. *New York Independent*, Oct. 7, 1867, p. 1.

127. Ibid., October 14, 1867, p. 1.

128. *Cincinnati Commercial*, January 1, 1868, p. 2 (Mack).

129. *Congressional Globe*, 40th Cong., 2d Sess., 1955 (1868).

130. Ibid., 1971.

131. *Springfield Republican*, October 15, 1867, p. 2.

132. Ibid., March 19, 1868, p. 2 (Van).

133. *Springfield Republican*, October 14, 1867, p. 2; January 3, 1868, p. 2.

134. *Cincinnati Commercial*, January 10, 1868, p. 4.

135. *Springfield Republican*, October 12, 1867, p. 4. See also *Cincinnati Commercial*, November 18, 1867, p. 1 (Mack).

136. *New York Times*, April 13, 1868, p. 4.

137. *Cincinnati Commercial*, May 14, 1868, p. 4.

138. *Springfield Republican*, April 9, 1868, p. 2.

139. For detailed accounts of the impeachment proceedings, see Michael Les Benedict, *The Impeachment and Trial of Andrew Johnson* (New York, 1973); Hans L. Trefousse, *Impeachment of a President: Andrew Johnson, the Blacks, and Reconstruction* (Knoxville, 1975).

140. Martin E. Mantell, *Johnson, Grant and the Politics of Reconstruction* (New York, 1973), 69–70, 98–99.

141. *New York Independent*, May 21, 1868, p. 4; *National Anti-Slavery Standard*, May 9, 1868, p. 2.

142. Donald B. Johnson, ed., *National Party Platforms*, vol. 1 (Urbana, 1978), 39.

143. Resolutions prepared for Massachusetts Anti-Slavery Society, reported in *Cincinnati Commercial*, May 30, 1868, p. 2.

144. *Boston Commonwealth*, June 6, 1868, p. 2 (letter of Carl Rosser).

145. *Springfield Republican*, May 23, 1868, p. 4. See also *Cincinnati Commercial*, May 23, 1868, p. 4; *Nation*, May 28, 1868, p. 425.

146. *Cincinnati Commercial*, June 24, 1868, p. 4; June 17, 1868, p. 2 (speech of Will Cumback); *Nation*, May 28, 1868, p. 425.

147. *Congressional Globe*, 40th Cong., 2d Sess., 2138 (1868).

148. Ibid., 2211.

149. Ibid., 1818.
150. Ibid., 2216.
151. Ibid.
152. Ibid., 2390.
153. Ibid., 2391–92.
154. Ibid., 2401.
155. Ibid., 2502, 2600.
156. Ibid., 2602.
157. Ibid., 2602–3. See also *Springfield Republican*, June 8, 1868, p. 4.
158. *Congressional Globe*, 40th Cong., 2d Sess., 2701, 2749–50 (1868).
159. Ibid., 2609.
160. Ibid., 2748.
161. Ibid., 2901, 2904.
162. Ibid., 3029, 3096.
163. Mantell, *Johnson, Grant and the Politics of Reconstruction*, ch. 8.
164. Democratic Platform of 1868, in Johnson, *National Party Platforms*, 1:38.
165. Speech of Daniel Voorhees, *Cincinnati Commercial*, June 13, 1868, p. 1; speech of John Reid, ibid., June 20, 1868, p. 2; speech of Allan Thurman, ibid., July 20, 1868, pp. 2–3; *Philadelphia Age*, May 23, 1868, p. 2.
166. *Philadelphia Age*, May 26, 1868, p. 2.
167. Ibid., June 3, 1868, p. 2.
168. *Cincinnati Commercial*, June 13, 1868, p. 1 (speech of Michael Kerr); ibid., July 22, 1868, p. 2 (speech of A. K. Bradley).
169. Ibid., August 1, 1868, p. 2 (speech of George Pendleton).
170. Mantell, *Johnson, Grant and the Politics of Reconstruction*, ch. 9.

CHAPTER 9. THE COMING OF
THE FIFTEENTH AMENDMENT

1. *Cincinnati Commercial*, November 9, 1868, p. 4; *Harper's Weekly*, November 28, 1868, p. 754; *National Anti-Slavery Standard*, November 14, 1868, p. 3 (Asmodeus).
2. The uncertainties surrounding this question are illustrated by two statements made by Frederick Frelinguysen of New Jersey—*Congressional Globe*, 40th Cong., 3d Sess., 1629, 1631 (1869). For various estimates of Republican strength in the new Congress, see *Cincinnati Commercial*, February 3, 1869, p. 2 (D. P.); February 22, 1869, p. 2; *National Anti-Slavery Standard*, January 9, 1869, p. 2; *Philadelphia North American and United States Gazette*, February 24, 1869, p. 2; March 4, 1869, p. 2.
3. *National Anti-Slavery Standard*, November 28, 1868, p. 1 (Griffen); *Philadelphia North American and United States Gazette*, February 6, 1869, p. 2.
4. *Congressional Globe*, 40th Cong., 3d Sess., 1628 (1868).
5. James G. Blaine, *Twenty Years of Congress: From Lincoln to Garfield with a Review of the Events Which Led to the Political Revolution of 1860*, vol. 2 (Norwich, Conn., 1884–86), 412–13. See also *Congressional Globe*, 40th Cong., 3d Sess., 912 (Senator Willey) (1869); and app. 99 (Congressman Shellabarger).

6. *Congressional Globe*, 40th Cong., 3d Sess., 983. See also ibid., 912 (Senator Willey) and app. 99 (Congressman Shellabarger); *Cincinnati Commercial*, November 9, 1868, p. 4; *Nation*, January 28, 1869, p. 64; *National Anti-Slavery Standard*, May 9, 1868, p. 2.

7. See LaWanda Cox and John H. Cox, "Negro Suffrage and Republican Politics: The Problem of Motivation in Reconstruction Historiography," *Journal of Southern History* 33 (1967): 303.

8. See, e.g., *Congressional Globe*, 40th Cong., 3d Sess., 1314–15 (1869).

9. *Nation*, May 28, 1868, p. 425.

10. Ibid., January 28, 1869, p. 124; *National Anti-Slavery Standard*, October 17, 1868, p. 1 (letter of Charles Moss); *New York Times*, November 25, 1868, p. 4.

11. *Philadelphia Press*, February 5, 1869, p. 2.

12. *Philadelphia North American and United States Gazette*, February 1, 1869, p. 2.

13. William Gillette, *The Right to Vote: Politics and the Passage of the Fifteenth Amendment* (Baltimore, 1965), argues that this perception provided the primary impetus for Republican advocacy of a black-suffrage amendment.

14. *Cincinnati Commercial*, April 6, 1867, p. 4; *National Anti-Slavery Standard*, May 11, 1867, p. 1 (letter from Charles Sumner); *Philadelphia North American and United States Gazette*, February 1, 1869, p. 2; *Philadelphia Press*, February 3, 1869, p. 2 (letter from "Occasional").

15. *Congressional Globe*, 40th Cong., 3d Sess., 991 (1869). See also ibid., 912 (Senator Willey); *Cincinnati Commercial*, November 13, 1868, p. 4; *New York Times*, November 19, 1868, p. 4.

16. William. M. Stewart, *Reminiscences of Senator William M. Stewart of Nevada* (New York, 1908), 232.

17. *Congressional Globe*, 40th Cong., 3d Sess., 668 (1869).

18. Ibid., 1010 (Senator Doolittle); and app. 287 (Senator Davis).

19. Ibid., 995 (Senator Davis); and 1639 (Senator Buckalew).

20. Ibid., 707 (Senator Dixon); and 1006 (Senator Hendricks).

21. Ibid., 1035.

22. For more detailed information on Stewart's life and career, see Russell R. Elliott, *Servant of Power: A Political Biography of William M. Stewart* (Reno, 1983); Stewart, *Reminiscences*.

23. *New York Times*, November 16, 1868, p. 2.

24. *Congressional Globe*, 40th Cong., 3d Sess., 904 (1869) (Senator Sumner). See also ibid., 561 (Congressman Boutwell); and 1001 (Senator Edmunds).

25. Ibid., 904.

26. Ibid.

27. Ibid., 902.

28. Ibid., 721 (Congressman Kelley); and 903 (Senator Sumner).

29. Ibid., 1004 (Senator Yates).

30. Ibid., 558–59 (Congressman Boutwell); and 1000 (Senator Edmunds).

31. Ibid., 723–24 (Senator Jones); and 1033 (Senator Fessenden).

32. Ibid., 1002 (Senator Drake); and 1003 (Senator Howard).

33. Ibid., 1041.

34. Ibid., 286.

35. Ibid., app. 97–99. See also ibid., 722 (Congressman Bingham); and 744 (Congressman Schenck).

36. Ibid., 728.

37. Ibid., 638.
38. Ibid., 744.
39. Ibid.
40. Ibid., 745.
41. Ibid., 668. The basic formulation adopted by the Senate Judiciary Committee was actually introduced by John Henderson of Missouri. Ibid., 542.
42. Ibid., 668.
43. Ibid., app. 155.
44. Ibid., 1039.
45. Ibid., 1038; see also 1037 (Senator Patterson).
46. Ibid., 1037; see also 1038 (Senator Conkling).
47. Ibid., 1029.
48. Ibid., 1040.
49. Ibid., 1042.
50. Ibid., 1044.
51. Ibid., 1224–26.
52. Ibid., 1224–25. Some historians have questioned Bingham's sincerity in supporting the Wilson proposal. Michael Les Benedict, *A Compromise of Principle: Congressional Republicans and Reconstruction 1863–1869* (New York, 1974), 333; Gillette, *The Right to Vote*, 62–63. In this regard it should be noted that though Bingham would have only required impartial suffrage as a condition for the restoration of the ex-Confederate states, he had supported universal suffrage in other contexts. *Congressional Globe*, 39th Cong., 1st Sess., 310 (1866) (District of Columbia); *Congressional Globe*, 40th Cong., 2d Sess., 3094 (1868).
53. *Congressional Globe*, 40th Cong., 3d Sess., 1225 (1869).
54. Ibid., 1226.
55. Ibid., 1225.
56. Ibid.
57. Ibid., 1226.
58. Ibid., 1284.
59. Ibid., 1296.
60. Ibid., 1296, 1299.
61. Ibid., 1299.
62. Ibid., 1295.
63. Ibid., 1300.
64. Ibid., 1306.
65. Ibid., 1318.
66. Ibid., 1426 (Congressmen Bingham, Shellabarger, and Logan); and 1427 (Congressman Lawrence).
67. Ibid., 1426.
68. *Germantown Telegraph*, March 3, 1869, p. 3.
69. *Congressional Globe*, 40th Cong., 3d Sess., 1428 (1869).
70. Ibid., 1426.
71. Ibid., 1428.
72. Gillette, *The Right to Vote*, 69.
73. Ibid.
74. *Congressional Globe*, 40th Cong., 3d Sess., 725 (1869) (Congressman Butler); and 726 (Congressman Boutwell).
75. Ibid., 1226, 1428.
76. See ibid., 728 (Congressman Garfield); and 1427 (Congressman Bingham).

77. *National Anti-Slavery Standard*, February 20, 1869, p. 2.

78. *Congressional Globe*, 40th Cong., 3d Sess., 1426 (1869).

79. Ibid., 1428.

80. Ibid.

81. Ibid., 1481.

82. *Chicago Tribune*, February 24, 1869, p. 1.

83. *Congressional Globe*, 40th Cong., 3d Sess., 1495 (1869).

84. Stewart, *Reminiscences*, 236.

85. *Congressional Globe*, 40th Cong., 3d Sess., 1626 (1869) (Senator Edmunds).

86. Ibid., 1563-64.

87. Ibid., 1623.

88. Ibid., 1627 (Senator Wilson); and 1629 (Senator Sawyer).

89. Ibid., 1625 (Senator Howard).

90. Ibid., 1306.

91. Ibid., 1626.

92. Ibid., 1641.

93. Ibid., 1009 (Senator Howard); and app. 97-98 (Congressman Shellabarger).

94. Ibid., 1010 (Senator Sawyer); and app. 97-99 (Congressman Shellabarger).

Selected Bibliography

PRIMARY SOURCES

Basler, Roy P., ed., *The Collected Works of Abraham Lincoln*. 8 vols. New Brunswick, N.J., 1953–1955.

Beale, Howard, K., ed. *The Diary of Edward Bates, 1859–1866*. Washington, D.C., 1933.

Blaine, James G. *Twenty Years of Congress: From Lincoln to Garfield with a Review of the Events Which Led to the Political Revolution of 1860*. 2 vols. Norwich, Conn., 1884–1886.

Boutwell, George. *Reminiscences of Sixty Years in Public Affairs*. 2 vols. New York, 1902.

Browne, Albert G., Jr. *Sketch of the Official Life of John A. Andrew as Governor of Massachusetts*. New York, 1868.

Cobb, Thomas, R. R. *An Inquiry into the Law of Negro Slavery in the United States*. N.p., 1858; reprint, New York, 1968.

Cooley, Thomas M. *A Treatise on the Constitutional Limitations Which Rest upon the Legislative Power of the States of the Union*. Boston, 1867.

Fleming, Walter. *Documentary History of Reconstruction*. Cleveland, 1906.

Hoar, George F. *Autobiography of Seventy Years*. 2 vols. New York, 1908.

Holmes, Oliver Wendell, ed. *Kent's Commentaries*. 4 vols. Boston, 1896.

Hutchinson, Robert D. *A Treatise on the Law of Carriers as Administered in the United States and England*. Chicago, 1880.

Johannsen, Robert W., ed. *The Lincoln-Douglas Debates of 1858*. New York, 1965.

Johnson, Donald B., ed. *National Party Platforms*. 2 vols. Urbana, 1978.

Edward McPherson Papers. *Civil Rights Scrapbook*. On file, Library of Congress.

————. *Fourteenth Amendment Scrapbook*. On file, Library of Congress.

Nicolay, John G., and John Hay. *Abraham Lincoln: A History*. 10 vols. New York, 1890.

Poore, Benjamin, ed. *The Federal and State Constitutions, Colonial Charters and Other Organic Laws of the United States*. 2 vols. Washington, D.C., 1877.

Stewart, William M. *Reminiscences of Senator William M. Stewart of Nevada*. New York, 1908

Story, Joseph. *Commentaries on the Constitution of the United States*. 2 vols. Boston, 1833.

Sumner, Charles. *His Complete Works*. 15 vols. Boston, 1870–83.

Swindler, William F., ed. *Sources and Documents of United States Consitutions*. 10 vols. Dobbs Ferry, N.Y., 1979.

Trumbull Papers. Library of Congress.

Tucker, St. George, ed. *Blackstone's Commentaries*. 5 vols. Philadelphia, 1803.

Wilson, Clyde N., ed. *Papers of John C. Calhoun*. 18 vols. Columbia, S.C., 1959–88.

Wilson, Henry. *History of the Rise and Fall of the Slave Power*. 3 vols. Boston, 1875–77.

LEGISLATIVE SOURCES

Congressional Globe. Thirty-fifth through Fortieth Congresses.
Debates and Proceedings of the Oregon Constitutional Convention of 1857.
Debates of the Constitutional Convention of the State of Maryland (1864).
Journal of the Missouri Constitutional Convention of 1863.
Kendrick, Benjamin B. *The Journal of the Joint Committee of Fifteen on Re-construction, 39th Congress, 1865–1867.* New York 1914.
Opinions of the Attorneys General of the United States.
Pennsylvania Legislative Record (1867).
Report of Maj. Gen. Carl Schurz on the Condition of the South, 39th Cong., 1st Sess., Senate Executive Document No. 2 (December 19, 1865).
Report of the Joint Committee on Reconstruction, 39th Cong., 1st Sess. (1866).
Reports to the General Assembly of Illinois, 24th Session.

NEWSPAPERS AND OTHER PERIODICALS

Boston Commonwealth
Charleston (S.C.) *Courier*
Chicago Tribune
Cincinnati Commercial
Germantown (Pa.) *Telegraph*
Harper's Weekly (New York)
Harrisburg (Pa.) *Daily Telegraph*
Ironton (Ohio) *Register*
Nation (New York)
National Anti-Slavery Standard (New York)
National Intelligencer (Washington, D.C.)
New York Independent
New York Times
New York Tribune
Philadelphia Age
Philadelphia North American and United States Gazette
Philadelphia Press
Raleigh (N.C.) *Sentinel*
Springfield (Mass.) *Republican*
Washington Chronicle

SECONDARY SOURCES

Avins, Alfred. "The Civil Rights Act of 1875: Some Reflected Light on the Four-teenth Amendment and Public Accommodations." *Columbia Law Review* 66 (1966): 873.
Baer, Judith A. *Equality under the Constitution: Reclaiming the Fourteenth Amendment.* Ithaca, 1983.
Beale, Howard K. *The Critical Year: A Study of Andrew Johnson and Recon-struction.* New York, 1930.
Beauregard, Erving E. "John A. Bingham and the Fourteenth Amendment." *Historian* 50 (November 1987): 67.

Belz, Herman. *A New Birth of Freedom: The Republican Party and Freedmen's Rights, 1861–1866.* Westport, Conn. 1976.

———. *Reconstructing the Union: Theory and Policy during the Civil War.* Westport, Conn., 1969.

Benedict, Michael Les. *A Compromise of Principle: Congressional Republicans and Reconstruction 1863–1869.* New York, 1974.

———. *The Impeachment and Trial of Andrew Johnson.* New York, 1973.

Berger, Raoul. *Government by Judiciary: The Transformation of the Fourteenth Amendment.* Cambridge, Mass., 1977.

Berry, Mary. *Military Necessity and Civil Rights Policy: Black Citizenship and the Constitution, 1861–1868.* Fort Washington, Pa. 1977.

Berwanger, Eugene. *The Frontier against Slavery: Western Anti-Negro Prejudice and the Slavery Extension Controversy.* Chicago, 1967.

Bestor, Albert. "State Sovereignty and Slavery: A Reinterpretation of Proslavery Constitutional Doctrine 1846–1860." *Journal of the Illinois State Historical Society* 54 (1961): 148.

Bickel, Alexander M. "The Original Understanding and the Segregation Decision." *Harvard Law Review* 69 (1955): 1.

Bowers, Claude. *The Tragic Era: The Revolution after Lincoln.* Cambridge, Mass., 1929.

Brock, William R. *An American Crisis: Congress and Reconstruction 1865–1867.* New York, 1963.

Buchanan, G. Sidney. *The Quest for Freedom: A Legal History of the Thirteenth Amendment.* Houston, 1976.

Burgess, John W. *Reconstruction and the Constitution, 1866–1876.* New York, 1902.

Castel, Albert. *The Presidency of Andrew Johnson.* Lawrence, Kans., 1979.

Cole, Arthur C. *Centennial History of Illinois: The Era of the Civil War 1848–1870.* Vol 3. Springfield, Ill., 1919.

Cornelius, J. *A History of Constitution-Making in Illinois.* Urbana, 1969.

Cox, LaWanda, and John H. Cox. "Negro Suffrage and Republican Politics: The Problem of Motivation in Reconstruction Historiography." *Journal of Southern History* 33 (1967): 303.

———. *Politics, Principle and Prejudice 1865–1866.* London, 1963.

Crosskey, Charles. "Charles Fairman, 'Legislative History' and the Constitutional Limitations on State Authority." *University of Chicago Law Review* 22 (1954): 1.

Curtis, Michael Kent. "The Fourteenth Amendment and the Bill of Rights." *Connecticut Law Review* 14 (1982): 237.

———. *No State Shall Abridge: The Fourteenth Amendment and the Bill of Rights.* Durham, N.C., 1986.

Donald, David. *Charles Sumner and the Coming of the Civil War.* New York, 1960.

———. *Charles Sumner and the Rights of Man.* New York, 1970.

———. *The Politics of Reconstruction.* Baton Rouge, 1965.

Dumond, Dwight L. *Antislavery: The Crusade for Freedom.* Ann Arbor, 1961.

Dunning, William A. *Essays on the Civil War and Reconstruction, and Related Topics.* New York, 1898.

Elliott, Russell R. *Servant of Power: A Political Biography of William M. Stewart.* Reno, 1983.

Fairman, Charles. "Does the Fourteenth Amendment Incorporate the Bill of Rights." *Stanford Law Review* 2 (1949): 5.

_____. *Reconstruction and Reunion 1864–1888, Part 1*. New York, 1971.

Fehrenbacher, Don E. *The Dred Scott Case: Its Significance in American Law and Politics*. New York, 1978.

_____. *Prelude to Greatness: Lincoln in the 1850s*. Stanford, 1962.

Finkelman, Paul. *An Imperfect Union: Slavery, Comity and Federalism*. Chapel Hill, 1981.

_____. "Prelude to the Fourteenth Amendment: Black Legal Rights in the Antebellum North." *Rutgers Law Journal* 17 (1986): 415.

_____. "Slavery and the Northwest Ordinance: A Study in Ambiguity." *Journal of the Early Republic* 6 (1986): 343.

Foner, Eric. *Free Soil, Free Labor, Free Men*. New York, 1970.

_____. *Nothing but Freedom: Emancipation and Its Legacy*. Baton Rouge, 1983.

_____. *Reconstruction: America's Unfinished Revolution, 1863–1877*. New York, 1988.

Franklin, John Hope. *Reconstruction: After the Civil War*. Chicago, 1961.

Freehling, William W. *Prelude to Civil War: The Nullification Controversy in South Carolina*. New York, 1966.

Gienapp, William E. "The Republican Party and the Slave Power." In *New Perspectives on Race and Slavery in America: Essays in Honor of Kenneth M. Stampp*. Edited by Robert H. Abzug and Stephen E. Maizlish. Lexington, Ky., 1986.

Gillette, William. *The Right to Vote: Politics and the Passage of the Fifteenth Amendment*. Baltimore, 1965.

Holt, Michael. *Slavery, Republicanism and the Republican Party*. New York, 1978.

Horwitz, Morton J. *The Transformation of American Law, 1780–1860*. Cambridge, Mass., 1977.

Hyman, Harold M. *A More Perfect Union: The Impact of the Civil War and Reconstruction on the Constitution*. New York, 1973.

Hyman, Harold M., and William M. Wiecek, *Equal Justice under Law: Constitutional Development 1835–1875*. New York, 1982.

Jaffa, Harry V. *Crisis of the House Divided: An Analysis of the Lincoln-Douglas Debates*. Garden City, N.Y., 1959.

James, Joseph B. *The Framing of the Fourteenth Amendment*. Urbana, 1956.

_____. *The Ratification of the Fourteenth Amendment*. Macon, Ga., 1984.

Kaczorowski, Robert J. *The Politics of Judicial Interpretation: The Federal Courts, Department of Justice and Civil Rights, 1866–1876*. New York, 1985.

_____. "Revolutionary Constitutionalism in the Era of the Civil War and Reconstruction." *New York University Law Review*, 61 (1986): 863.

Kettner, James H. *The Development of American Citizenship, 1608–1870*. Chapel Hill, 1978.

Kincaid, Larry G. "Victims of Circumstance: An Interpretation of Changing Attitudes toward Republican Policy Makers and Reconstruction." *Journal of American History* 57 (1970): 48.

Kohl, Robert. "The Civil Rights Act of 1866: Its Hour Come Round at Last: *Jones v. Albert Mayer Co.*" *Virginia Law Review* 55 (1969): 272.

Kousser, J. Morgan. " 'The Supremacy of Equal Rights': The Struggle against Racial Discrimination in Antebellum Massachusetts and the Foundations of the Fourteenth Amendment." *Northwestern University Law Review* 82 (1988): 941.

Levy, Leonard. *The Law of the Commonwealth and Chief Justice Shaw*. Cambridge, Mass., 1957.

Litwack, Leon F. *North of Slavery: The Negro in the Free States, 1790–1860*. Chicago, 1961.

McKitrick, Eric, ed. *Andrew Johnson: A Profile*. New York, 1969.

_____. *Andrew Johnson and Reconstruction*. Chicago, 1960.

McPherson, James M. *The Struggle for Equality: The Abolitionists and the Negro in the Civil War and Reconstruction*. Princeton, 1964.

Maltz, Earl M. "The Appeal of Originalism." *Utah Law Review* (1987): 773–805.

_____. "The Concept of Equal Protection of the Laws—A Historical Inquiry." *San Diego Law Review* 22 (1985): 499.

_____. "The Fourteenth Amendment as Political Compromise—Section One in the Joint Committee on Reconstruction." *Ohio State Law Journal* 45 (1984): 933.

_____. "Fourteenth Amendment Concepts in the Antebellum Era." *American Journal of Legal History* 32 (1988): 305.

_____. "Reconstruction without Revolution: Republican Civil Rights Theory in the Era of the Fourteenth Amendment." *Houston Law Review* 24 (1986): 221.

_____. " 'Separate But Equal' and the Law of Common Carriers in the Era of the Fourteenth Amendment." *Rutgers Law Journal* 17 (1986): 553.

Mantell, Martin E. *Johnson, Grant and the Politics of Reconstruction*. New York, 1973.

Morris, Thomas D. *Free Men All: The Personal Liberty Laws of the North 1780–1861*. Baltimore, 1974.

Mott, Rodney L. *Due Process of Law: A Historical and Analytical Treatise of the Principles and Methods Followed by the Courts in the Application of the Concept of the "Law of the Land."* Indianapolis, 1926.

Nelson, William E. *The Fourteenth Amendment: From Political Principle to Judicial Doctrine*. Cambridge, Mass., 1988.

Nye, Russell B. *Fettered Freedom*. East Lansing, 1949.

Onuf, Peter. *Statehood and Union: A History of the Northwest Ordinance*. Bloomington, 1987.

Paludan, Phillip S. *A Covenant with Death: The Constitution, Law and Equality in the Civil War Era*. Urbana, 1975.

Perman, Michael. *Reunion without Compromise: The South and Reconstruction*. Cambridge, England, 1973.

Riddleberger, Patrick. "The Break in the Radical Ranks: Radicals vs. Stalwarts in the Election of 1872." *Journal of Negro History* 44 (1959): 136.

Silbey, Joel H. *A Respectable Minority: The Democratic Party in the Civil War Era, 1860–1868*. New York, 1977.

Stampp, Kenneth M. *The Era of Reconstruction, 1865–1877*. New York, 1965.

Stephenson, W. H. *The Political Career of James H. Lane*. Topeka, 1930.

Swift, Donald C. "John A. Bingham and Reconstruction: The Dilemma of a Moderate." *Ohio History* 77 (1968): 81.

tenBroek, Jacobus. *The Antislavery Origins of the Fourteenth Amendment*. Berkeley, 1951.

Thornbrough, Emma Lou. *Indiana in the Civil War Era, 1850–1880*. Indianapolis, 1965.

Trask, David F. "Charles Sumner and the New Jersey Railroad Monopoly during the Civil War." *New Jersey State Historical Society Proceedings* 75 (1957): 259.

Trefousse, Hans L. *Impeachment of a President: Andrew Johnson, the Blacks, and Reconstruction.* Knoxville, 1975.

———. *The Radical Republicans: Lincoln's Vanguard for Racial Justice.* New York, 1969.

Van Alstyne, William. "The Fourteenth Amendment, The 'Right' to Vote, and the Understanding of the Thirty-Ninth Congress." In Philip B. Kurland, ed., *1965 Supreme Court Review.* Chicago, 1965.

Voegeli, V. Jacque. *Free But Not Equal: The Midwest and the Negro during the Civil War Era.* Chicago, 1967.

Weisberger, Bernard. "The Dark and Bloody Battle Ground of Reconstruction Historiography." *Journal of Southern History* 25 (1957): 427.

Wiecek, William M. *The Guarantee Clause of the U.S. Constitution.* Ithaca, 1972.

———. *The Sources of Anti-Slavery Constitutionalism in America, 1760–1848.* Ithaca, 1977.

Wilson, Theodore B. *The Black Codes of the South.* University, Ala., 1965.

Ziegler, Donald. "Reassessment of the *Younger* Doctrine in Light of the Legislative History of Reconstruction." *Duke Law Journal* (1983): 987.

Zilversmit, Arthur. *The First Emancipation: The Abolition of Slavery in the North.* Chicago, 1967.

Zuckert, Michael P. "Completing the Constitution: The Thirteenth Amendment." *Constitutional Commentary* 4 (1987): 259.

———. "Congressional Power under the Fourteenth Amendment—The Original Understanding of Section Five." *Constitutional Commentary* 3 (1986): 123.

Index